Rwanda

Rebuilding of a Nation

Editors
A. Ndahiro, J. Rwagatare, A. Nkusi

FOUNTAIN PUBLISHERS
www.fountainpublishers.co.ug

Fountain Publishers Rwanda Ltd
Opposite Cogebanque-Remera
P.O. Box 6567 Kigali
E-mail: sales@fountainpublishers.rwanda@gmail.com

Fountain Publishers
P.O. Box 488 Kampala, Uganda
E-mail: sales@fountainpublishers.co.ug
publishing@fountainpublishers.co.ug
Website: www.fountainpublishers.co.ug

© Rwanda Patriotic Front 2015
First published 2015

All rights reserved. No part of this publication may be reproduced, stored in a retrieval system or transmitted in any form or by any means electronic, mechanical, photocopying, recording or otherwise without the prior written permission of the publisher.

ISBN 978-10-92401-03-6

Photo Credits:
Timothy Kisambira, George Baryamwisaki, Rwanda Ministry of Agriculture, Ministry of Health, Ministry of Infrastructure, RPF Secretariat, New Vision, Uganda

Contents

List of Abbreviations .... *vii*
Foreword .... *x*
Acknowledgements .... *xii*
Introduction .... *xiii*
Maps .... *xv*

Part 1 1

Historical Background 1

Chapter 1. Pre-colonial Period 3
Origin of Rwanda 3
Formation and Expansion of the Kingdom of Rwanda 4

Chapter 2. Rwanda under Colonial Rule 11
Rule for Exploitation 11
Belgian Rule: 1916-1962 13

Chapter 3. Post-colonial Rwanda 17
First Republic: 1962-1973 17
Second Republic: 1973-1994 19

Part 2 23

Liberation Struggle 23

Chapter 4. Liberation Struggle 25
Precursor to the Rwanda Patriotic Front (RPF) 25

Chapter 5. RPF Military Struggle 29
Rationale for the struggle 29
Why Option Z? 30
Launch of the Liberation Struggle 32
Reactions from Various Actors 33
Military Operations and Diplomacy 35
Blocking and Delaying Tactics 38
Negotiations and Genocide Preparations 39

Chapter 6.	**Genocide Against the Tutsi and its Aftermath ... 49**
	Preparations of the Genocide 49
	Planning of the Genocide 50
	Execution of the Genocide..57
	Stopping the Genocide 58
	International Betrayal..62
	Aftermath of the Genocide against the Tutsi.....................62
	Resilience of a nation..66
	Rwanda Policies to Contain Genocide 67

Part 3 71

Post-Genocide Transitional Government (1994-2003)...........71

Chapter 7.	**Facing the Immediate Challenges after 1994...... 73**
	Establishing the Government of National Unity...............73
	Pressing Challenges in Key Sectors 75
Chapter 8.	**Insurgency and the Congo Wars........................81**
	Facing Security threats 81
	First Congo War...83
	Second Congo War..83
	Lusaka Ceasefire Agreement and its Implementation 84
	Pretoria Accord..85
	Withdrawal of Rwandan Troops From DRC......................85
Chapter 9.	**Urugwiro Consultations.................................... 87**
	Consensus Building 87
	Purpose...88
	People 88
	Process..89
	Highlights of the Consultations 89
	Recommendations from Urugwiro Consultations 92
Chapter 10.	**Setting the Transformational Agenda 99**
	New national direction..99
	Prioritising Unity and Reconciliation.................................99
	Catalysing Long-Term Development: Vision 2020.......... 101
	Constitution Making Process.. 106

Part 4 ....**109**

Deepening Socio-Economic Transformation **109**

Chapter 11. **Good Governance** **111**
  Where Rwanda has come from 111
  Consensual Democracy and Power-sharing 112
  Implementing Decentralisation 117
  Gender Equality 119
  Empowering Youth 121
  Empowering Civil Society Organisations 123
  Reforming the Media Sector 124
  Security for Stability and Sustainable Development 125
  International Relations and Cooperation 127
  Peacekeeping 129
  Home-grown Solutions in Governance 130

Chapter 12. **Justice** **135**
  Rebuilding the justice system 135
  Separation of Powers within the Judiciary 135
  National Prosecution Authority 136
  Restructuring of the Court System 137
  Capacity Building for Public Trust 138
  Infrastructure 139
  Strengthening the Human Rights Commission 139
  Fighting Genocide and its Ideology 141
  Home-grown Solutions 142

Chapter 13. **Economic Development** **145**
  Reviving the Economy 145
  Agriculture for Sustainable Development 145
  Infrastructure Development 160
  Information Communication Technology (ICT) 165
  Urban and Rural Settlement 169
  Industrial Development 172
  Doing Business and Attracting Investment 174
  Trade Development 176
  SME Development and Job Creation 177
  Rwanda Cooperative Movement 178
  Tourism Development 180
  Emerging Mining Industry 183
  Conserving the Environment 185
  Home-grown Solutions 188

Chapter 14.	**Social Welfare** **207**
	People First 207
	Education 207
	Healthcare for All 212
	Improvement of Health Services 215
	Social Security 218
	Sports for a Healthy Nation 221
	Home-grown Solutions 223
Chapter 15.	**Journey Ahead: Thinking Big** **225**
	Vision 2020 for Economic Transformation 225
	Regional Integration 226
	Confronting Challenges 232
Bibliography *255*
Index *261*

List of Abbreviations

AgDF	Agaciro Development Fund
AGER	Association Génerale des Etudiants Rwandais
APROSOMA	Association pour la Promotion Sociale de la Masse
ASM	Agence de Santé Maternelle
AUCC	African Union anti-Corruption Convention
BBTG	Broad-Based Transitional Government
BBTP	Broad-Based Transitional Parliament
C-MNH	Community Maternal and Newborn Healthcare
C-PBF	Community Performance-Based Financing
CBNP	Community-Based Nutrition Programme
CDR	Coalition pour la Défense de la République
CEEAC	Communauté Economique des Etats de l'Afrique Centrale
CEPGL	Communauté Economique des Pays des Grands Lacs
CHP	Community Health Programme
CHU	University Central Hospital
CHUB	Centre Hospitalier Universitaire de Butare
CHUK	Centre Hospitalier Universitaire de Kigali
CHWC	Community Health Workers' Cooperatives
CHWs	Community Health Workers
CNLG	Commission Nationale de Lutte Contre le Genocide
COMESA	Common Market for Eastern and Southern Africa
CRC	Citizen Report Card
DAU.V	Desert Gold Ventures Inc.
DDRR	Demobilisation, Disarmament, Rehabilitation and Re-Integration
DHS	Demographic and Health Survey
DRC	Democratic Republic of Congo
EAC	East African Community
EAPCCO	Eastern Africa Police Chief Cooperation Organisation
EDPRS	Economic Development and Poverty Reduction Strategy
EICV	Enquête Intégrale sur les Conditions de Vie des Ménages (Integrated Household Living Conditions Survey)

FAO	Food and Agriculture Organisation
FAR	Forces Armées Rwandaises
FDLR	Forces Démocratiques de Libération du Rwanda (Democratic Forces for the Liberation of Rwanda)
GHI	Global Hunger Index
GoR	Government of Rwanda
HIMO	Haute Intensité de Main d'Oeuvre
IDPs	Internally Displaced Persons
IFPRI	International Food Policy Research Institute
ICCM	Integrated Community Case Management
INATEK	Institute of Agriculture, Technology and Education of Kibungo
IPAR	Institute of Policy Analysis and Research
ISAE	Institute of Agriculture and Animal Husbandry
KIM	Kigali Institute of Management
MAJ	Maison d'Accès à la Justice
MDR	Mouvement Démocratique Républicain
MINADEF	Ministry of Defence
MINAGRI	Ministry of Agriculture and Animal Resource
MINALOC	Ministry of Local Government
MINECOFIN	Ministry of Finance and Economic Planning
MINICOM	Ministry of Trade and Industry
MINIRENA	Ministry of Natural Resources
MONUC	United Nations Peacekeeping Mission to Congo
MONUSCO	United Nations Stabilisation Mission in the Democratic Republic of the Congo
MRND	Mouvement Révolutionnaire National pour le Développement
NCDs	Non-communicable Diseases
NEC	National Electral Commission
NICI	National Information and Communication Infrastructure
NISR	National Institute of Statistics of Rwanda
OSCE	Organisation for Security and Cooperation in Europe
PARMEHUTU	Parti du Mouvement de l'Emancipation Hutu (Party of the Bahutu Emancipation Movement)
PDC	Parti Démocrate Chretien

PDI	Parti Démocratique Idéal
PL	Parti Libéral
PSD	Parti Social D'emocrate
PSR	Parti Socialiste Rwandais
PTSD	Post Traumatic Stress Disorder
RADER	Rassemblement Démocratique Rwandais
RANU	Rwanda Alliance for National Unity
RDF	Rwanda Defence Force
RDRC	Rwanda Demobilisation and Reintegration Commission
RGAC	Rwanda Governance Advisory Council
RGB	Rwanda Governance Board
RGS	Rwanda Governance Scorecard
RPA	Rwanda Patriotic Army
RPF	Rwanda Patriotic Front
RTDA	Rwanda Transport Development Agency
SGD.V	Simba Gold Corp
TIG	Travail d'Intérêt Général
TVET	Technical and Vocational Education and Training
UDPR	Union Démocratique du Peuple Rwandais
UNAMIR	United Nations Assistance Mission for Rwanda
UNAR	Union Nationale Rwandaise
UNCAC	United Nations Convention against Corruption
UNTOC	UN Convention against Transnational Organised Crime
UR	University of Rwanda
WHO	World Health Organisation

Foreword

Rwanda is undergoing rapid transformation and Rwandans know that the renewal and reconstruction of the country is real, even though it is not without complication. This is in large measure because they have all made a contribution.

Together, we have had to think big and long-term and endeavour to correct the mistakes of the past, including divisive politics and systemic governance failures that culminated in the Genocide against the Tutsi. Where necessary and relevant, we have had to draw on specific aspects of our culture and traditional practices to steer our development process. This way we were able to tailor our programmes to the context and needs of our country. This is how our home-grown solutions were born and have turned out to be very useful tools as we continue to confront our challenges.

Since 1994, we have practiced a system of inclusive politics that promotes dialogue and participation.

Rather than dampen our hopes and aspirations, our recent tragic history served as an awakening and galvanized each and every Rwandan to tap their innermost resources to build the country we deserve.

Today, Rwandans share unity of purpose and palpable optimism about the country's future; and there is good reason for that. Over the last decade, Rwanda's economy has been growing steadily at an average of 8% per annum. Between 2006 and 2011, one million of our citizens climbed out of poverty and, ultimately, the goal is to eradicate it altogether. We should also be happy that our country continues to be one of Africa's most attractive places to do business. Also, a woman's voice has now found its rightful place in our society.

Rwandans now live longer and happier lives: 98 % of our people have access to health care and all our children benefit from free primary and secondary education.

There is no doubt that the rebuilding of Rwanda has relied on the implementation of sound policies, but the success registered in the last twenty years is not solely technocratic. Our achievements are also a function of the political convictions that constitute the thinking of the Rwanda Patriotic Front and the universal values of fairness, justice and freedom that have guided us throughout the liberation struggle.

This book is intended to give that part of the Rwandan story, without which it would be difficult to fully appreciate how the country and our leadership have managed to deliver.

As we look to the future, we can say with confidence that Rwanda will continue to make further progress. The immense challenges that we have confronted and the turnaround that we have seen give us hope that we can shape the future and build a united and prosperous nation, one that we will be happy to bequeath future generations.

H.E. Paul KAGAME
President of the Republic of Rwanda,
Chairman FPR - Inkotanyi

Acknowledgements

The Editors would like to thank the Rwanda Patriotic Front for providing the resources that were vital for the research and compilation of material that has gone into the production of this book.

We also wish to thank Fountain Publishers for accepting to publish it and for their professional advice all along. Needless to say, the Editors take responsibility for the final product.

A number of Government institutions and departments availed important information that constitutes a sizeable part of this book. We are also greatly indebted to the various RPF cadres whose contributions made the publication of this book possible. Many more individuals had significant input and they should all understand that we are grateful to them and acknowledge their invaluable contributions. They are all authors who are well-versed in Rwanda's history, or active participants and witnesses of the events described in these pages.

The Editors

Introduction

Rwanda: Rebuilding of a Nation was written to set the record correct for the People and the Nation of Rwanda.

The story of Rwanda, as told in this book, is intertwined with the story of the Rwanda Patriotic Front (RPF). *Rwanda: Rebuilding of a Nation* details the birth and growth of RPF: how a group of oppressed refugees united and sacrificed all that they had, including their lives, to liberate their motherland from the shackles of brutal and genocidal regimes. They all shared the dream of rebuilding a new nation that would give equal opportunities to all its citizens.

The book is divided in four parts, each grouping an uneven number of chapters presenting a common theme. The chronological and logical sequence invites the reader on a journey of liberation struggle, reconciliation, reconstruction and rebuilding of a nation.

Part One traces the formation of the Kingdom of Rwanda through the centuries, giving the historical background of the socio-economic institutions that characterised the pre-colonial society. Rwanda was a strong united and feared nation. The colonial era and the post-independence regimes that followed were all marked by division, injustice and discrimination meted out on citizens. All this culminated in the 1994 Genocide against the Tutsi that threatened to wipe out Rwanda as a nation.

Part Two covers the rise of the Rwanda Patriotic Front and the Liberation struggle that also ended the Genocide. This Genocide potrayed in Chapters 5 and 6 depicts Rwanda as a near-failed state. Rwanda struggled to stand again on its feet and began a new journey, one of unity, reconciliation and reconstruction.

Part Three focuses on the Post-Genocide strategies, the real phase of rebuilding the nation. The Transitional Government faced the challenges of repatriation of millions of Rwandan refugees and maintaining security, both internal and external, while pursuing economic recovery.

The repatriation was followed by years of rebuilding institutions, finding ways to achieve reconciliation in a nation that was still deeply grieving, and restoring confidence and a sense of security among its people. A people who had known nothing but despair and privation for decades acquired a sense of purposeful living within the borders of their motherland.

Part Four concentrates on specific interventions undertaken to ensure faster economic recovery. Under the strong leadership of RPF, the new united democratic Rwanda, undergoes deep unprecedented economic, industrial and technological transformation in all key sectors as well as experiencing the continued improvement of the social welfare of its citizens.

The last section discusses in detail the four key pillars of Governance, Justice, Economic Development and Social Welfare, the very foundations on which the new nation is being rebuilt. Each Chapter from 11 to 15 focuses on the specific interventions, with emphasis on peculiar mechanisms drawn from the home-grown solutions that trace their resilience back to the very cherished fundamental values of Rwandan society.

The emphasis on health, social security, education and economic transformation shows RPF's commitment to a holistic approach in improving the lives of all Rwandans.

All these strides aside, the RPF-led government has set ambitious goals to drive economic growth and reduce poverty, through the Second Economic Development and Poverty Reduction Strategy (EDPRS II), which set Rwanda firmly on the path to achieving the objectives of Vision 2020.

The newly rebuilt Rwanda remains a nation on the move, refusing to dwell in the past but instead recognising the opportunities of regional integration and determined to ensure a promising future for all who call Rwanda 'home'.

Introduction xv

Maps

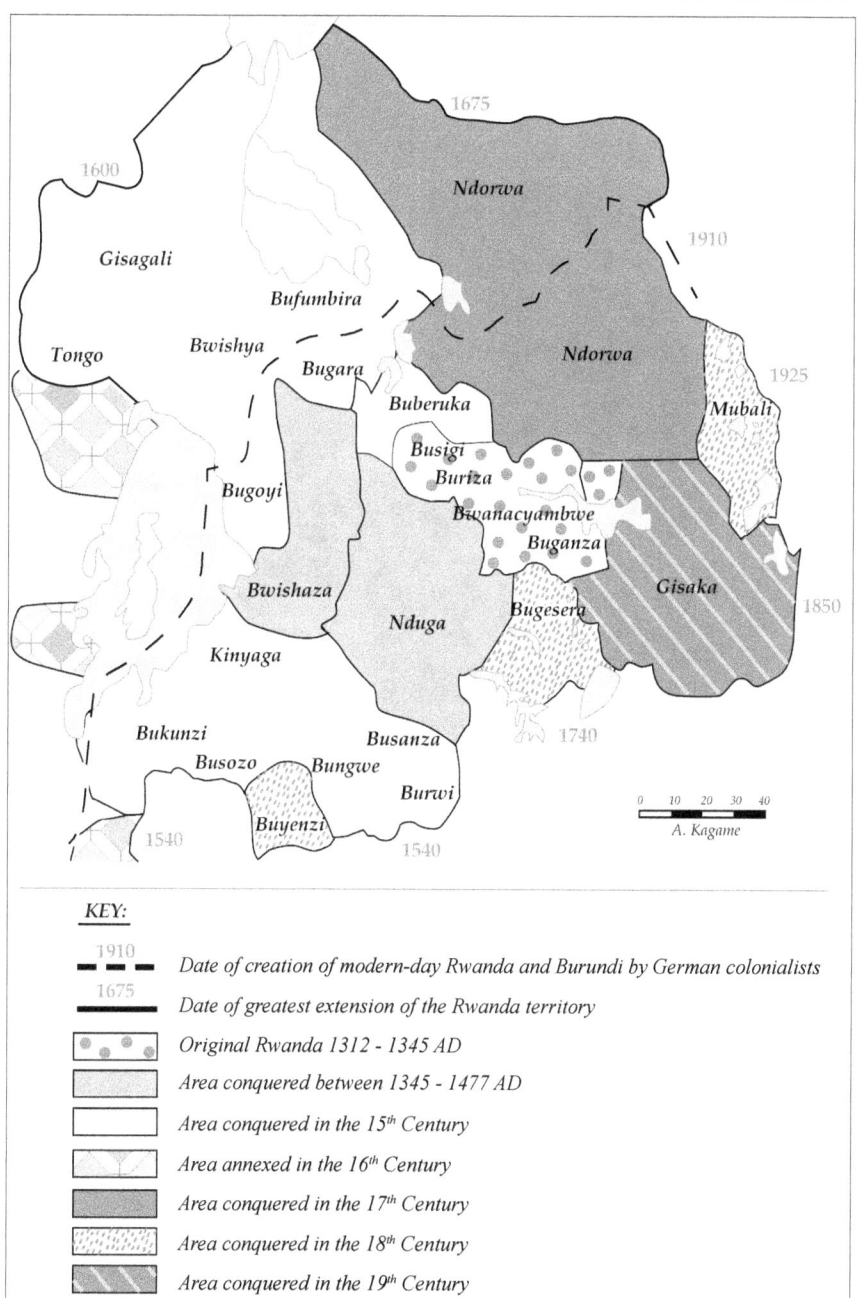

KEY:
- - - - Date of creation of modern-day Rwanda and Burundi by German colonialists
——— Date of greatest extension of the Rwanda territory
Original Rwanda 1312 - 1345 AD
Area conquered between 1345 - 1477 AD
Area conquered in the 15th Century
Area annexed in the 16th Century
Area conquered in the 17th Century
Area conquered in the 18th Century
Area conquered in the 19th Century

Map showing expansion of Rwanda

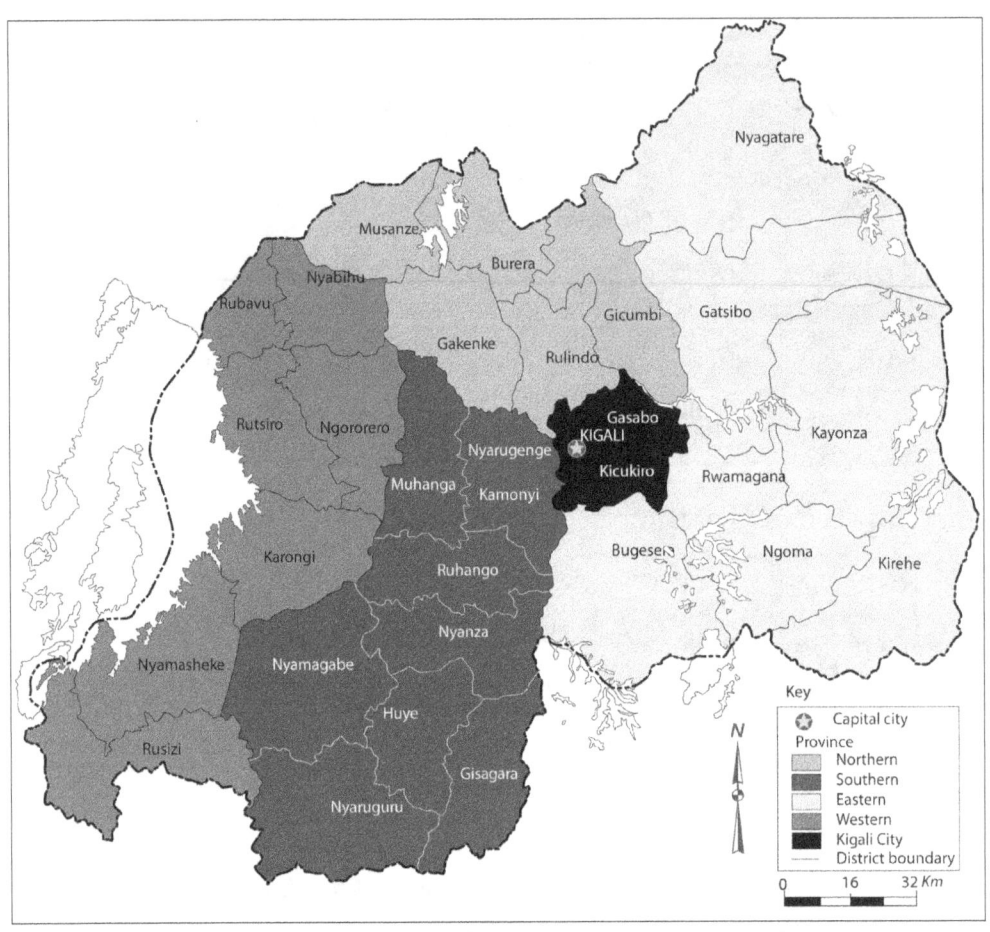

Administrative division map of present-day Rwanda

Part 1

Historical Background

1

Pre-colonial Period

After climbing a great hill one only finds that there are many more hills to climb.
Nelson Mandela

Origin of Rwanda

Like in most African societies, oral traditions present several myths about the origin of Rwandans. These myths tend to vary from one region to another even though they all seem to agree that the first ancestor of Rwandans — referred to by various names such as Kigwa, Shyerezo, Sebantu, etc. — dropped from the sky and is believed to have landed at a place known as Mubari (North-East Rwanda). There he is said to have found the Abasangwa-butaka clans: Abazigaba, Abagesera and Abacyaba.

A new narrative brought by Europeans at the turn of the 19th century would have it that three different races or ethnic groups came from different areas at different times. They were distinguished by their physique and occupation. These were: Abatwa who are supposed to have come first, followed by Abahutu from West Africa (Tchad) and Abatutsi, who came later grazing their herds of cattle from Abyssinia (Pagès, 2000; Sebasoni, 1933). The chronology of these migrations has, however, been questioned by new information that has emerged over time. Indeed many archaeological and anthropological documents show that groups that settled in the Great Lakes Region, including Rwanda, before AD were speakers of Bantu languages, central and eastern Sudanese languages, and Nilo-Saherian and Cushitic languages. All these groups progressively evolved mixed cultures, selecting the elements needed for a better life in this region. Those who settled in today's Rwanda formed territories which they later integrated to make up Rwanda (Chrétien, 2000; Kanimba, 2002).

Formation and Expansion of the Kingdom of Rwanda

The original country of Rwanda which is referred to as "the Rwanda of Gasabo" (*u Rwanda rwa Gasabo)* was composed of a small territorial entity located in the present district of Gasabo, in the valley of Nyabugogo along Lake Muhazi. When the period of historical kings (*abami b'ibitekerezo),* unfolded, Rwanda came under the reign of King Ruganzu Bwimba who became the first king, one among a series of historical kings who ruled from the 14th to the 20th centuries. These kings *(abami)* belonged to one of the clans called *Abanyiginya* (Kagame, 1943; Vansina, 2001).

According to tradition, the original Rwandan kingdom peacefully coexisted with neighbouring political entities with which she formed a «confederation» of sorts. At that time, these were small-sized entities which can be considered as chieftaincies referred to at that time as «countries» *(Ibihugu).* These chiefdoms were composed of *Buganza, Bwanacyambwe, Buriza, Busigi and Busarasi.* Rwanda first incorporated those neighbouring kingdoms, before extending its conquest to other clan-based chiefdoms. Later on the annexed territory included: Gisaka, Nduga, Bukunzi, Busozo, Bunyambiriri, Bwanamukari, Burwi, Bugoyi, Bufumbira, Mubali, Bugesera, Ndorwa, Bwishya, Busigi, Bufundu, Buyenzi, etc. (see map below).

The great expansion started from King Cyirima Rujugira to King Kigeli Rwabugiri. Cyirima Rujugira was the most powerful king in the 18th century. He introduced a lot of innovation in the administration and the army. To contain the threat from the neighbouring kingdom of Burundi, he created military units in charge of guarding the country's borders, particularly along the Akanyaru River, which marks the present boundary between Rwanda and Burundi. Some of the guarded borders included: Mututu (in Muyira), Gakoma (in Mayaga), Buhanga-Ndara (in Kirarambogo), Imvejuru (in Nyaruhengeri/Shyanda), Nyakare (in Kigembe), Bashumba (Nyakizu), and Nyaruguru. As for Muyaga, it was to defend the kingdom against invasion from Gisaka while other companies were stationed at Gakura and Rutare to defend the kingdom against invasion from Mubali or Ndorwa (Kagame, 1972; Muzungu, 2003).

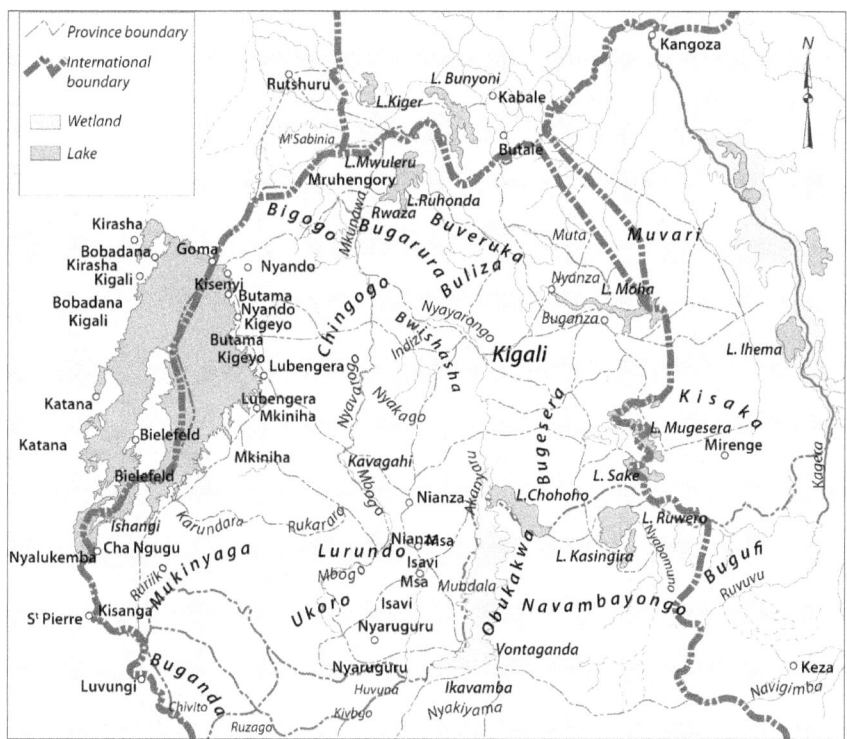

Boundaries of Colonial Rwanda

King Kigeli Rwabugiri is famous for a lot of military campaigns, particularly on Idjwi Island and in Bunyabungo (present-day Bushi in South Kivu, Democratic Republic of Congo-DRC). His other achievements include structuring and re-organising the administration, fighting people and groups opposing him and empowering royal leadership in areas recently conquered through standing army units to guard them. He also promoted diplomatic relationships with foreigners. He refused to have dealings with slave traders like Rumaliza (an agent of notorious slave trader Tip Tip) and refused him entry into Rwanda from Burundi through Bugarama. By contrast, he received, in 1894, Count Adolf Von Gotzen, a German officer with a force of approximately 700 men in Kageyo (present-day Ngorero district).

Socio-political Institutions

Many factors contributed to the expansion and development of the kingdom of Rwanda, notably the cultural institutions and the administrative structures. Rwanda's political system revolved around the king who ruled jointly with the queen-mother and the court. Several cultural institutions and practices reinforced one another to ensure the authority of the king permeated every level in Rwanda. Some of these institutions were: *Ubwiru* (institution for the management of the court), *Ingabo* (the army), *Ubuhake* (social contract based on cattle), *Ubusizi* (royal poetry and historiography), *Ubucurabwenge* (the royal genealogy), *Ibitekerezo by'Imiryango* (family historical narratives), etc. These cultural institutions inculcated among the people the spirit of patriotism.

The king lived inseparably in the company of the royal drum which was the symbol of authority. He was believed to enjoy divine attributes. The queen-mother was very powerful in court leadership and her power was equal to that of the king. She supervised royal civil servants, agricultural and livestock activities, was able to raise armies, and could even dispense wealth and power *(kugaba)*.

Surrounding the king and the queen-mother were several people playing various roles in the royal court. These included: dancers, blacksmiths, carpenters, religious leaders, poets, musicians, drummers, cooks, royal herdsmen, potters, etc.

In the northern parts of the country, the administration was in the hands of family or clan leaders, and they paid tribute to the court (*ikoro*) as evidence of allegiance to the king. Some other parts of the country also enjoyed administrative autonomy. They included parts administered by keepers of the esoteric code such as Bumbogo, and the small kingdoms of Bukunzi and Busozo. Clearly, the administration was not the same everywhere: but the king was the final reference.

National Army

The other important institution in the kingdom was the army (*Ingabo*). The organisation of army units changed over time and the most important change occurred during the reign of Cyirima Rujugira. The army recruited and trained youths sent to the royal court by their families. They defended the nation under attack or during military campaigns to conquer new territory. Every new king created new battalions from his age group/generation. During peace times, the army was involved in social activities.

Senior chiefs or military commanders were appointed by the king to administer parts of the country or the militarised zones. Starting with the reign of Yuhi Gahindiro, the day-to-day administration of Rwanda kingdom was vested in the hands of three leaders: the one in charge of farming (*umutware w'ubutaka*), another in charge of livestock (*umutware w'umukenke*) and another in charge of the army (*umutware w'ingabo*).

Exchange and Trade

Before the arrival of Europeans, barter trade or exchange of goods and services existed among families and in different regions in the country. The traded commodities included food, animals, braided-fibre, leg bracelets, copper bracelets, hoes, etc. Some of these commodities originated from countries neighbouring Rwanda (salt from Lake Katwe in Uganda, copper from Shaba, pearls from Butembo, hoes from Buvira in the DRC). Clothing from Karagwe was common during the reign of Yuhi Gahindiro and was widespread among chiefs during subsequent years. Commodities from Europe or Asia appeared during the reign of Yuhi Mazimhaka. This was the Rwanda on the eve of the colonial era.

Top: Mwami Kigeli IV Rwabugiri, the tireless conqueror of the 19th century whose 'sword name' was Inkotanyi-cyane — the name later adopted by the RPF

Bottom: Back row L-R: Rwidegembya, Kanuma, Kabare, Mwami Yuhi V Musinga, Nkwaya, Mushigati, Cyitatire and Nyagatana

Top: Mwami Musinga, centre, and Queen Mother receiving Major Declerck, then Resident of Rwanda, at the royal court.

Middle: The Royal couple - King Mutara III Rudahigwa and Queen Rosalie Gicanda

Bottom: Young men dressed in traditional dress

2

Rwanda under Colonial Rule

Historically, our people were living alongside one another, but outside forces manipulated these communal ties and provoked division, hatred and conflict.
President Paul Kagame

Rule for Exploitation

The first explorers (Speke, Stanley, Bauman, Von Gotzen) came to Rwanda in the search of the River Nile, which had been an obsession that went back many years. Secondly, they wanted to exploit opportunities to carry out commerce and evangelisation. The German colonialists came at the end of the nineteenth century and this marked the start of the disruption of Rwandan society that was to go on for a period of 60 years. This was later followed by Belgian colonialism, both of which thrived on the ideology of 'divide and rule'.

Although they were impressed by the social and political organisation that prevailed in Rwandan society, they were quick to introduce division amongst the Rwandan people based on the false assumption that the Batutsi were superior to the rest.

The so-called superiority of the Tutsi is the reason why they were chosen to be auxiliaries of the colonisers. For a long time, these false assumptions were propagated by Europeans and accepted by some of the Rwandan elites as a fact, despite their lack of scientific grounding.

German Rule: 1987-1916

Following the Berlin Conference (1884-1885), Rwanda was annexed to German East Africa. From the beginning of the Protectorate (1897), German rule was characterised by respect for the administration of Rwandan monarchs.

In 1907, Rwanda and Burundi were separated and each country had its own resident administrator. The first civilian Resident in Rwanda was Dr. Richard Kandt (called Kanayoge by Rwandans) and he established the colonial capital in Kigali in 1908.

The next big event was the Accord signed on 14 May 1910 that resolved the border issue which had fuelled conflicts among Germany, Belgium and Britain. In that settlement, Rwanda lost some of its territories, namely: Bufumbira, Bwishya, Gishari and Idjwi. King Musinga was not happy about that, but he had no choice. The Germans had helped him to fight a local rebellion.

The German administration had the following objectives: to support the Rwandan king and defend him in case of war, to help extend and strengthen Batutsi leadership, to support all the institutions created by the monarchy except those that were an obstacle to colonial rule, and to protect Christian missions (Catholic and Protestant).

Because of the short presence of Germans in Rwanda (19 years), a number of planned projects were never implemented, especially the railway project to link Tabora and Rusumo due to World War I (1914-1918). Nonetheless, some changes took place. Germany opened Rwanda to regional trade, linking it to the Indian Ocean, and created new markets close to administrative and trade centres. In general, Rwandans' outlook changed and their needs increased. Trade in hides and skins grew steadily.

It was also during this period that new religions came to Rwanda for the first time. Islam was the first to be introduced by Muslims accompanying explorers and German officers and later by Arab traders. It was limited to a few places and a few converts among Rwandans because of the discrimination from the Christian colonial rulers.

The next were the Missionaries of Africa (also known as White Fathers and founded by Cardinal Lavigerie in 1868) who arrived in Rwanda in February 1900, under the leadership of Bishop J. Hirth. By the start of the First World War, they had already founded over ten missions. The Protestants arrived in 1907. Christian missions became centres for the dissemination of the new ideas, values and behaviour brought in by Europeans.

Teachings by the missionaries were mostly informed by ways in which they negatively portrayed black people in general: as unintelligent, unable to reflect in a rational manner, naturally lazy, holding primitive beliefs, etc. Their immediate objective was to convert Batutsi leaders first for them to be able to convert the whole country to Christianity. They also wanted to replace the traditional beliefs, considered as pagan, by new cultural beliefs from Europe. Like the colonialists, the missionaries used a combination of force and persuasion in their effort to achieve their objectives.

Belgian Rule: 1916-1962

The First World War (October 1914 to May 1916 in Rwanda) brought about Belgian colonial rule, taking over from the Germans.

At the end of this war (1918), Rwanda was placed under Belgian trusteeship by the League of Nations. At the time, the country was in the midst of a severe famine (Rumanura 1916-1918), partly resulting from the war which had devastated a big part of the country.

Political and Administrative Reforms

Belgian administration from 1916 to 1924 was characterised by opposition to King Musinga's rule. Musinga was forced to give up his absolute power including his right as supreme judge and his right to appoint and dismiss administrative chiefs. Furthermore, the institution of *Ubwiru* and all the ceremonies associated with it at the royal court (including *umuganura* or celebration of first harvest) were abolished, as well as *itorero*, a mixed cultural and military training 'school' for the youth.

The monarchy as it had existed till then finally came to an end when Musinga was deposed in 1931 and deported to Kamembe (Rusizi District) and subsequently to Moba in the DRC. He was succeeded by his son Mutara III Rudahigwa, who governed according to the imposed Belgian administration.

The administrative reforms that were instituted between 1926 and 1933 had a big impact on the country's political and social life. Belgian administration changed the administrative structure: the traditional head of agriculture, the head of livestock, and the military commanders were removed and were replaced by chiefs and sub-chiefs. These new chiefs had gone to Catholic schools or Nyanza Government School. They had to be baptised in the Catholic Church or willing to do so and pay allegiance to the Belgian administration.

Under centralised Belgian administration, the new king effectively lost authority over his kingdom. The only role he had was to relay the message that Belgian orders had to be obeyed.

The Belgian administration divided Rwandans into three distinct groups: Abahutu, Abatutsi, and Abatwa. They used terms of race, castes, and tribes to classify these groups although traditionally, these were used to denote fluid socio-economic classes.

Socio-economic Reforms

Another feature of Belgian rule was harsh policies against Rwandans. This included forced labour *(akazi)*, statutory work *(uburetwa)* and heavy taxation. These compulsory activities attracted tough penalties, including imprisonment and flogging *(ikiboko)*, for those who did not perform them to the letter.

The ordinary citizens suffered a lot of harassment and ill-treatment at the hands of administrators. Thus, some level of animosity was created between the people and the chiefs appointed by the Belgian administration.

Some of the many consequences following forced labour included hard times caused by lack of food: famines known to Rwandans as Gakwege (1924-25), Rwakayihura (1928-29), and Ruzagayura (1943-45). Many Rwandans were forced to flee to Congo, Uganda and Tanzania, fearing the forced labour, taxes and punishment *(ikiboko)*.

All along, the Catholic Church collaborated and entrenched the above reforms. In consequence, the church enjoyed a privileged position in the appointment of chiefs and in running education institutions and used this to coerce Rwandan society to convert to the Catholic faith, starting with King Mutara III Rudahigwa.

Towards Independence

After World War II, the UN pressured the Belgian authorities to improve their policies in preparation for an autonomous and independent Rwanda. As a result, Belgium launched a ten-year development plan to improve the economy and the standard of life. In July 1952, councils were created at all levels up to the National High Council.

These councils, however, turned out to be consultative as most of their members were auxiliaries of the colonial administration. In 1955, King Mutara III Rudahigwa and the National High Council asked the Belgian Government to revise the law of 14 July 1952 to empower organs representing the population through free and direct elections. The aim was to give Rwandans a greater role in the affairs of their country. No substantial feedback was given. Instead, the Belgian administration suspected that the king and some of the chiefs wanted to get rid of the Belgian rule and regain national independence.

Subsequently, Rwandans addressed their petitions directly to the UN, denouncing the harsh treatment at the hands of the Belgian administration and reiterating their desire for independence.

In 1957, the National High Council issued the document - *Mise au point* - asking the Belgian administration to include Rwandans in the management of their country. The Belgian administration reacted negatively to the document. Another document - *Le Manifeste des Bahutu* - was also issued to the Belgian Government by a group of Bahutu intellectuals asserting that they were the spokespersons of all Bahutu. This one asserted that independence and emancipation from Belgium was not the problem. For them, the immediate problem was the emancipation of the Bahutu from perceived Batutsi oppression.

From then on, the Hutu/Tutsi issue came to the fore, overshadowing the debate on all other problems facing Rwandans. For example, André Perraudin, the Bishop of Kabgayi, authored a document asserting that the conflict between the 'racial groups' was the real problem facing the nation. By contrast, Aloys Bigirumwami, the Bishop of Nyundo, asserted that social, economic and political problems were the central issue. Because of the decision by Catholic missionaries and Belgian rulers to support the Bahutu elites, the social analysis which would have been more appropriate to understand the local realities was put aside in favour of the "racialist" approach. Thus the Belgian policy of divide and rule became further entrenched.

As fate would have it, while Rwandan elites were on the verge of conflict, King Mutara III Rudahigwa died on 25 July 1959 in Bujumbura, Burundi. This unexpected death had an adverse effect on the events that followed. These included the immediate enthronement of Jean Baptiste Ndahindurwa, as Kigeli V, against the wishes of the Belgian authorities. The political party, Union Nationale Rwandaise (UNAR), emerged and claimed immediate independence. In reaction, the Belgians supported the formation of two political parties: Parti du Mouvement de l'Emancipation Hutu (Parmehutu) and Association pour la Promotion Sociale de la Masse (Aprosoma).

The colonial administration, especially under Colonel Guy Logiest, Special Resident of Rwanda, supported the Parmehutu leaders. What followed were widespread killings of the Batutsi in 1959 which were manipulated to serve political interests. Logiest claimed that the killings were instigated by UNAR and that he would fight them. Then, he proceeded to remove the Batutsi chiefs and sub-chiefs and replaced them with the Bahutu from the Parmehutu and Aprosoma parties. These violent activities were the first pogroms against the Batutsi, which Logiest and Parmehutu called a revolution. The other outcome of this violence was the flight of a large number of Rwandans into exile in neighbouring countries.

Elections were then hurriedly conducted at the Commune (1960) and Parliament (1961) levels. Logiest declared Parmehutu Party the winners. These elections took place while the Batutsi were being massacred. It is under these conditions of violence and social crisis that Rwanda's independence was granted by the colonisers on 1 July 1962 and the Parmehutu party acceded to power.

Independence ushered in many changes. The country got new leaders and new institutions came into existence. However, the period also set off a new set of challenges, some of which persisted for many years and characterised the turbulent post-independence history of Rwanda. Some of these problems included the continued massive displacement of people inside the country, and thousands of others being forced to become refugees in other countries. A campaign of hate among Rwandans, and the impunity of killing people on the basis of ethnicity, became widespread.

3

Post-colonial Rwanda

Rwandans learned their sense of self-worth from being deprived of it for so long.
President Paul Kagame

First Republic: 1962-1973

Rwanda became independent without a proper Constitution. The Constitution of 28 January 1961, cobbled together by the Parmehutu Party in Gitarama and with the help of Colonel Logiest, was never respected. This, it will be recalled, was after the King had been removed and a Republic declared. It is later, on 24 November 1962, that the constitution was adopted after being approved by 40 Members of the first Parliament (Reyntjens, 1985).

This constitution emphasised that the monarchy was a bygone institution and that it had been replaced by a Republican constitution. It also made it clear that it supported Christian values (the Catholic Church particularly) because it outlawed polygamy and the propagation of a communist ideology. This constitution vested in the President of the Republic so much power that legal scholars equated President Grégoire Kayibanda's rule with that of a monarch's.

The judiciary did not play its role for fear of coming into conflict with the President of the Republic. This was in spite of the freedom the judges had been entrusted with by the law. The fear of using this freedom gave the President of the Republic unlimited power to modify the law according to his own will.

The First Republic went through eight governments. The first government (1962-1963) was the only one that included all the major political parties. The 1962 Constitution, Article 10, gave Rwandans the right to create political parties. By 1963, Mouvement Démocratique Républicain -Parmehutu (MDR) had taken exclusive control of all leadership positions in the country. This fact was confirmed by the election of President Kayibanda in 1965 when he won by 98%. This overwhelming victory was repeated in 1969. For Parmehutu leaders to achieve this supremacy, they persecuted all the other political parties, undermining them (Aprosoma) or killing their leaders as in the case of UNAR and Rassemblement Démocratique Rwandais (RADER). This happened following the December 1963 attack in Bugesera by a group of Batutsi refugees called *Inyenzi,* from neighbouring countries.

The attacks by Inyenzi, composed of mainly young refugees unwilling to remain in exile, started in 1961. Their objectives were to fight Belgian authorities and Parmehutu leaders. These attacks were of various kinds: commando attacks with a few people, guerrilla attacks which targeted the borders, especially in Byumba Province, and major attacks, like the ones in Birunga (July 1962), Bugesera (December 1963), Bugarama (1964) and Bweyeye (1966).

The Inyenzi infiltrations gave Kayibanda's government a pretext, in his propaganda, to define the Batutsi as the 'enemy' within and outside the country. The government used the excuse to persecute and kill the Batutsi inside Rwanda, displace some of them within Rwanda and force others to flee the country. The massacres that followed the Bugesera attack in 1963-64 led some eyewitnesses to call them genocide (Lemarchand, 1970). To date, no one responsible for these killings has ever been punished for these crimes.

By 1967, Inyenzi attacks had come to an end. Their defeat was due to various factors including: lack of unified leadership and clear political ideology, and lack of a unified military command.

The ruling Parmehutu Party failed to offer all Rwandans better living conditions because it had never planned to do so. Its ideology was fundamentally exclusive and discriminatory. As a result, only very few of the Bahutu it purported to work for really developed economically. The absence of a sound political programme was obvious, particularly after the Inyenzi scapegoat was over. Conflicts within the party arose as time went by. The 1964 National Assembly Report brought to public knowledge the conflict within Parmehutu, saying that injustice was rampant in the country. A commission that was set up in 1966 to settle internal problems in the party was not successful. Instead, it brought to the surface deep-seated intrigue among party leaders, besides regional conflicts.

In 1968, another report by the National Assembly re-examined the acute problems facing Parmehutu. Subsequently, some members of the party resigned in protest against the rampant social injustices (Mugesera, 2004).

As Parmehutu was being ripped apart by conflicts, its leadership base was narrowing to a group of a few people from the same province, Gitarama. This group planned and implemented the 1973 massacres of the Batutsi, as well as their expulsion from secondary and higher institutions of education and from public and private jobs. They falsely argued that there were too many Batutsi in these positions, and that they had taken positions which by right should go to the majority - the Bahutu.

One of the causes of the renewed persecution of the Batutsi by Kayibanda was his failed attempt to engineer the overthrow of the Burundi Batutsi military regime, using the few Bahutu who were in the army.

In addition, Kayibanda's regime was weakened by internal dissent within Parmehutu and he had failed to unite the Bahutu as he had done in 1959. He hoped that by massacring the Batutsi he would strengthen his party and restore its cohesion.

It is during this period that he revised the constitution to make himself a life president. The army commander, Juvenal Habyarimana, and his ten military companions opposed this attempt and overthrew him on 5 July 1973.

Second Republic: 1973-1994

In their announcement, the officers who had removed Kayibanda's government accused its members of being tired and also a threat to the population's peace and security. They banned all Parmehutu organs, all political activities and repealed the constitution. All but three members of the military Committee for Peace and National Unity came from Ruhengeri and Gisenyi provinces.

Inspired by the Mouvement Populaire de la Revolution (MPR) party of President Joseph Desire Mobutu of Zaire (DRC), J. Habyarimana founded the Mouvement Revolutionnaire Nationale pour le Developpement (MRND), one single party which was supposed to include all Rwandans. The party and the government were essentially one, and the Party chairman who was also the President of the Republic, usurped all powers of the state: he was Prime Minister, the Supreme Army Commander, the Minister of Defence, Chairman of the High Commission of Magistrates and the Chairman of the Constitutional Court (Nkunzumwami, 1996).

The MRND became a vehicle for its leaders to control and manipulate Rwandans. Its policy on the allocation of jobs and development projects, and admission into schools, was based on ethnic and regional quotas, despite the fact that no population census had been carried out. This policy of discrimination had been initiated by Kayibanda. Habyarimana perfected it to suit his agenda, giving it more force, to the extent that it affected more people.

Throughout this entire period, no government — be it Kayibanda's or Habyarimana's — ever tried to address the political problems engendered by the genocidal violence of 1959. They maintained the divisive ideology underlying these events. The main preoccupation of leaders of both republics was the property left behind by refugees which they shared among themselves, especially land. A law was enacted preventing returning refugees from ever claiming any of the property they had left behind (Mugesera, 2004).

This was coupled with regulations that were put in place to deter refugees wishing to return home. The wish constantly expressed in various documents by leaders in the Second Republic was for refugees to stay where they were in exile and settle there as Rwanda was too small and overpopulated to accommodate them (Mugesera, 2004). For them, refugees were enemies of the nation and they were not accepted as Rwandans. This was one of the unresolved problems that eventually triggered the liberation war.

Top: Grégoire Kayibanda (R), first President of independent Rwanda with Bishop André Perraudin of the Catholic Church (L)

Middle: Juvenal Habyarimana, second President of independent Rwanda

Bottom: President Julius Nyerere of Tanzania chatting with President Jean-Baptiste Bagaza of Burundi. Looking on is President Habyarimana, 1984

Part 2
Liberation Struggle

4

Liberation Struggle

When we have African problems, we ourselves have a duty to solve our problems.
Mwalimu Julius Nyerere

Precursor to the Rwanda Patriotic Front (RPF)

By 1968, the last training camp for Inyenzi had closed in the Rwenzori Mountains in Western Uganda. The initial Inyenzi groups were in total disarray, to the extent that their leaders were no longer on talking terms. Worse still, they started betraying each other to the host authorities, who, naturally, were worried about their own relations with the Rwandan Government.

On the ground in refugee camps, the youth were increasingly being blocked from schools and employment, mostly in Uganda and Burundi. Earlier, skilled refugees in these countries had had access to employment but that became increasingly difficult as more and more of the host nationals completed training and acquired education. This was to be expected but the refugees, desperate as they were, could only see it as rejection and this was hard to take, particularly in Burundi where the Batutsi refugees considered themselves kin and kith of the Burundi ruling class.

Young refugees started moving around the region looking for better opportunities in education and employment. Some went abroad, mainly to Europe, USA and Canada. Problems of appropriate or choice employment hit professionals as well and this provoked debates about possible solutions. Groups started to form around the themes of return and self-help. Among the institutions set up as vehicles to address the challenges of education were the Rwandese Refugees Welfare Foundation (RRWF) in Uganda and College Saint Albert in Bukavu and Bujumbura. Later the institutions were to become the hotbeds of "return" politics, and they provided a large number of cadres for the Rwandese Alliance for National Unity (RANU) and the Rwanda Patriotic Front (RPF).

A minority of cadres advanced the notion that Rwandan refugees should renounce their right to return to Rwanda and seek citizenship of their host countries, or be recognised by Rwanda as citizens and get Rwandan passports to enable them continue living abroad. This view was hotly and inconclusively debated at the Washington meeting in 1988 and in other fora. On the other hand, and throughout the long exile, the King of Rwanda, Kigeli V Ndahindurwa, kept promising the older people that he would take his people back home to Rwanda some day.

By 1979, it was clear to the first generation of educated refugees who had witnessed struggles in Africa, such as the liberation wars in Southern Africa, Eritrea and Ethiopia, that there was no magic formula for a solution to their country's problems. Consequently, social and cultural associations mushroomed and became strong tools for mobilising and raising the consciousness of refugees about their plight.

It was in this context that a Rwandan refugee group at an initial meeting held at Lenana School in Nairobi in June 1979 resolved to organise themselves into a political movement. This is how RANU, a precursor political organisation to the RPF, was born.

The decision to form the political organisation was reached after long soul-searching among themselves and with many other Rwandans, both in Kenya and beyond, as to what constituted the fundamental problem that faced Rwanda as a nation.

It was agreed that although the Rwandan refugee problem was a serious one, it would never be resolved in isolation from the decades-old fundamental problems of governance that the country faced. It was a political problem that had to be put in its real historical perspective.

It was also agreed at the outset that the endemic Rwandan refugee problem, like many other symptoms of the anti-people politics in Rwanda, would only be solved by Rwandans themselves, united under a progressive organisation that sought to rally all Rwandan nationals around a common national vision, irrespective of their "ethnic" backgrounds and other divisions characteristic of the colonial legacy of Rwanda.

The successful liberation of Uganda by the National Resistance Army (NRA) in 1986 was of particular importance not only for RANU members but for most Rwandans as well. The sheer numbers of Rwandans in the ranks of NRA and their role in liberating Uganda was a source of pride and renewed hope. Nevertheless, challenges lingered within the Rwandan exiled communities linked to their past experience and condition.

Many Rwandan refugees had lost hope and were reluctant to join any political organisation due to past failures of the early attempts to regain the country, spearheaded by Inyenzi. Because of solidarity among the newly independent African states and international laws governing the hosting of refugees, no regime in the region would tolerate any Rwandan liberation movement on its territory.

Besides, the ever suspicious Juvenal Habyarimana regime was aware that the young refugees were mobilising. President Habyarimana often countered this in public fora by attempting to convince the world that Rwanda was too small to allow refugees to return and that for all intents and purposes, children of refugees born outside Rwanda could not be his responsibility. It was therefore necessary to keep RANU activities covert to avoid detection and ensure the survival of the movement.

Transition from RANU to RPF

In December 1987, during the 4th RANU Congress, the participants decided to change, not only its name to the Rwanda Patriotic Front/Inkotanyi (RPF-Inkotanyi) but its philosophy as well. The transformation of RANU to RPF with its Eight Point-political Programme and the establishment of the military wing – Rwanda Patriotic Army (RPA) – in Mbuya, Kampala, was a significant leap in the history of the Rwandan liberation movement with a protracted people's war of liberation as its strategy.

The RPF's struggle and political programme were based on the following principles:
- Re-establishing national unity as a foundation for building peace and development in Rwanda;
- Putting an end to segregation and abuse of human rights among Rwandans;

- Giving the people the right to choose their leaders as a basis for true democracy and development;
- Committing to the resolution of Rwanda's political and economic problems.

The Eight-point Political Programme was based on these principles. Later a ninth point dealing with the genocide ideology was added. Below are the nine points:

- Restoration of unity among Rwandans;
- Defending the sovereignty of the country and ensuring the security of the people and their property;
- Establishing democratic leadership;
- Promoting an economy based on the country's resources;
- Elimination of corruption, favouritism and embezzlement;
- Promoting social welfare;
- Eliminating all reasons for fleeing the country and enabling the return of Rwandan refugees;
- Promoting international relations based on mutual respect, cooperation and mutual economic exchange.
- Preventing Genocide and its ideology.

As noted earlier, Rwandans participated in the liberation struggle of Uganda from 1978. This experience would later be of great value to their own liberation struggle. The interaction with Ugandan liberators and the presence of some Rwandan patriots within the high ranks of the Ugandan liberators, notably Fred Rwigema and Charles Musitu, was not only encouraging but it was also positively exploited.

The National Resistance Movement, under Yoweri Museveni, included in its leadership Rwigema and Paul Kagame. These two played a crucial role in the leadership of RPF and the liberation of Rwanda. Several other groups of Rwandans joined them on their own, especially after the 1982 expulsion of Rwandan refugees and Ugandans of Rwandan origin from Uganda by the Obote regime.

Soon it became clear that the affairs of the RPF would have to be entrusted to the most experienced military cadre, Rwigema, who was given powers to restructure the RPF and to re-organise the leadership. When on 2 October 1990 Major General Rwigema was mortally wounded in battle, the leadership had to be re-organised.

5

RPF Military Struggle

During the liberation struggle we were strengthened by the validity of our cause. The prize was freedom and respect for our rights.
President Paul Kagame

Rationale for the struggle

As stated in the previous chapter, the top leadership of the RPF, in particular Fred Rwigema and Paul Kagame, used their positions in the NRA to mobilise cadres and recruit soldiers in preparation for the liberation struggle. This helped them to acquire the much needed military training and combat experience.

The statelessness for decades of close to one million Rwandans in the region and abroad was simply compelling enough to make mobilisation for the war effort easy in the region and beyond. This situation was compounded by the recurrent expulsions and persecution of the Batutsi, denial of access to higher education, lack of employment opportunities, as well as the 1982 denial of fundamental human rights and many other forms of injustice.

As persecution against the Batutsi inside the country escalated, victims fled to join their already exiled families. Waves of new refugees were reconnecting with their families and the RPF, keenly aware of this background, had to develop an ideology which focused on transformation of the social, economic and political order in Rwanda rather than focusing solely on the refugee problem. This ideology guided the RPF struggle, its subsequent negotiations with the government of Rwanda, and its eventual programme when it came to power in 1994.

Why Option Z?

From its inception, the RPF was committed to the resolution of Rwanda's problems through political and peaceful means. However, it was also conscious of the futility of liberating the country through political means alone. In the first place, the Kayibanda and Habyarimana regimes were viciously opposed to any opponents. That is why it was decided to keep military confrontation as an option and prepare for it, albeit as a last resort, hence the name 'Option Z'.

Rwanda, under Habyarimana and the MRND, was a military dictatorship, with a president who controlled both the military and the party, disregarding numerous calls from inside and outside the country demanding political reforms, especially to allow other parties to exist in the country.

There was, in addition, a host of restless refugees in very unstable and increasingly hostile neighbouring countries. The regime, however, was unresponsive to all these signs of its own fragility.

In 1982, for example, when the government of Uganda, under President Milton Obote, expelled Rwandan refugees, the government of Rwanda denied responsibility for them and chased them back, claiming there was no space for them in Rwanda. When four years later (1986), after the victory of the NRM in Uganda, President Museveni contacted President Habyarimana on the question of Banyarwanda refugees in Uganda, the latter replied cynically that Rwanda was like a glass full of water to which one could not add a drop.

Rwandans in Uganda and other countries were declared economic refugees who should remain wherever they were making their living, and were not to dream of returning to Rwanda. These declarations and many others were made at the time Habyarimana and his government had sensed that something was afoot but never expected it to be serious. They had not felt the extent of discontent among Rwandans both inside and outside the country. Just like Parmehutu felt they had vanquished political opponents and Inyenzi in 1963, Habyarimana and the MRND felt comfortable after liquidating the Parmehutu leadership in the 1973 coup.

At the same time, the military within Rwanda became restive and as allegations of treason and coup plots became frequent, officers like Colonel Alexis Kanyarengwe, who later became the RPF Chairman, fled into exile in 1980 and the Intelligence Chief, Major Theoneste Lizinde, and others were in the same year thrown behind bars, later to be rescued by the RPF from the Ruhengeri maximum prison. Even Colonel Mayuya, who commanded the Kanombe elite military base and who was reputedly close to Habyarimana, was murdered in 1988.

Sections of the population began to publicly denounce and clamour for more rights and democracy. Students abroad were also organising themselves to challenge the Habyarimana regime, including those on government scholarships in Europe and Canada, such as the Association Générale des Etudiants Rwandais (AGER) in Europe and ARG in Burundi. They organised discussions and weekend meetings and wrote newspaper articles that were very critical of the Habyarimana regime. The refugees had also taken an open stand rejecting their continued exile and the indifference of the Rwanda government and the international community to their plight.

Even President Francois Mitterrand of France, at a summit with African heads of state and government in June 1990, called on African countries to heed what was happening in Eastern Europe, meaning the breakdown of the Soviet Union and Yugoslavia, ushering in a change from dictatorship to democratic rule. The message was that there cannot be development without democracy, and no democracy without development. While other countries under the control of military regimes attempted to find a way out through 'Les Conferences Nationales', Habyarimana was happy to lead a protest at La Baule, rejecting the proposed reforms. Surprisingly, President Mitterrand never followed up Habyarimana on possible repatriation of Rwandan refugees.

All the above mentioned signs and developments made Option Z inevitable for the RPF. It offered the requisite leadership to the voices of dissent and spearheaded the liberation of Rwanda.

Launch of the Liberation Struggle

As soon as the RPF was formed in 1987, recruitment into RPF from all over the region mainly from Uganda, Kenya, Burundi, the then Zaire, Tanzania and to a small extent from Rwanda itself, intensified. In Rwanda, special attention was paid to the recruitment of members, intelligence gatherers, guides and listening posts along the border points. It was clear at this point in time that the RPF was preparing for Option Z.

Members had a lot of confidence in seasoned commanders like Rwigema and Kagame who had not only formidable experience from other armed liberation movements, but had also demonstrated excellent leadership in the RPF with unprecedented revolutionary discipline. Rigorous structural changes were set up and clandestine methods of work in most regions were instituted especially in Uganda, where most military activities were taking place. Clandestine RPF political schools sprang up from early 1986 and cadres began working full time for the RPF, particularly devoting their time to political mobilisation and development of cadreship throughout Eastern African countries, Burundi, Rwanda, the Democratic Republic of Congo, and Belgium.

The Rwandan officers who held responsible positions in the NRA started mapping out where the RPA officers and men were located in NRA units and preparing for withdrawal to attack Rwanda. Crucial military equipment and materials were gathered and stored in strategic locations close to the Rwandan border.

On the night of 30 September 1990, RPA troops withdrew from all NRA units across the country and assembled near Kagitumba, where on 1 October 1990, they launched the first attack.

This launch of the war triggered a lot of diplomatic activity. The RPF leadership and cadres unleashed a widespread diplomatic offensive while concurrently mobilising all Rwandans in exile to support the war effort with much needed logistics. At the same time, able-bodied men and women including doctors, nurses and other medics joined the war effort. This opened the way for all Rwandans to be part of their own liberation.

Reactions from Various Actors

Rwandans in Exile and Inside Rwanda

There was excitement among Rwandans both inside and outside Rwanda. The prospect of joining the RPF liberation struggle was heightened as the war progressed. Mobilisation to support the war effort was deepened in the region and abroad and recruitment into the RPA intensified. A lot of money, medicine, food and clothing were mobilised on a continuous basis in support of the war.

However, inside Rwanda, there were mixed reactions. Some people, mainly sympathisers of the RPF, who had been taken as second class citizens, felt the time had come for their rescue, and joined the struggle through different neighbouring countries. Others were worried about the reaction of the Habyarimana regime. As for the regime extremists, this was a time to rally behind their own government, which they claimed was under attack by foreigners, not Rwandans. For example, the regime feigned an attack on Kigali to create a pretext for hunting down RPA infiltrators in and around Kigali, and shortly afterwards in many other parts of the country.

Government of Rwanda and her Allies

After the launch of the armed struggle on 1 October 1990, Habyarimana maintained that he had been invaded by neighbouring Anglophone Uganda and mobilised his closest allies to come to assist him militarily and diplomatically. Consequently, France, Belgium and the then Zaire (now DR Congo) under Mobutu Sese Seko sent in troops. On 4 October 1990, the French military was the first to intervene alongside Habyarimana's troops under the pretext of protecting French nationals in Rwanda. Between 200 and 300 French troops were deployed against the RPA in what they called "Operation Naroit".

However, this did not deter the capture of Nyagatare town by RPA's 9th battalion. On the following day, 5 October 1990, around 535 soldiers from Belgium with additional troops from DR Congo were sent in and fought alongside the FAR in Mutara. They were humiliated by the RPA in three battles for Gabiro and went back with most of their soldiers dead or injured, leaving to the RPA all their military equipment and other military supplies. RPA's 4th battalion captured Gabiro military barracks during the battles of 6 and 7 October 1990.

The Belgian troops were withdrawn by 1 November in response to domestic political pressure that was also partly due to the RPF's diplomatic success.

However, the French maintained their troops under the pretext of protecting their citizens. Their role was purportedly to prevent the capture of the airport but in actual fact they were directly assisting the regime, supplying plenty of arms and ammunition and manning roadblocks, giving a hand to those who were committing massacres against the Batutsi.

Immediately after the attack, security forces rounded up alleged collaborators of the RPF, particularly in Kigali. In an apparently pre-planned action, on 4 and 5 October, 10,000 of them were lined up in Nyamirambo Stadium. Most were tortured and imprisoned without trial as collaborators of the RPF while others were killed by government agents.

A desperate Habyarimana decided to send a Batutsi delegation to Nairobi in December 1990, consisting of Fr Mahame, a Catholic Jesuit Priest, Mr Shamukiga, an owner of a construction company and Mr Maharagari, who was a banker. Their mission was to talk to some elders whom they suspected to be the natural leaders of the RPF. Michel Kayihura and others directed them to the RPF office in Brussels where a small delegation was meeting, and the stated purpose of the visit was to persuade the RPF to stop the war so that the northern trade routes through Gatuna and Kagitumba could open. The reason Habyarimana gave was that the Rwandan people were starving, and there was a veiled threat that the Batutsi inside the country would face the consequences.

For Habyarimana, the war was a Bahutu/Batutsi war and the Batutsi inside the country were hostages. This was emphasised by Paul Dijoud, a director in the French Foreign Affairs Ministry to Kagame who had led an RPF delegation to France. The warning was: "If you do not stop the war, all your people will be finished by the time you win."

During the same period, the Rwanda government sent a delegation to meet the OAU Secretary General, Dr Salim Ahmed Salim, in December 1990 to request that he contact the RPF and propose indirect negotiations because there was no way the government would sit face-to-face to negotiate with foreigners.

Throughout the war, President Habyarimana maintained that the refugees were no longer Rwandans, and that RPF members, in particular, were Ugandans. The RPF delegation assured the OAU Secretary General that they would cooperate with him and that the government of Rwanda's objection to meeting RPF was unfortunate.

Reactions from the Region

The heads of state of the region, Presidents Ali Hassan Mwinyi (Tanzania); Yoweri K. Museveni (Uganda); Pierre Buyoya (Burundi); Mobutu Sese Seko (Zaire); and Juvenal Habyarimana (Rwanda) met in Dar-es-Salaam on 19

February 1991, and mandated Mobutu Sese Seko, to "take immediate and urgent measures" likely to start a dialogue leading to a ceasefire between the GoR and RPF. Following this, President Mobutu Sese Seko organised several meetings in Zaire, in Gbadolite, Goma, and finally N'sele, which led to the N'sele Ceasefire Agreement (29 March 1991).

Even at that point, the GoR delegation objected to direct talks until Mobutu informed them that this was unacceptable after he lost a Colonel of his army, the FAZ (Forces Armées Zairoises), during the fighting in Rwanda.

Military Operations and Diplomacy

On the second day of the war, RPA lost its overall commander and chairman of RPF, Major General Fred Rwigema, in action. A few days later, operation commander Major Chris Bunyenyezi as well as Major Peter Bayingana and others were killed. These tragedies had several effects, including loss of command and control, leading to subsequent disorganisation on the part of the RPA. The Habyarimana government falsely thought it had won the war and began celebrating. The RPF cadres became apprehensive, thinking the RPA was crippled.

It did not take long, however, for Major Kagame to arrive in the morning of 15 October 1990 from the USA, where he had gone for a military course. He reorganised the forces, instilling morale and discipline. His approach was to change the fighting strategy of RPA, moving away from conventional warfare and using more of guerrilla warfare. He moved the fighters from the plains to the highlands. As a result, on 3 January 1991, the RPA captured Gatuna border post and Kaniga Hills as well as Murindi and the surrounding hills in a total demonstration of strength at the very time the Habyarimana government was celebrating the obliteration of the rebellion.

The forces continued to manoeuvre inside and along the Rwanda-Uganda border in the volcanic mountains, specifically in Gahinga. From here, an attack on the key northwest town of Ruhengeri, in present-day Musanze, was launched on 23 January 1991 and prisoners were released, most of whom joined the RPA at their tactical headquarters in Gahinga.

The RPA started carrying out very successful operations against the FAR, which essentially lost all subsequent battles. As a result, the morale of the

RPF cadres was high, and many men and women were recruited into its ranks. It did not take long for the RPA to re-take Mutara region and Byumba.

In the meantime, the Rwanda Forces (FAR) were boosted by French aviation and artillery, and Zaire's motorised infantry and tried to push back the RPA, but in vain. The GoR had thought it had an upper hand in the war but realised this wasn't the case and was forced to abandon its intransigence because the military pressure worried the region and the international community, including the OAU and the UN. The January attack on Ruhengeri confirmed to the world that the RPF had not been defeated, despite major setbacks at the beginning.

This realisation led to the Dar-es-Salaam regional summit, to which the RPF was not invited. It should, however, be emphasised that the RPF never sought recognition in the tradition of liberation movements, insisting instead on being accepted as an unavoidable partner in seeking a resolution to the Rwanda crisis. It is on this basis that the RPF encouraged Mobutu to take on the role of mediator, which partly made him withdraw his forces from the war theatre in Rwanda.

The GoR signed and broke the N'sele Ceasefire almost immediately. Its forces, after signing the N'sele Ceasefire Agreement, declared that there were no enemy forces left on its soil, claiming that the RPF was a Ugandan Army which had been defeated by the *Inzirabwoba* (the fearless) national army. The GoR intensified the harassment of the suspected collaborators of the RPF, mainly the Batutsi in Kigali and other towns. Government forces proceeded to attack RPA positions in the mountains by helicopter and artillery. All this was in violation of the terms of the N'sele Ceasefire Agreement.

The RPF response was swift and emphatic. In less than three months, it led an offensive against the government forces and extended its front from the Volcanic Mountains to the Mutara area, regaining all lost ground in the northeast and the entire northern frontier. With an increasingly restive population within government-controlled areas, the RPF simultaneously undertook limited repatriation of refugees returning from Uganda while securing the Internally Displaced Persons (IDPs) within its controlled areas.

Having accepted the GoR hypothesis that the RPA forces were firstly, Ugandans and secondly, not on Rwandan territory, the UN proposed a UN patrol mission along the Uganda-Rwanda border, dubbed the United

Nations Observer Mission Uganda-Rwanda (UNOMUR). To everyone's surprise this did not elicit any protest from the RPF or disrupt any of its operations. The UN accepted to deploy a buffer force along the border to prevent the RPA infiltrating fighters, armament, and provisions into Rwandan territory from Uganda.

In the meantime, the RPF approached Rwanda's Western partners explaining to them that they should not ignore the democratisation agenda for Rwanda which was one of the key demands of Rwandans. The Habyarimana regime succumbed to both military and diplomatic pressure and the Constitution was amended in June 1991 to allow a multi-party dispensation.

The result was devastating for the regime but it won RPF lasting political partners. Habyarimana's rule, like that of his predecessor Kayibanda, was premised on the false claim of being representative of the Bahutu majority, and a one-party state was the ultimate expression of this 'ethnic political oneness'. When the Constitution was amended, over eight political parties were formed within the first month, including the MDR-Parmehutu, returning as MDR, the party Kayibanda founded in 1957.

For the RPF, this was a political victory since they had been building pressure for the change, which created political space for others and themselves. Thus the RPF was vindicated in its argument that politics in Rwanda should move away from divisive ideologies. Those who set up and or joined the new parties came out of MRND, and were able to vent their frustration against the MRND one-party stint in power.

The fast moving events in the political arena and persistent military pressure by the RPA pushed the regime further to the brink. Subsequent battles, like in Byumba, the creation of the demilitarised zone, and finally the battle to stop genocide all brought about positive change. In the process, the regime lost all the military, diplomatic, and political battles.

Blocking and Delaying Tactics

The opening up of the political space forced the Habyarimana regime to attempt to woo back the dispersed Bahutu forces. He was forced to form a coalition with the MDR-Parmehutu whose leaders he had murdered, the Social Democratic Party (PSD), the Liberal Party (PL) and the Christian

Democratic Party (PDC). The government would be coordinated by a Prime Minister nominated by MDR, but who needed the approval and support of the President.

In the period between 1991 and 1994, Rwanda had three prime ministers, Sylvester Nsanzimana (12 October 1991 to 2 April 1992), Dr Dismas Nsengiyaremye (2 April 1992 to 18 July 1993), and Agathe Uwilingiyimana (18 July 1993 to 7 April 1994). This frequent removal or rejection of prime ministers was used to destabilise the arch-enemy of the MRND, which was the MDR.

According to the National Human Rights Commission, this period was also used by MRND to prepare for genocide. MRND had a congress on 28 April 1991 at which Habyarimana talked of a final solution to the Batutsi question, after which the hate literature flared up. The Prime Minister was removed and MDR went through another divisive search for a replacement (see Genocide Chronology).

In the meantime, recruitment of *Interahamwe* (those who work together) began in the six Communes of Byumba (Kinyami, Rushaki, Muhura, Muvumba, Bwisige and Ngarama) and spread across the entire country. This was described by the government as the 'MRND youth movement'. They started to take part in killings as early as 1992 and were later the main perpetrators of the genocide. Their name is a reminder of the slogan of the 1959 massacres, *"Tujye gukora akazi"*, "Let us go and do the work". By year-end, the FAR, under the command of Col. Deogratias Nsabimana launched a military campaign against the RPF code-named 'Ratissage Combiné (RC) as the final push against the RPA headquarters. It literally means to comb territory with a combination of weapons and tactics, such as infantry, motorised units, artillery and air support. It failed not only to dislodge the RPA but also lost many positions in Umutara Region.

The anti-Batutsi propaganda was intensified by an extremist Bahutu political party, the Coalition for the Defence of the Republic (CDR), that was created in March 1992, and media pamphlets such as *Nyiramacibiri and Kangura*. Throughout this period (March 1991 to July 1992) there were no negotiations after the collapse of the N'sele Ceasefire Agreement. This forced the RPF into action and the capture of Byumba shook the international community, particularly as it closely coincided with a meeting of the coalition parties with RPF in Brussels. The ensuing communiqué by political parties opposed to Habyarimana was a big setback to the MRND because the parties called for mass action and outright condemnation of manipulation of their parties by Habyarimana, MRND and CDR.

Under pressure from the Western powers, the GoR and the RPF met in Paris to chart the way forward. However, there were key difficulties for both sides. The RPF was opposed to the French involvement in the negotiations since they were already fighting on the government side. Furthermore, the RPF leader, who was the RPF Vice-Chairman and Commander-in-Chief of the RPA, Major Paul Kagame, had been humiliated by the French Government while on a diplomatic mission to Paris in January 1992 (saoti. over-blog.com).

The coalition government needed to push the political agenda since they had no control of the military and in that way they could show Rwandans that their engagement with Habyarimana was not to support his agenda, but to seek an end to the war and thus be able to play a major role in the political future of Rwanda. The Foreign Minister, Boniface Ngurinzira had clear instructions to achieve a resumption of negotiations. So, the RPF's proposal to shift meetings to Tanzania was readily accepted and a timetable was set.

Negotiations and Genocide Preparations

In order to resume negotiations, the N'sele Ceasefire Agreement was renewed on 12 July 1992 in Tanzania's northern town of Arusha, with the RPF committing itself to a permanent ceasefire and deciding to turn itself from an armed movement into a political party. Unfortunately, this was followed by hostile extremist rhetoric by Bahutu extremists who defined the Batutsi as the enemy, depicted them as snakes and the anti-Christ. The extremists declared that any Bahutu who married Batutsi, or did business with Batutsi, were traitors to the cause of the majority Bahutu. Bahutu extremists advocated for what they called a 'final solution' to the Batutsi problem. This dehumanisation of the Batutsi was intentionally meant to prepare the genocide against them.

As a result of the negotiations, a power-sharing protocol was signed on 30 October, 1992. Shortly after, President Habyarimana rejected the protocol and, on 17 November 1992, threatened to call on his *Interahamwe* to descend on the country and sow havoc. The situation was very tense despite the signing of the protocol. It was around this time that Léon Mugesera, a member of the MRND Central Committee, made his infamous speech at an MRND rally, in Kabaya in present day Nyabihu in November 1992, saying the Batutsi should be dismembered and thrown into River Nyabarongo to float back to Ethiopia where they allegedly came from.

The second Protocol was signed on 9 January 1993. But contrary to its provisions, widespread massacres were carried out against the Bagogwe, in Gisenyi, Kibuye and other areas. The Bagogwe are pastoralists who inhabit the high hills between Gisenyi and Ruhengeri, known as Crête Congo-Nil. The home of Bagogwe covered Northern Kibuye and Southern Gisenyi, the central part of Gisenyi, through the volcanoes up to Jomba and Masisi both in DRC. They had been subjected to massacres in 1991, at the same time as the massacres of Kibirira and Bugesera. Hate language continued to increase and power factions wrecked the MDR and PL. Statements like the one made by Amandin Rugira who was a former MP and a senior member of MRND, that "Batutsi are weeds and if one needs to destroy them one has to gather them" became more frequent. The euphemism referred to the fact that Batutsi in exile had returned to a trap from which they would never have a chance to escape.

The RPF response to the violation of the protocol was the launch of the famous 8 February 1993 offensive on a number of fronts, almost encircling Kigali, the capital. The offensive was very swift and emphatic, and it was a warning to the MRND government, that RPF could not allow the GoR to continue using negotiations as a cover to blackmail the RPF in the eyes of the international community and Rwandan population, while creating elbow room to kill the Batutsi. In ensuing battles, once again the FAR lost ground and face, and the territory gained by the RPF grew larger. The RPF's captured areas extended as far as Kisaro, Miyove, Base and Shyorongi just about 9km from Kigali.

The international community, including Rwanda's neighbours, prevailed on the RPF to pull back its troops. The RPF agreed to do that, but refused to cede any of the territory it had gained back to the FAR thus a demilitarised zone was created between the RPA and the FAR.

Within a month, at the request of opposition political parties and civil society organisations, including the clergy, meetings were held in Bujumbura and then in Dar-es-Salaam with the regional leaders. The RPF agreed to resume negotiations. The final protocols of the Arusha Peace Agreement were signed on 4 August 1993, and arrangements were made for the United Nations Assistance Mission for Rwanda (UNAMIR) to come in and secure the country for the implementation of the Arusha Peace Agreement. Subsequently, UNAMIR commander General Romeo Dallaire and his headquarters staff arrived in Rwanda on 17 August 1993. The UN flag was raised at Kinihira in the Demilitarised Zone on 1 November 1993. A transition government was put together on paper and the principle of a joint army accepted. All Batutsi refugees would be allowed to return to Rwanda and "ethnic" designation would no longer be included on national identity cards. However, Col. Theoniste Bagosora of the FAR, had earlier on left the Arusha Conference room, saying to those who had asked where he was going: "To Kigali, to prepare the apocalypse."

Such statements by senior military officers of the FAR clearly indicated that some officials within Habyarimana's government were totally opposed to the Arusha Peace Agreement and were instead bent on preparing genocide against the Batutsi. This is well illustrated by Dallaire in his book *Shake Hands with the Devil* (Dallaire, 2003). Gen. Dallaire says in the book that instead of enforcing peace, the peace-keepers watched the devil take control of paradise on earth and feed on the blood of the people they were supposed to protect. Habyarimana, after being sworn in as President of the Transition Government, frustrated all efforts to put in place other institutions such as Parliament and the Cabinet. The *Interahamwe* militia were being recruited and armed, assassinations became routine and no one could do anything about it.

Gen. Dallaire was all along reporting the new developments on ground, but the UN never showed any political or military will to intervene. The UN had an adequate force to frustrate Habyarimana but it did not want to, which is evidenced by the infamous cable that came to be dubbed the "genocide cable", sent by Gen. Dallaire on 1 October, 1993. This cable warned the UN headquarters in New York of preparations by the Habyarimana government to systematically exterminate Batutsi. In response to the cable, the UN ordered Gen. Dallaire not to take any action. The United Nations Department of Peace-keeping Operations determines the nature of missions and in most cases they do not recommend use of dissuasive force, and normally the UN Security Council goes along. All these were signs of the possibility of the collapse of Arusha Peace Agreement, on which many had hinged their hope for a new peaceful Rwanda.

By the time Habyarimana died in a plane crash on the night of 6 April, 1994, Rwanda had no Transition Government as provided for in the Arusha Peace Agreement and this proved to be the last nail in its coffin. The plane which was carrying President Habyarimana and the President of Burundi, Cyprien Ntaryamira, was shot down as it came to land in Kigali. Immediately, widespread massacres of Batutsi started, carried out by *Interahamwe* militia, assisted by all state security agencies like the army, police and gendarmes. On 7 April 1994, the Prime Minister, Agathe Uwilingiyimana was murdered, as well as her ministers from the opposition parties. Those who were not killed were busy hunting their colleagues to have them killed.

The 1994 genocide against the Batutsi seems to have been carried out in an apparent power vacuum, but the truth was that the worst mass murder the world has ever witnessed had been carefully planned over a period of months by cold-blooded killers. After the Belgian contingent to the UNAMIR lost 10 officers who were trying to save Prime Minster Uwilingiyimana, Belgium decided to pull out, in spite of the importance of their role, being in charge of Mission Headquarters and Kigali. They left on 12 April 1994.

After the collapse of the Arusha Agreement and the UN Mission, the only hope of rescuing Rwanda lay with the RPF and its army. Following the assassination of the prime minister and with massacres going on in several parts of Kigali city, the RPA Commander-in-Chief at his headquarters in Mulindi and his commanders took the sole responsibility to draw up the RPA's campaign plan to defeat the murderous regime and stop the genocide. However, this was a very tense and confused situation that called for strong and focused leadership. The RPF provided this. They swung into action across the country to defeat the murderous regime, rescue survivors and stop the fastest genocide that the world has ever witnessed: one million people killed in 100 days!

Major Paul Kagame, leader of the liberation struggle from October 1990

Top: RPA soldiers singing at a parade, 1991

Middle: Major General Paul Kagame addressing journalists

Bottom: RPA, Delta Mobile Force, 1992

Top: RPA soldiers marching at a parade, 1992

Middle: RPA soldiers in training, 1992

Bottom: Final inspection on 28 December 1993 at Mulindi of the 600 soldiers assigned to go to Kigali

Top: RPA combatants, 1994

Bottom: Major Paul Kagame giving instructions to his soldiers during the struggle

Top: RPF chairman Alexis Kanyarengwe (R), Major Paul Kagame (L) during the signing of the government - RPF Peace Accord in Arusha, August, 1993

Bottom: Former Rwandan President Juvenal Habyarimana (back to camera) exchanging copies of the Arusha Peace Accord with RPF chairman Alexis Kanyarengwe, August 1993

6

Genocide Against the Tutsi and its Aftermath

I knew I wanted to be part of the healing of a nation of brave and courageous people.
Pastor Rick Warren

Preparations of the Genocide

The genocide against the Tutsi in 1994 and its ferocity shocked the world. But it was not the first attempt by the government of Rwanda to wipe out sections of the population they believed were opposed to their politics. As we saw earlier, the first massacres of the Batutsi in Rwanda took place in 1959. Thereafter, periodic killings of the Batutsi became a common practice. Throughout the 1960s, the Kayibanda government launched vicious attacks on Rwanda's Batutsi population, resulting in a mass exodus into neighbouring Burundi, Tanzania, Uganda, Kenya and DR Congo.

Massacres re-occurred in 1973 and 1979. In 1990, after the start of the liberation struggle by the Rwanda Patriotic Front (RPF), the government launched yet another cycle of pogroms.

Between 1990 and 1994, the Bagogwe people of northern Rwanda were targeted by the Habyarimana regime, resulting in tens of thousands of deaths. There were similar attacks orchestrated against the people of Kibuye, Butare and elsewhere in Rwanda.

The First Republic, under President Grégoire Kayibanda, institutionalised discrimination against the Batutsi and periodically used massacres against this targeted population as a means of perpetuating discrimination and retaining power.

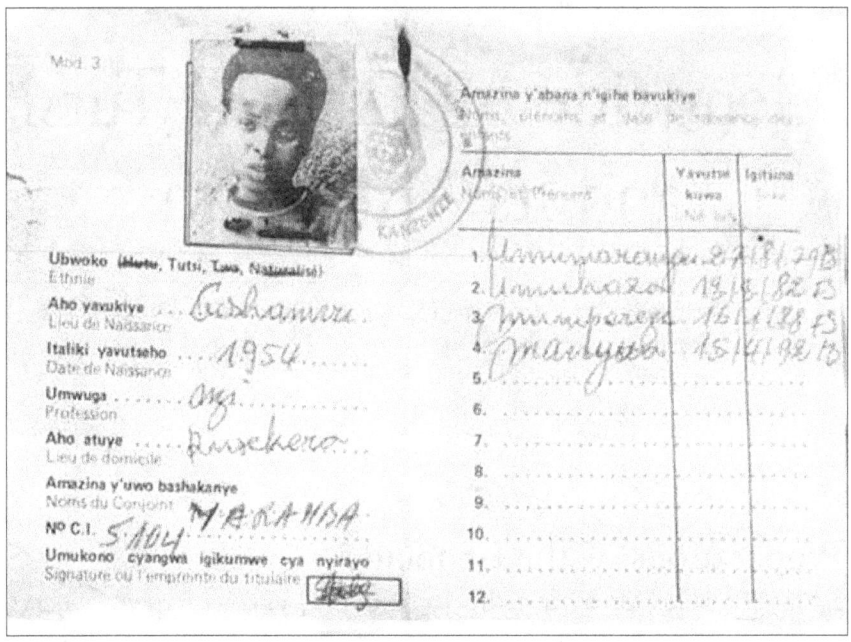

Ethnic identity card used during the colonial era, the First and Second Republics

Planning of the Genocide

The French academic and historian, Gerard Prunier, has noted that "tragedies do not occur in a vacuum". Similar to a harvest, the seeds are planted well beforehand. Given time and the right conditions they are able to develop and grow (Prunier, 1995). In the case of Rwanda, the seeds were planted in early colonial times and allowed to manifest through various policies, ideologies and overt segregation, eventually culminating in the 1994 Genocide against the Tutsi.

Between April and July 1994, over one million Batutsi were killed by the genocidal regime. Many people were involved in the killings. Those who planned and organised the genocide include President Juvenal Habyarimana, top government officials, including members of the

Provisional Government, the Presidential Guard, the National Gendarmerie, the Rwanda Armed Forces (FAR), the MRND-CDR militia (*Interahamwe*), local officials, and many Bahutu in the general population. As Melvern (2000) says,

> The massacres of Batutsi were the result of a chain of command, the result of a prepared strategy. The genocide was a conspiracy at national level, but without the complicity of the local and national civil and military authorities, the large-scale massacres would not have occurred.

Proliferation of Propaganda

Professor Gregory Stanton (2013) outlines the "The Ten Stages of Genocide" as classification, symbolisation, discrimination, dehumanisation, organisation, polarisation, preparation, persecution, extermination, and denial.

In the case of Rwanda, as we have seen, the first three stages were already in motion. Persecution was in full effect with a 1993 report indicating that more than 10,000 Batutsi had been detained and a further 2,000 killed from as early as 1990. The organisation, preparation and extermination were to follow. The connection, however, was found in the dehumanisation and polarisation phases.

Stanton argues further that dehumanisation is where one group denies the humanity of the other. Its effect is overriding because dehumanisation allows for the normal human revulsion against murder to be overcome. Similarly, polarisation is used by extremist groups to drive the groups further apart. In both cases, and as we will see, hate propaganda, amplified in the media, is used to vilify and marginalise the victim group.

In December 1990, the Bahutu paper *Kangura* ("Wake Up!") published the "Ten Commandments of the Bahutu" - a set of instructions that extremists hoped to see imposed on the minority Batutsi. It denounced the Batutsi as inferior, appealed for unity and solidarity amongst all Bahutu, called for the proliferation of Bahutu ideology, and promulgated segregation at every level of politics, business and social life.

In June 1993, a new radio station called Radio-Télévision Libre des Mille Collines (RTLM) began broadcasting in Rwanda. In its own way it was extremely effective and popular. It used street slang, played popular music, broadcast obscene jokes and had a far-reaching audience. RTLM was set up and financed by hard-liner Bahutu extremists (some connected to the Habyarimana family) who were fiercely loyal to the Bahutu cause. From the outset RTLM pushed an increasingly sectarian agenda.

In the months leading up to the genocide, RTLM contributed to creating an atmosphere of fear and hatred, repeatedly conveying the message that the Batutsi were the enemy.

Once the killings started, RTLM went beyond just espousing hate; they took an active role in the slaughter. The RTLM called for the Bahutu to 'cut down the tall trees', a code phrase used to excite the Bahutu to start killing the Batutsi. During broadcasts, RTLM often used the term *inyenzi* ('cockroach') when referring to Batutsi and then told Bahutu to "crush the cockroaches".

Rwanda's media outlets were not the only ones responsible for disseminating propaganda. In 1992, a senior member of Habyarimana's political party addressed a gathering of the National Revolutionary Movement for Development (MRND) saying: "The fatal mistake we made in 1959 was to let the Batutsi get out... We have to act. Wipe them out!" (Mugesera Léon in a speech given in Kabaya in 1992: http://clg.portalxm.com/library/keytext.cfm?keytext_id=190 accessed 20.4.2015)!

Political extremism was nothing new but the rhetoric that emerged in political circles in the early 1990s was almost desperate in its rallying efforts. The total support of the Bahutu masses was needed and for this to be effective, the government not only had to reinforce its power and authority, but also instil fear. After years of war and the emergence of a despised peace agreement, the Bahutu loyalists and other extremist groups had all the ammunition they needed and slowly began to use propaganda as a weapon.

Agreeing to Peace but Preparing for War

By 1992, Bahutu militia had purchased, stockpiled, and begun distributing an estimated eighty-five tonnes of munitions. In 1993, the Rwandan government had imported an estimated US$750,000 worth of new machetes from China. A December 1993 CIA study found that some four million tonnes of small arms had been transferred from Poland to Rwanda, via Belgium. For a country entering into a peace-sharing agreement, this represented an enormous amount of weaponry.

By 1993, death lists had become so widely known that there were reports that individuals had begun paying local militias to have their name removed. Local militia were being armed and trained at an alarming rate. In January 1994, UNAMIR contingent commander General Romeo Dallaire relayed to the UN headquarters in New York that one of his informants was claiming that Bahutu extremists had "been ordered to register all Batutsi in Kigali". "He suspects it is for their extermination," Dallaire wrote, adding that the informant claimed in 20 minutes his personnel could kill up to 1,000 Batutsi (United Nations, Department of Peace Keeping Operations, 1994),

Dallaire's UNAMIR were woefully ill-equipped. In addition, RTLM had begun denouncing UN peacekeepers as Batutsi accomplices. On 23 February 1994, Gen. Dallaire reported that he was drowning in information about death squad target lists.

The existence of clandestine networks, including the Zero Network, AMASASU, and death squads was evidence of conspiracy and planning of the genocide against the Batutsi.

Definition of the Enemy

Having convened and presided over a meeting of high-ranking military officers at ESM (Ecole Supérieure Militaire) on 4 December 1991, President Habyarimana set up a military commission with the mandate "to further study and respond to the question: What must be done in order to defeat the enemy militarily, in the media, and politically". Colonel Theoneste Bagosora chaired the commission (the Enemy Commission), which sat until about 20 December 1991. The Commission's report was originally given limited distribution. However, on 21 September 1992, the Rwandan chief of staff, Deogratias Nsabimana, sent a letter to all OPS Sector Commanders, enclosing excerpts of the report, *Définition et Identification de l'ENI* (Ennemi), (ICTR, 2008) The commanders were asked to "circulate this document widely, highlighting in particular the chapters concerning the definition, identification and recruiting grounds of the enemy". The following is an excerpt from that report;

A. Definition of the Enemy

The enemy can be subdivided into two categories:
- the primary enemy
- enemy supporters

1. The primary enemy are the extremist Batutsi within the country and abroad who are nostalgic for power and who have NEVER acknowledged and STILL DO NOT acknowledge the realities of the Social Revolution of 1959, and who wish to regain power in RWANDA by all possible means, including the use of weapons.

2. Enemy supporters are all who lend support to the primary enemy. [...] Political opponents who desire power or peaceful and democratic change in the current political regime in RWANDA are NOT to be confused with the ENEMY or supporters of the ENEMY.

B. Identification of the Enemy

The ENEMY, or their accomplices, be they Rwandan or foreign nationals within the country or abroad, can be identified in particular by any of the following acts:

- Taking up arms and attacking RWANDA;
- Purchasing arms for enemy soldiers;
- Contributing money to support the ENEMY;
- Providing any form of material support to the ENEMY;
- Spreading propaganda favourable to the ENEMY;
- Recruiting for the ENEMY;
- Contaminating public opinion by spreading false rumours and information;
- Spying for the ENEMY;
- Divulging military secrets to the ENEMY;
- Acting as a liaison officer or runner for the ENEMY;
- Organising or performing acts of terrorism and sabotage in support of ENEMY activities;
- Organising or inciting revolts, strikes or any form of disorder to support ENEMY activities;
- Refusing to fight the ENEMY;
- Refusing to comply with war requisitions.

The ENI document was used by senior military officers to promote ethnic hatred and violence.

Death Squads

From as early as 1990, prominent anti-Batutsi civilians and military officials joined forces to pursue a strategy of ethnic division and incitement to violence.

The Death Squad was a group of powerful people from President Habyarimana's region in Gisenyi who did not want regime change. It existed from the advent of multi-party politics, and had been sent to eliminate innocent people. Several clandestine groups worked in close association with these death squads. The death squads were distinguished from Zero Network, as a "small group apparently of well-trained people who were in charge of executing the decisions of the members of the networks".

In particular, the death squads executed the orders of the Dragons. The Dragons, that is the *Abakozi*, were the masterminds behind activities directed at accomplices of the enemy, the enemy in this case being the Batutsi and the Bahutu who did not espouse the genocide ideology (ICTR, 2008).

Additional evidence of investigations into the existence of death squads in Rwanda was presented through the August 1993 report of United Nations' Special Rapporteur, Bacre Waly Ndiaye. The report documented the groups' aims as creating terror and discrediting democratic reforms through, for example, assassinations and provoking riots in collaboration with militias and members of the armed forces in civilian attire.

Preparation and Use of Lists

As part of the conspiracy to exterminate Batutsi, civilian and military authorities and militia prepared lists of persons to be eliminated. As early as October 1990, lists were used for mass arrests.

The lists included persons to be arrested, such as intellectuals, business and ordinary people.

At one of the meetings in 1992, Col. Bagosora instructed the two chiefs of staff in charge of the army and gendarmerie to create lists of the "enemy and its accomplices", which had been defined earlier in the "Enemy Document". The army intelligence bureau (G-2) prepared and updated these lists under the supervision of Colonel Nsengiyumva and later Aloys Ntiwiragabo. One of these lists was found in the vehicle of Deogratias Nsabimana, the army chief of staff, after a traffic accident in 1993. On 10 January 1994, an *Interahamwe* leader informed UNAMIR that he had received orders to prepare lists of Batutsi to be eliminated. From 7 April to late July 1994, the military and *Interahamwe* used these pre-established lists to massacre Batutsi and moderate Bahutu.

Creation of Civilian Militia

Various political parties in Rwanda created youth wings: the most prominent were the *Interahamwe* for the MRND and the *Impuzamugambi* for the CDR. They were trained and armed to serve as a complementary force to the Rwandan army and ensure the extermination of the 'enemy' and its 'accomplices'.

Network Zero and Amasasu

Some senior military and political figures in Rwanda also belonged to a secret group called the "Network Zero" close to President Habyarimana, which exercised influence within Rwanda. It was closely linked to other clandestine groups and used a secret radio network.

This network was a secret clique, which stood out as the "leading defender" of President Habyarimana, thereby representing a barrier to change. Its members were referred to as a "hardcore of people", who pervaded the "entire national life at the political, military, financial, agricultural, scientific, scholarly, family and even religious levels".

The people in this Network used unconventional means to keep President Habyarimana in power. They were affiliated to death squads and other clandestine groups to sabotage the political change including the Arusha peace process.

A similar group known as Amasasu, *Alliance des Militaires Agacés par les Séculaires Actes Sournois des Unaristes* (Alliance of Soldiers Annoyed by the Underhand Secular acts of the Unarists) also recruited prominent civilian and military figures who shared an extremist Bahutu ideology. Their activities included plotting the genocide and distributing weapons to execute it.

Execution of the Genocide

One hundred Days of Slaughter

The Genocide against the Tutsi was a carefully planned and executed exercise to annihilate Rwanda's Batutsi population and Bahutu who did not agree with the prevailing extremist politics of the Habyarimana regime.

The speed and ferocity of the killings leave little doubt that the genocide had been planned as noted above. The Batutsi and Bahutu in opposition had been meticulously listed; their homes were marked, and only a few of those condemned to die had little chance to hide.

During 100 days, over one million Rwandan men, women and children lost their lives. The killers used ordinary weapons such as knives or machetes, spears, batons and clubs. Some used guns and grenades.

The killings began in Rwanda's capital city of Kigali in the night of 6 April, shortly after the downing of President Habyarimana's plane. During that night, roadblocks were set up and rampant killing started. The Presidential Guard units, together with the *Interahamwe* and *Impuzamugambi*, eliminated the Batutsi priority targets.

In the early morning of 7 April a core group gave the green light and ordered the systematic killings across the country. On the night of 7 April 1994, the Bahutu extremists began purging the government of their political opponents. That night Prime Minister Agathe Uwilingiyimana was killed together with 10 Belgian peacekeepers who were guarding her.

Over the next few days and weeks, the genocide spread with brutal efficiency to the rest of the country. In rural areas, the local government hierarchy was also in most cases the chain of command for the execution of the genocide. Governors of each province, acting on orders from Kigali, disseminated instructions to the district leaders (bourgmestres), who in turn issued directions to the leaders of the sectors, cells and villages within their districts. The majority of the actual killings in the countryside were carried out by ordinary civilians, under orders from the leaders.

Since Rwandans carried identity cards that labelled them Batutsi, Bahutu, or Batwa, the killers, in most cases neighbours, were able to go door to door, slaughtering the Batutsi. Men, women, and children were indiscriminately butchered using hand weapons, often machetes and clubs. Many were tortured before they were killed; women were raped or dismembered in the presence of their relatives. In fact, sexual violence was used as a means to dehumanise their victims although in the process they too were dehumanised.

Slaughter inside Churches, Hospitals and Schools

Thousands of Batutsi tried to escape the slaughter by hiding in churches, hospitals, schools, and government offices. These places, which historically have been places of refuge, were turned into places of mass murder during the genocide.

One of the worst massacres of the genocide took place on 15 -16 April 1994 at the Nyarubuye Roman Catholic Church, located about 60 miles east of Kigali. Here, the mayor of the town, a Muhutu, encouraged Batutsi to seek sanctuary inside the church by assuring them they would be safe there. Then the mayor directed the Bahutu extremists to kill, using grenades and guns first, but soon changing to machetes and clubs. In this particular church, it took two days to kill the thousands of Batutsi who were inside. Similar massacres took place in several churches all over Rwanda, with many of the worst ones occurring between 11 April and the beginning of May. To further degrade the Batutsi, Bahutu extremists would not allow the Batutsi dead to be buried. Their bodies were left where they were slaughtered, allowed to decompose or eaten by rats and dogs. The sight and the stench of thousands of decomposing bodies and those floating in rivers, lakes, and streams depicted the extent of the horror of the genocide against the Tutsi.

Stopping the Genocide

Following the killing of President Habyarimana by Hutu extremists in a plane crash at around 20h30, on 6 April 1994, the final phase of the Genocide was unleashed targeting Tutsi and opposition politicians in Kigali. On 07 April 1994, genocide started countrywide with the military, Interahamwe, Impuzamugambi and other Hutu gangs establishing roadblocks, hunting and mass killing Tutsi and moderate Hutu. Key opposition politicians and personalities that would obstruct the genocidal plan and form the transitional government were immediately hunted down and killed. These included the Prime Minister Agathe Uwilingiyimana, Information Minister Faustin Rucogoza, President of the Constitutional Court Joseph

Kavaruganda, President of PL Landouard Ndasingwa, PSD leaders Fréderic Nzamurambaho and Félicien Ngango, just to name a few.

CND building that was home to RPF politicians guarded by the RPA 3rd Battalion, was attacked including areas where civilians had fled to for protection such as Amahoro Stadium, churches and schools. The UN and Western embassies evacuated their citizens and UN forces after 10 Belgian peacekeepers were killed on 7 April 1994, abandoning vulnerable Tutsi and moderate Hutu at the hands of the genocidaires.

On 7 April 1994 at around 15h00, the Chairman of RPA High Command, Gen Paul Kagame, convened an emergency meeting of RPA High Command at Mulindi Headquarters. He gave them the Order "to stop the Genocide, defeat the genocidal forces (FAR and militias) and rescue genocide survivors".

Rescuing civilians was the main objective of the Campaign against Genocide. During the 100 days of the Genocide against the Tutsi, the Rwandan Patriotic Army saved tens of thousands of people through rescue operations conducted across the country. Many of these rescue missions were conducted behind enemy lines by men and women who risked their lives to save innocent people trapped in churches, schools, swamps, forests and other places.

The Chairman of High Command ordered Alpha Combined Mobile Force (CMF), Bravo CMF and 59th Battalion to urgently advance and link up with 3rd Battalion in the Kigali operations. The three battalions advanced through Byumba-Kigali Ngali-Kigali City as the main Central Axis, linking up with 3rd Battalion on 11 April 1994. They were joined by 101 CMF and 21st Battalion. 7th Battalion and 157th Battalion were ordered to advance on the South-Eastern axis. Charlie CMF was ordered to advance on the North-Western axis. The RPA forces advanced fighting the genocidal forces and conducting rescue operations to save genocide survivors.

The battles in Kigali began when 3rd Battalion was given orders on 7 April 1994, to break out of its initial positions in CND in order to defend itself and rescue the Genocide survivors in its vicinity. The Force advanced towards Remera and rescued people trapped in Amahoro Stadium who were attacked by FAR and militias after killing the refugees at Centre Christus. One Company was tasked to block the Para Comando forces attacking from Camp Kanombe. Another Company advanced and contained the

Presidential Guards (GP) that were attacking from Camp GP at Kimihurura. Two Companies were tasked with blocking attacks from Camp Kacyiru (Gendarmerie) and Camp Kami (Military Police) respectively. 3rd Battalion managed to contain the attacking genocidal forces and rescued people within the vicinity until they got reinforcement from other RPA forces from the north on the 4th day (11 April 1994). After link up with forces from the north, RPA forces captured Mont Rebero, opening rescue corridors in the southern part of the city (CND-Kicukiro-Nyanza-Rebero). After capturing Mont Rebero on 12 April 1994 and Nyanza two days after, more rescue missions were subsequently carried out in areas of Nyamirambo, Gikondo, Kicukiro, Gahanga, St. André, St Paul and Ste. Famille and other areas of Kigali.

On the Central axis, the RPA forces were able to link up with the 600 Force of 3rd Battalion and engage in rescue operations in Kigali. The main military victories in the central axis include the capture of Kanombe airport and barracks, the fall of Mont Jali, Shyorongi and other enemy positions in Kigali. The fall of Mont Kigali enemy position led to the eventual fall of the Capital City on 4 July 1994.

The RPA forces along the South-Eastern axis engaged the enemy, overrunning and destroying enemy positions and rescuing thousands of people along the axis. At Kayonza, 7th Battalion advanced along Kayonza-Rwamagana-Musha-Kabuga while 157th Battalion continued the advance to Kibungo-Rusumo-Bugesera-Mayaga. Notable among the strong enemy positions overrun include: Ngarama, Nyagatare, Gabiro, Kiziguro, Rukara, Kayonza, Rwamagana, Kibungo, Rusumo, Rukumberi, Gashora, Gako, Rwabusoro bridge, Ruhango, Nyanza, Kabgayi, Gitarama and finally Butare.

Along the North-Western axis, the RPA forces engaged in battles that liberated the towns of Ruhengeri on 14 July 1994 and Gisenyi on 17 July 1994, including the enemy barracks of Mukamira and Bigogwe which were overrun leading to the enemy defeat and withdraw to Zaire.

The 1994 Campaign Plan by the RPA forces to stop the Genocide against Tutsi was conducted in three phases of military operations - Phase 1: Advance and link-up with 3rd Battalion in Kigali (6-11 April 1994); Phase 2: Decisive Operations to defeat the genocide forces (12Apr-4July 94) and Phase 3: RPA Pursuit of genocide forces (5 July– 22 August 1994) until the genocide forces fled to former Zaire, and in Turquoise zone. The Campaign to stop the Genocide involved both military and political, humanitarian, diplomatic and media activities to achieve different set objectives all culminating into the effective stopping of the Genocide.

The Genocide was stopped on 4 July 1994 when the genocidal forces were defeated and Kigali liberated. The struggle for liberation and stopping genocide continued countrywide until 17 July 1994. Eventually, areas that were controlled by the French forces under 'Zone Turquoise' (Gikongoro, Cyangugu and Kibuye) were also liberated at a later stage, leading to a total liberation of Rwanda.

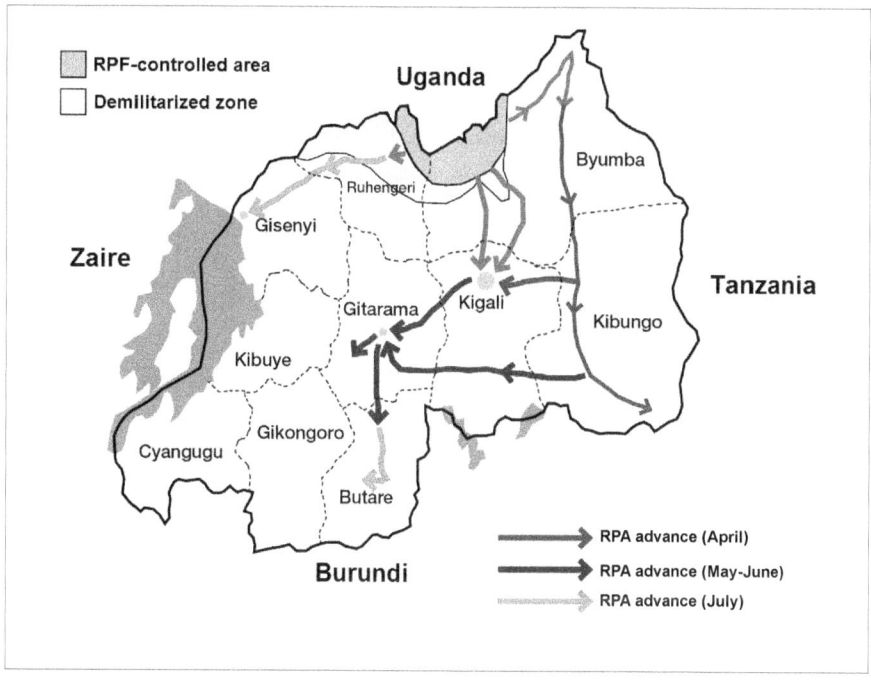

Map of Rwanda showing the RPA advances in stopping the genocide 1994

International Betrayal

When the genocide began, the United Nations had a peacekeeping force — the United Nations Assistance Mission for Rwanda (UNAMIR) — of about 2,500 troops in Rwanda. The first reaction of the United Nations, and indeed of other nations that had their own nationals in Rwanda, was to withdraw their troops and their nationals, respectively.

Rwandans were deliberately abandoned by the international community, among them the United Nations agencies and especially the office of the UN Secretary-General, during the genocide.

The United States and the United Kingdom were informed well in advance of the preparations of the genocide but they did not react. France's role and involvement in the genocide started from 1990 and continued until Opération Turquoise. If the international community had reacted, with the presence of UNAMIR, the genocide could have been prevented, or stopped.

The report of the Independent Inquiry into the actions of the UN during the 1994 genocide against the Tutsi in Rwanda, published in December 1999, called the genocide one of the most abhorrent events of the twentieth century. The report left no doubt that each part of the UN system, and in particular the Secretary-General, the Secretariat, the Security Council and the member states, had to assume and acknowledge their responsibility in the failure to prevent genocide (United Nations,1999).

Aftermath of the Genocide against the Tutsi

The social, economic and political impact of the 1994 genocide against the Batutsi on Rwanda has been devastating. Not only were more than one million innocent lives lost, but the social fabric of society was also destroyed. Thousands of children were orphaned and 250,000 women became widows with many suffering from HIV/AIDS as a result of rape. Mass murderers who needed to be arrested and brought to justice were still roaming the countryside. The economy was totally destroyed and the treasury looted by the defeated government. The political landscape was divided between genocidal killers, allied extremists with similar genocide ideology, and those that fought against the genocide forces and liberal political parties.

Sexual Violence and Gender Identity

During the genocide, many Rwandan social myths and taboos were broken. Family values, motherhood in particular, and the concept of women being non-violent could not hold any more in the face of the violence committed by women and mothers. For a country that placed a premium on cultural traditions, genocide was a social and family calamity.

The usual belief about women as victims in conflicts was therefore shattered during the genocide against the Tutsi, where women played an important role as agents of genocide. This active participation of women has had very negative repercussions. Today, within the Rwanda family, many children are in constant conflict with their own mothers, while other children had to grow up without their mothers because the latter were in jail or had been killed during the genocide. The post-genocide generation is made up in large part of orphans from both ethnic groups, a situation that can create long lasting trans-generational trauma.

Tutsi women were also sexually tortured with the intent of destroying their reproductive capabilities. When talking about their ordeal, many survivors of sexual torture simply say, "we are no longer women" or "we lost our femininity". Such survivors' testimonies show clearly the correlation between sexual torture and gender identity.

Although the physical and psychological repercussions from rape are similar for women and men, male victims are more reluctant to talk about their suffering or to report their victimisation because such torture directly affects their dignity in a society where masculinity is highly valued.

According to survivors' testimonies, only a few men were victims of genocidal rape. However, this does not mean that they were spared from other forms of sexual violence such as mutilation of the genitals which were then displayed as trophies in public, anal impalement, and castration, especially for pre-pubescent boys. Statistics about the number of men who were raped may never be known because most eyewitnesses and survivors reported only the rape of women and girls.

Consequences of Sexual Violence During the Genocide

The post-genocide generation is made up to a large extent of orphans and widows from all sections of Rwandan society, a situation that has created long-lasting trans-generational trauma. In 2000, the OAU's International

Panel of Eminent Personalities reported that, "we can be certain that almost all females who survived the genocide were direct victims of rape or other sexual violence, or were profoundly affected by it." (Organisation of African Unity, 2000).

Those effects are still being felt even 20 years later. Amnesty International estimates that 67% of the women raped during this period developed HIV (Amnesty International, 2004).

In the aftermath of the genocide, the children of rape, or rather 'the children of the devil' as they were referred to at the time, were a constant reminder of rape. In some cases they were resented by the surviving relatives and sometimes by the mothers themselves. Some women even decided to abort using unsafe methods that damaged them physically and psychologically.

The government of Rwanda decided to aggressively fight against gender-based violence and all other consequences of genocide by creating institutions and structures such as the Human Rights Commission, the Unity and Reconciliation Commission, and the National Commission to Fight against Genocide. In 2008, the 'Prevention and Protection Against Gender-Based Violence Act' was passed and officially became a law in 2009. The law seeks to avert the kind of atrocities that women experienced during the 1994 genocide.

New Gender Roles

After the genocide, there were fewer men than women and 70% of Rwandan households were headed by women. They became the major breadwinners for their families, roles previously reserved for men.

Women also took on other new, non-traditional roles. They formed organisations to work for peace, reconciliation, and for their human rights and economic well-being. These organisations, along with special constitutional provisions, gave women political power in unprecedented numbers. This is how they have played a central role in the economic and social transformation of the country.

Assisting Genocide Survivors to Cope

Following the genocide, the issue of lasting trauma among the survivors of genocidal rape and other forms of violence arose. Whatever mental health infrastructure and human resource pool that existed was destroyed during the genocide and there was only one general health provider, a nurse, remaining at the only psychiatric hospital in the country at the time — Ndera Hospital. Data collected by UNICEF in 1995 showed that 69% of Rwandans had witnessed someone being killed or injured during the genocide, and 31% had witnessed rape or sexual assault. The 1995 National Trauma Survey showed that at least 58% of youth survivors (8-19 years) were suffering from PTSD, with girls more affected than boys (Neugebauer R. et al 2009). (see bibliography)

In the years before the Genocide, there was no structured mental health system, with the exception of one psychiatric hospital (Ndera). There was minimal mental health treatment provided and a reliance on traditional healers.

In 1995, the Ministry of Health issued a National Mental Health Policy, and developed a programme and an implementation plan. A National Trauma Recovery Centre was built with the collaboration of UNICEF in 1995, but funding was abruptly pulled off only three years later. The Ministry of Health responded by establishing "Service de Consultations Psychosociales" (SCPS), which now serves as the Mental Health Department of Rwanda's central referral hospital, Kigali University Teaching Hospital (CHUK) It focuses on common neuropsychiatric conditions such as trauma, depression, anxiety, epilepsy and psychotic disorders. Another initiative focuses on drug and alcohol use and abuse. This includes education initiatives through sensitisation literature as well as radio and television shows and outreach programmes to schools.

A focus of the new system included the use of non-specialists such as primary care physicians and thousands of community health workers to assist in the implementation of mental health interventions and increase access to appropriate treatment. These non-specialists were located throughout the country and thus mental health care was no longer only provided in the capital of Kigali at Ndera and SCPS.

The Ministry of Education has also developed training programmes for psychiatric nurses and psychologists. Currently, psychiatrist doctors, clinical psychologists and mental health nurses are being trained at the University of Rwanda and INATEK (Institute of Agriculture, Education and Technology). In order to ensure that district hospitals have mental health capacity, two general medical practitioners and two general nurses from each district hospital are trained each year in psychiatric care. Now, 462 health centres (out of 468) have one or more general nurses trained in mental health.

Genocide Denial

During and after every genocide, the perpetrators deny they committed the crime. They portray the murders as justified killing during war or repression of terrorism. They dig up and dispose of the bodies and try to minimise the number of victims. They try to blame the victims, often claiming that the victims' own behaviour provoked the killing. They portray the murders as spontaneous outbreaks in response to the victims' actions, or as the actions of rogue army commanders, rather than as intentional government policy.

They challenge the veracity of the eye-witnesses and assassinate the character of their accusers. The perpetrators claim to have been powerless to prevent the killings by others, and even have the audacity to claim they assisted their victims.

All of these strategies of denial operated during and after the genocide against the Tutsi. The presence of the Rwandan government representative at the UN Security Council meetings that considered the situation provided an ideal forum for such denial. Since the genocide, despite massive evidence against them, this denial by perpetrators has continued both at the International Criminal Tribunal for Rwanda and in Rwandan courts and prisons.

Resilience of a nation

Over a million people died in the genocide, thousands of individuals' bodies and souls were broken and families were decimated and torn to pieces. And obviously, the damage reaches much further. Communities were split and the social fabric that had tied people together was ruptured. Therein lay the challenge as rebuilding the social fabric and making possible the development of new ties between people was an essential and yet almost insurmountable task.

It is in the paradox of seeking to restore communities amidst deep brokenness and supporting the recovery of genocide victims in the face of their immense psychological, physical, economic and social wounds that the possibility of true recovery and healing lies.

While suffering is widespread, resilience is also a feature that follows trauma. The atmosphere in Rwanda today is inspiring. There is a tremendous momentum towards rebuilding the nation and the resilience of many people is visible. In the relatively short time since the genocide, much has been achieved and the Rwandan people can be proud of that. However, it is important to remember that resilience coexists with suffering and that resilience does not mean that a person is no longer troubled by their experiences.

Despite all this, much has been achieved in the 20 years since the genocide. Different schemes have been developed to help survivors and a considerable number of trauma counsellors have been trained.

Rwanda Policies to Contain Genocide

Rwanda has put in place polices and laws to fight genocide, to ensure that the 1994 genocide against the Tutsi does not occur again. These laws and policies are in place while the threat from genocidal forces, as described above is politically and militarily unrelenting. Other kinds of pressures to undo the progress made so far surface in an attempt to return the country to the 1994 period.

Although 20 years may seem a long time, it is a short period indeed in comparison with other countries that have known genocide. It is important to note that 60 years after the Jewish Holocaust, the world is still enacting laws and policies on anti-Semitism, discrimination and denial of the holocaust. In 1992, the United Nations declared that anti-Semitism has to be recognised as a danger that must be fought by legal means. The Organisation for Security and Cooperation in Europe (OSCE), under the Cordoba Declaration of June 2005, calls upon its member countries to enact legislation designed to combat anti-Semitism. The majority of countries in Europe now have laws in their penal codes and other legislations on anti-Semitism, using Nazi symbols, denial and minimisation of the holocaust. Likewise policies and laws to contain genocide in Rwanda are still in the process of being formulated, enacted and revised.

The penal code has provisions punishing genocide, genocide ideology and other related offences as provided for under Articles 135, 497 and others. The draft law on genocide and genocide ideology is in advanced stages in Parliament.

Besides, dedicated institutions have been established by the Constitution and Government to address the causes and consequences of the genocide. They include the Human Rights Commission; the Unity and Reconciliation Commission; the Commission to Fight Against Genocide; the Gacaca Commission and Gacaca Courts.

The Specialised Chamber in the High Court has been equipped to international legal standards to receive genocide suspects from ICTR and Western countries. The Rwanda Demobilisation and Reintegration Commission (RDRC) was established to be a dedicated national commission on Demobilisation, Disarmament, Rehabilitation and Re-Integration (DDRR). A comprehensive DDRR programme has been in place for over 15 years now.

The RDRC, established in 1997, has had three programmes all funded by the World Bank and donors. Currently the Kingdom of Netherlands, Sweden and Germany sit on the trust fund with the Rwanda Government and the World Bank. Other partners have included the DR Congo and MONUSCO, particularly on media and sensitisation, reception and repatriation of members of armed groups from the DR Congo to Rwanda.

The Mutobo Demobilisation Centre received 46 intakes from 2001 to April 2013, and has rehabilitated 10,277 ex-armed group members since its inception. They include 8,564 from mainstream FDLR and those that have been serving in their allied groups.

Top-left: Rwandan refugees cross Rusumo border into Tanzania, 1994

Top-right: Rwandan refugees flee from Rwanda to DRC as corpses of genocide victims are strewn all over

Bottom: A lady breaks down while viewing skulls of genocide victims at a memorial site

RPA fighters dance to celebrate victory in 1994

Part 3

Post-Genocide Transitional Government (1994-2003)

7

Facing the Immediate Challenges after 1994

Rebuilding a nation's social fabric cannot follow any predetermined guidelines and it will only succeed if it is owned by citizens.
President Paul Kagame

Establishing the Government of National Unity

A post-genocide Rwanda required focused and tolerant leadership, which RPF provided. After stopping the 1994 genocide against the Tutsi and defeating the genocidal forces and their allies, the RPF/RPA had the option and capacity to govern alone. However, it did not do it because this would have been against its founding democratic principles and the other values it stood for.

RPF believed and continues to believe in fundamental change. It strongly believed in reconciling Rwandans as a necessary prerequisite for socio-economic development, establishment of peace in the country and restoration of dignity to all Rwandans.

The post-genocide phase was certainly difficult because of the nature of challenges that resulted from a long period of misrule by divisive regimes. Decades of divisive policies had seriously entrenched sectarianism in the Rwandan population.

Despite the fact that the country had lost more than one million lives during the one hundred days of genocide, and that more than two million other Rwandans had fled to neighbouring countries, the RPF never hesitated to form a government that was all inclusive as was envisaged in the Arusha Peace Agreement which had been signed on 4 August 1993.

To kick-start the revival and spirit of the Arusha Agreement, the RPF made a declaration on 17 July 1994, commonly known as 'The RPF Declaration'. In that declaration, the RPF made it categorically clear that it would not share power with parties and political organisations that had committed genocide. Subsequently, these parties were accordingly outlawed.

It reiterated its commitment to a broad-based transitional government, the rule of law, the formation of a national army open to all Rwandans and dedicated to serve their interests. In that spirit, the RPF announced that it was ready to share power with the Mouvement Démocratique Républicain (MDR), the Parti Démocrate Chretien (PDC), the Parti Démocratique Islamique (PDI), the Parti Libéral (PL), the Parti Socialiste Démocratique (PSD), the Parti Socialiste Rwandais (PSR) and the Union Démocratique du Peuple Rwandais (UDPR).

Following the declaration, the parties that were part of the Arusha Peace agreement formed a Broad-Based Transitional Government (BBTG) in accordance with the provisions of the agreement. Accordingly, members of this Broad-Based Transitional Government took oath of office on 19 July 1994.

Since all arms of the government had to be established, on 14 November 1994, the RPF signed an agreement with other political parties governing the sharing of parliamentary seats. Thirteen seats were reserved for each of the major parties, namely: RPF, MDR, PSD and PL, then PDC was given six seats while the other small parties — PSR and UDPR — had two each. These political parties agreed to have the national army represented in Parliament and they were allocated six seats. Guided by the spirit of power sharing, the PSD took the office of the Speaker of the Broad-Based Transitional Parliament (BBTP) and the two Deputy Speakers came from the RPF and the PDI. All these arms of the government had their legal basis in the Arusha Peace Agreement, the RPF Declaration, the Constitution of 1991, as well as on the RPF Eight-point programme.

Following the establishment of the Government and Parliament, it was imperative to staff various government departments with competent technocrats for the smooth running of the transitional institutions.

Therefore, civil service appointments were made on a competitive basis using the UNDP to conduct interviews and award points to individual applicants according to merit. Through these transparent means of recruitment and appointments, the RPF demonstrated that it was not hungry for power but was indeed a pro-people political organisation that held all Rwandans equal.

Pressing Challenges in Key Sectors

Rwanda was deeply damaged and had enormous social challenges. The devastation was so great, and the legacy of the genocide so painful that some regarded it as a failed state. Besides, since Rwanda's social fabric had fractured due to the divisive politics that preceded the genocide, suspicion and mistrust characterised the population, and to a large extent also existed amongst the leaders in the Broad Based Transitional Government (BBTG) of national unity.

This posed a serious challenge to the functioning of institutions because the RPF's vision was not shared by all stakeholders. In spite of all this, the RPF believed that Rwanda was not dead but that it could be reborn and re-built. To reach that goal, the RPF advocated strongly for unity and reconciliation despite the enormous challenges.

Security

Although the RPF had captured power and a transitional government had been established, the security situation was still fluid, with former government forces and *Interahamwe* militia still carrying out genocide in various parts of the country. A French buffer area in western Rwanda, known as the Turquoise Zone, had become a safe haven for genocidal forces. In addition, infiltrators from refugee camps across the border continued to cross and destabilise the country. It should be noted that the ex-FAR and *Interahamwe* were allowed to retain their weapons and to mix with the civilian refugees. Other sympathisers of the former regime continued to give support, notably the DR Congo (then Zaire) under President Mobutu Sese Seko. All these proved to be security challenges for a country that had been hit by one of the worst human tragedies of the 20th century.

The Broad-Based Transitional Government under RPF leadership had to devise means to address insecurity in the whole country and regain a semblance of normalcy so that Rwandans could begin the task of rebuilding the nation.

Resettlement of Refugees and Survivors

The RPF strived to restore Rwanda as a country for all Rwandans and provided a homeland to which million of Rwandan refugees could return. Tens of thousands of internally displaced people, especially genocide survivors whose homes had been destroyed were resettled and provided with basic housing facilities. About three million Rwandan refugees who had been taken hostage by fleeing genocidal forces in the DR Congo and some in Tanzania were brought back home by the transitional government. This humanitarian exercise was largely successful despite the failure of the international community to address their plight in refugee camps. About two million older refugees (of 1959 and subsequent years) were also resettled peacefully across the country.

Health

In the health sector, the picture was equally bleak. This sector had always been weak in Rwanda. Health workers in this sector were few and poorly trained. This was a result of chronically poor human resource development strategies that characterised the colonial and post-colonial Rwanda. This situation was greatly exacerbated by the genocide in which a large number of health workers had participated and fled the country or had been killed. The few that had returned from exile settled in Kigali, which had some infrastructure and was also safer to live in.

To mitigate the health crisis, a number of NGOs and the army came in and tried to make a difference, but the task was overwhelming since the number of the injured and the sick was very high. Statistics indicate that immunisation coverage for children had dropped to 27% as a result of war and mismanagement.

Malnutrition levels were also very high. Child as well as maternal mortality rates were equally high due to poor health service delivery. The prevalence of water-borne diseases and other conditions related to poor sanitation was among the highest in Africa at that time. Equally worrying was the high infection rate of transmittable diseases, especially HIV and AIDS which had been made worse during the genocide in which rape was used as a weapon of war. The bad situation was worsened by the very high fertility rate, coupled with ignorance. Malaria was hyper endemic in some parts of the country, especially in the current east and southern provinces (Amnesty International, 2004).

Education

The education sub-sector was also a casualty of consecutive regimes that lacked the right vision for the country and was worsened by war and genocide. Poor and discriminatory education policies, coupled with an education system that did not respond to the socio-economic needs of the country, only served to perpetuate massive ignorance in the country. Even the few that went to school could not translate their knowledge into productive activities to improve the standard of living of the Rwandan people. This already catastrophic situation was worsened by the genocide, during which most of the education infrastructure was destroyed and human capital decimated.

In the eastern part of the country, schools were not only few and far between, but in some areas they did not exist at all. There were only a few colleges to train teachers in the conventional sense. Overall, the primary and secondary enrolment and completion rates were low and education was probably among the worst hit by discrimination policies. Science was only taught in very few schools and there was visible deficiency of technical and vocational schools. Higher education was not only quantitatively low but was also a privilege of the few favoured ones. Not even the quota system worked. For instance, in the period between 1963 and 1994, only about 2,000 Rwandans had completed university education.

Economy

The Rwandan economic and political situation before 1994 was marked by economic stagnation and high levels of poverty, mainly attributed to lack of vision and poor economic planning by the leadership of the time. They emphasised state control of the economy by a clique who benefited from the existing system.

As a result, post-genocide Rwanda faced a number of economic challenges, including an unstable macroeconomic environment. For example in 1994, the economy shrank by 50% and inflation rose to 64%. Between 1985 and 1994, the GDP growth rate was a mere 2.2%, against a population growth rate of 3.2%, meaning there was an annual decline of -1% of per capita GDP (Ryan, 2004).

This was mainly due to the fact that the economy was characterised by low productivity in all sectors, but most especially in agriculture, yet this is a sector on which more than 90% of the population depended for their livelihood. Of course without a visionary leadership to avert the situation, this resulted in a very weak export base coupled with a narrow revenue collection base. This implied limited internally generated resources to fund social services like education and health.

In addition, there was low private investment and as such, the country lacked a serious and vibrant private sector to drive economic growth. In the public sector too, there was a highly unskilled labour force. For example, in 1994, at least 79% of civil servants in the country did not have qualifications higher than secondary school. To make matters worse, skilled professionals had been particularly targeted in the genocide.

Justice

The transitional government inherited a broken justice sector. As earlier mentioned, more than 140,000 genocide suspects had been arrested yet there was insufficient prison infrastructure to hold them. Their upkeep became a huge challenge in terms of feeding, and provision of medical and other services. To make matters worse, there was an inadequate number of trained lawyers to handle the large number of perpetrators of genocide and this was also true for other crimes that were being committed in the country.

The laws were also outdated, obscure and inadequate. According to legal experts, the multiple national courts system which was in existence had very low productivity and high rates of consumption of the meagre national resources. Judicial and prosecution institutions did not have independence as they served under the executive arm of Government. In general, the Judiciary was characterised by delays, interference, poor services rendered to the people, gross violations of human rights and unskilled personnel.

For example, according to records of the Supreme Court, out of 702 judges in 2003, only 74 possessed a bachelor's degree in Law (Republic of Rwanda, 2010).

Nonetheless, justice had to be delivered. And despite the meagre resources that were available, the government did everything possible, and in a short period of time, the judicial institutions were revived and started their operations.

8

Insurgency and the Congo Wars

For Rwandans, stability is not an abstraction. It's a reality that abides in the minds and hearts of the people.
President Paul Kagame

Facing Security threats

As mentioned above, the defeated genocidal forces fled to Eastern Congo, taking with them over two million refugees and quickly regrouped. This situation posed a number of serious security challenges for the newly established transitional government of national unity in Kigali. First, the international community was indifferent to the threat they posed. Second, the UN agencies and other international organisations did not separate the armed militias from innocent civilians, thus allowing the militia to benefit from the humanitarian assistance provided by these international organisations. This enabled the ex-FAR and militia to maintain their military organisation even within the refugee camps while enjoying assistance from the international community and political support from the Mobutu regime. They established effective political and military structures a stone's throw away from Rwanda's border with the DR Congo. This is how the Rassemblement Démocratique pour le Rwanda (RDR), which vowed to overthrow the new government in Rwanda and continue the genocide, was born and established its military structures within the refugee camps. It is also the reason they were able to continue to make armed incursions into Rwanda.

Inside the refugee camps, the plight of Rwandan refugees held hostage increasingly deteriorated. According to some UN reports, refugees were forced to pay about US$10 monthly in what became a 'war tax'. Additionally, refugees were forced to contribute food received from international humanitarian agencies to support ex- FAR and *Interahamwe* militia. Equally, the DR Congo government violated an international arms embargo and continued supplying them with weapons (United States Committee for Refugees and Immigrants, 1997).

Months before the first Congo war erupted, Paul Kagame, then Vice President and Minister of Defence, warned the international community of the consequences of their continued inaction amidst the escalating humanitarian and security situation. He expressed Rwanda's resolve to act unilaterally to free Rwandans and dismantle the militia camps if the situation remained unresolved. The international community did not appreciate the resolve of the new government to deal with this security threat from just across its border.

In the same interview, President Kagame is quoted as saying that he and other Rwandan officials had attempted to persuade the United Nations and Western countries to demilitarise the refugee camps and separate the genocidal forces from the innocent civilians. He adds that the international community remained "insensitive" (Kinzer, 2008).

Security threats against Rwanda continued to escalate, with the now organised forces in refugee camps launching constant raids on the northern and western provinces of Rwanda, causing deaths in a population already haunted by the genocide. The situation continued to deteriorate as Rwandan refugees held hostage in the camps continued to suffer due to increased militarisation of the camps and death by disease.

Faced with this complex security situation in the aftermath of the genocide, and with Rwanda's pleas to the international community for action against Ex-FAR militia and *Interahamwe* falling on deaf ears, the new government resolved to cross into Eastern Congo to resolve the situation.

First Congo War

The first objective of the invasion by Rwanda was to free and repatriate the over two million Rwandan refugees held hostage by ex-FAR and *Interahamwe* militia.

The continued presence of these two million refugees in Eastern Congo guaranteed ex-FAR government forces and *Interahamwe* a substantial recruitment base and justification for continued support by the international community.

The second objective was to help the Congolese people liberate their country. The dictatorial government of President Mobutu, not only threatened Rwanda, but also allowed the genocidal forces to target a cross-section of Congolese people, particularly the Kinyarwanda speaking ones.

These objectives were accomplished. The RPA dismantled ex-FAR and *Interahamwe* militia camps, thereby freeing and repatriating Rwandan refugees back to their country. The Rwandan involvement also led to the overthrow of President Mobutu on May 17, 1997. Subsequently, a new government led by President Laurent Desire Kabila, who had led an armed Congolese rebellion, was established in Kinshasa.

Second Congo War

Despite the success of the operations that overthrew Mobutu and freed Rwandan refugees, security threats continued. Within a year, President Laurent Kabila had established a close alliance with the same genocidal forces that had led to the first war and his assumption of the presidency. These forces simply changed names while maintaining their original genocide ideology and intent of overthrowing the Rwandan government. The RDR simply changed into Armée pour la Libération du Rwanda (ALiR), composed of the *Interahamwe* and ex-FAR soldiers that had committed genocide. President Kabila expelled Rwandan troops from Congo in July 1998, thus creating room for genocidal forces to operate freely in Eastern Congo.

Militarily, the Government of National Unity, led by the RPF had made a strategic decision to secure Rwanda by pursuing the genocidal forces inside their areas of operation within Eastern Congo. President Kabila's decision to facilitate these forces, offering them support to attack Rwanda resulted in what was called 'Africa's First World War' since it attracted about eight African countries, some fighting on the side of Kabila, and others fighting on the side of a number of armed rebellions that were struggling to overthrow the Kabila regime. In 2000, the ALiR forces, took eight Western tourists hostage, including Americans. This group was eventually classified as a terrorist organisation by the US State Department. It then changed its name to Forces Démocratiques de Libération du Rwanda (Democratic Forces for the Liberation of Rwanda) [FDLR]. For the next several years, the battlelines stabilised and the war stagnated. However, the Rwandan government under RPF maintained that her security concerns due to the presence of *Interahamwe* and ex-FAR genocidal forces had forced her to maintain troops inside the Democratic Republic of Congo.

Lusaka Ceasefire Agreement and its Implementation

Politically and militarily, the Rwandan government made it clear that it was not ready to withdraw its troops from the DR Congo when *Interahamwe* and ex-FAR forces were being supported and openly attacking Rwanda. This political and military deadlock later ended in political negotiations sponsored by the Southern African Development Community (SADC) and the then Organisation of African Unity (OAU), involving all warring parties. This resulted in the Lusaka Ceasefire Agreement, which aimed at ending the second Congo war through a ceasefire, releasing prisoners of war, and the deploying of an international peacekeeping force under the auspices of the United Nations.

To Rwanda's satisfaction, Article 2 of the Agreement stressed that all involved parties were to commit themselves to immediately addressing the security concerns of the DR Congo and her neighbouring countries. In that sense, it looked like Rwanda's concerns had been taken care of. Article 3 dealt with issues relating to the request for the deployment of a UN peacekeeping mission in the Congo, withdrawal of foreign troops and the disarmament of militias and armed groups, amongst other issues.

Annex A contained 13 articles and was fully devoted to the modalities for the implementation of the Agreement. Central to the implementation was the request for the deployment of a UN Peacekeeping force under Chapter

VII, which would give that force a mission to conduct peace enforcement activities that would include: tracking down and disarming armed groups in DRC, screening mass killers, perpetrators of crimes against humanity and war criminals as well as handing over Rwandan genocide suspects to the International Criminal Tribunal for Rwanda (ICTR).

The Agreement recognised for the first time the security threat posed by *Interahamwe* and ex-FAR genocidal forces and called for a regional response. To Rwanda that had stationed about 20,000 troops in the DRC since 1998, this was both a military and political victory since all her concerns were addressed by the agreement. The Lusaka Ceasefire Agreement was signed on 10 July, 1999 by the Heads of State of Rwanda, Angola, Democratic Republic of Congo, Namibia, Uganda, Zambia and Zimbabwe.

However, as the United Nations failed to deploy a fully-fledged peacekeeping force that would enforce peace and disarm the militia, including the *Interahamwe* and ex-FAR, Rwanda maintained troops in the DR Congo as a buffer against attacks on the country.

Pretoria Accord

Failure to implement the Lusaka Agreement in full led to further negotiations between the Governments of Rwanda and the DR Congo. These new talks were sponsored by the African Union. The five-day talks held in Pretoria, South Africa, culminated in the Pretoria Accord in July 2002 that was supposed to end the second Congo War.

Rwanda agreed to withdraw her troops from the DRC after international commitment to disarm *Interahamwe* and ex-FAR forces and to hand over genocide suspects to either the International Criminal Tribunal for Rwanda or to Rwandan domestic courts.

Withdrawal of Rwandan Troops From DRC

In September 2002, Rwandan troops started to withdraw from the DR Congo. By October 2002, the 20,000 Rwandan troops had returned home through Goma and Bukavu.

In a dispatch by IRIN News Service (Humanitarian news and analysis service from the UN Office for the Coordination of Humanitarian Affairs) of 18 September 2002, the then Rwandan Foreign Affairs Minister, Andre

Bumaya, is quoted as saying that the withdrawal was "motivated by our desire to conform to the letter and spirit of the Pretoria Accord". On 5 October 2002, Rwanda announced the completion of its withdrawal, while the United Nations Peacekeeping Mission to Congo (MONUC) confirmed the departure of Rwandan soldiers.

Despite Rwanda's commitment since the Lusaka Ceasefire Agreement and the Pretoria Accord, Eastern DR Congo continued to be a base for FDLR and a source of threat to Rwanda's national security and that of the region.

9

Urugwiro Consultations

The business of government is to draw up development goals and priorities, and design ways of achieving them in collaboration with the citizens.
President Paul Kagame

Consensus Building

Democracy, dialogue and consensus building are among the RPF's core political values. It believes that they are the foundation of shared ownership by the people of the country's political, economic and social destiny.

Thus after repatriating most of the refugees, resettling the internally displaced, treating the injured and generally improving the welfare of the population as well as carrying out significant rehabilitation of basic infrastructure, Rwandans had to have a conversation on the future of their country.

It is in this spirit that the Government of National Unity under the leadership of the RPF made a historic decision to consult Rwandans on critical challenges the country was facing. This decision was also made at a time when the stipulated transition period, according to the Arusha Peace Agreement, was nearing its end.

Every Saturday, from May 1998 to March 1999, the Government of National Unity under the RPF conducted discussions and consultations in Urugwiro Village (where the offices of the Head of State are located), to hammer out a common vision for a new Rwanda. These consultations, which later became the foundation of a new Rwanda, were subsequently referred to as the Urugwiro Consultations.

Purpose

The rationale behind the consultations was for the Government to get views from a cross section of Rwandans on important challenges the country was facing as well as consensus on how to tackle these challenges. In the process, Rwandans would own the roadmap to the recovery and development of the country.

The major challenges discussed included: national unity and reconciliation after a long period of divisions amongst Rwandans that culminated in the war and genocide against the Batutsi in 1994; establishing democratic governance after decades of dictatorship; rebuilding the justice system in view of the immense problems that this sector faced, including a large number of genocide suspects, putting the economy back on its feet, and addressing the challenging security situation in the country, especially in the northern, southern and western parts of the country.

People

In order to get a wide range of views, the consultations attracted a cross section of Rwandans serving in various positions of responsibility in the country at the time or who had been in such positions in previous regimes. All in all, the consultations included: the President of the Republic, Vice President of the Republic, the prime minister and all members of cabinet; the speaker and the two deputy speakers of parliament, as well as chairpersons of parliamentary standing committees; the presidents of all political parties registered in the country; the members of the bureau of the supreme court; the governors of the 12 provinces in the country; the commanders of the national army and gendarmerie; advisors of the President and those of the Vice-President, as well as advisors in the prime minister's office. Invited were also individuals who had served in political positions in previous regimes from the time when Rwanda was a kingdom in colonial times, and those who had served in the post-colonial regimes who were still able to contribute. Others included technicians and experts in various fields such as law, finance, academia, civil society and military and intelligence services as well as members of the public who had useful knowledge to contribute to debates and consultations.

Process

To facilitate open and sincere debates, participants with special expertise in a particular field would be constituted into working commissions to study a given problem and report back to the larger meeting. As mentioned above, critical national issues discussed over a period of almost a whole year included: reconciliation, democracy, justice, the economy, and peace and security.

These five issues therefore constituted what the RPF leadership felt still presented a number of challenges, whose solutions needed to be debated and a way forward agreed upon by all stakeholders so that together, the government and the people could address them.

Highlights of the Consultations

Unity and Reconciliation

After a thorough analysis by all participants, it was agreed that the root causes of disunity amongst Rwandans began with the advent of the colonialists, who introduced their divide and rule policy, dividing a people who shared everything, including language, culture, and geographical settlement. They further agreed that there had never been wars among the social groups in Rwanda and that Rwandans lived in harmony although they had different occupations. It is worth recollecting that after 1973 the divisions took another turn, creating hostility between the Northerners and especially the Southerners and, to a certain extent between religions.

It was generally agreed that unless one clearly understood the genesis of the divisions among the Rwandan people, it would be difficult to carry out a meaningful national reconciliation effort.

Democracy and Governance

In the consultations, democracy was generally understood to be about leadership, including how leadership is put in place, and how leaders relate to the people they lead in terms of accountability. Democracy was also understood to be about how institutions of leadership are put in place or removed. Hence Rwandans understood that democracy is about leadership that is given by the people, determined by the people and works in the interest of the people, and that democracy is characterised by free participation of the people, representation of the people in institutions of leadership (not monopolised by some) and accountability of people's representatives to those they represent.

Participants at the consultations agreed that in pre-colonial Rwanda, there was no democracy. However, there was always a level of consensus in making major decisions, especially through the institutions of leadership that existed then. These institutions were:

- *Abatware b'Umukenke* (chiefs in charge of livestock)
- *Abatware bashinzwe iby'ubutaka* (chiefs in charge of agriculture)
- *Abatware bashinzwe iby'ingabo* (chiefs in charge of the army)

It was thus agreed that a lot more needed to be done to introduce democracy in Rwanda.

Already, the Government of National Unity (GNU) and the Broad Based Transitional Parliament (BBTP), since their inception, had begun to champion the principle of consensus building in decision-making. This was reflected in the search for constructive ideas from many people through discussions. The Urugwiro consultations were also built on the same principle. The participants appreciated that this was an important beginning of democratic governance and a fundamental departure from the past regimes.

Economy

During the consultations it was discovered and agreed that past regimes had mismanaged Rwanda's economy to the extent that about 90% of Rwandans had no direct role in the country's economy. It was observed that those in charge of running the country's economy would most of the time take arbitrary decisions to the detriment of economic growth that would have benefited the population, while others had plundered the country's economy for their personal gain. By 1980 Rwanda's external debt had sky-rocketed to US$150 million and in 1990 it had gone up to more than US$ 1 billion.

This poor economic state had been further exacerbated by the 1994 genocide against the Tutsi which left more than one million people killed, taking away human resources which were the cornerstone of the country's economy. Many Rwandans who had survived the genocide saw no need to engage again in economic activities since they had no hope for the future. A large percentage of these Rwandans had been left helpless and very vulnerable and were depending on government assistance to survive. In post-genocide Rwanda, most of the funds to finance development projects in the country were from external sources. At the same time, Rwanda had an external trade deficit that stood at about US$ 250 million annually since the country's exports were valued at about US$70 million while her imports were at US$ 350 million. Rwanda had to rely mainly on foreign aid for her developmental needs, which was not sustainable.

Justice

After decades of corrupt regimes, misrule had become entrenched in Rwandan society. The justice system in the country needed a total overhaul. This sector lacked qualified personnel. As outlined above, out of 702 judges, only 74 had university law degrees across the country (Republic of Rwanda, 2010).

Impunity and injustice were recognised as impediments to the reconciliation efforts that the Government of National Unity was determined to carry out. The consultative meetings classified the challenges that faced the Justice Sector into two categories: challenges in the ordinary practice of justice in Rwanda and the challenges that had been brought about by the aftermath of the 1994 genocide against Tutsi.

It was also agreed that the 1994 genocide had resulted in unprecedented numbers of perpetrators, posing a heavy burden on the already weakened justice sector. The challenges ranged from personnel, equipment and infrastructure to handling the overwhelming number of alleged perpetrators throughout the country, which made investigations into the crimes an uphill task, yet justice had to be done.

During the consultations, participants appreciated that the justice sector had complex challenges that required appropriate solutions in

Peace and Security

At the consultations, it was observed that despite RPF/RPA single-handedly stopping the genocide and repatriating millions of Rwandans from neighbouring countries, there was still mistrust among the population. At that point in time some even believed that genocide could easily recur. This had been worsened by the insurgency in Northern, Western and Central Rwanda by some members of *Interahamwe* and ex-FAR who would attack and kill people randomly.

Some politicians were even sowing seeds of hatred and mistrust among the population, and this posed a big challenge to the efforts of unity and reconciliation. A number of politicians were fleeing the country and going into self-imposed exile, thus creating more confusion among the population.

Some Rwandans believed that the Government of National Unity was a Batutsi government that was planning to exterminate Bahutu at some point in time. This false belief was supported by those in the jungles of DR Congo and other countries, who used this propaganda so as to keep Rwandans divided along Bahutu-Batutsi lines. Another great threat to peace and security that was highlighted at the consultations was the settlement policy that wasn't clear and rampant land wrangles which were causing mistrust among the people.

Despite the challenges highlighted above, the RPF-led Government of National Unity was credited for fighting the insurgency and dismantling the refugee camps in neighbouring DR Congo, which had been turned into military bases for ex-FAR and *Interahamwe*. This had resulted in the return of relative peace and security in many parts of the country, more particularly the northern part. It was further highlighted that many Rwandans were no longer sympathisers of those armed groups.

Recommendations from Urugwiro Consultations

From Urugwiro Consultations emerged key recommendations, all in line with the prevailing challenges and the vision that the RPF had for the country.

Unity and Reconciliation

Participants observed and recommended that the correct version of the history of Rwanda and its people needed to be understood, including the distortions created by the colonialists whose aim was to divide and rule Rwandans.

They also agreed that the covered history should be taught in schools in order to undo the colonial damage. However, it was noted that the road to unity was still long as the Bahutu and Batutsi were still apart although they worked and lived together. Mistrust and suspicion were still pervasive. It was further noted that fighting against the divisive politics that had characterised Rwanda for decades and eradication genocide ideology of the needed long term relevant and strategic programmes to eradicate it had to be put in place.

Property and land issues needed to be resolved because they had not been fully tackled. It was also recommended that people whose residences had been destroyed needed to be assisted to acquire houses.

Since some political parties in coalition with RPF had never publicly denounced sectarian politics, participants recommended that this issue needed to be addressed because the image of those parties had never changed and citizens remained suspicious of them. For a united Rwanda to be realised, it was also recommended that all leaders in government, parliament and political parties should combine efforts to find out how to reconcile Rwandans in order to build a strong foundation for social, political and economic transformation.

Much emphasis was also put on the character of all leaders and it was recommended that leadership at all levels has to be good and must fight against anything that threatens the unity of Rwandans.

On this note, they recommended that a political school be established to teach Rwandans politics and good governance. It was further resolved that a leadership code of conduct be established to guide the behaviour and conduct of leaders in the country; that it must be respected by all and should indicate sanctions against any leader who violates it.

To strengthen national unity and reconciliation, it was recommended that a National Unity and Reconciliation Commission (NURC) be established and its main mission would be to explain to Rwandans the origins of their disunity and what needed to be done to restore it and to fight against anything that would obstruct reconciliation efforts. Since RPF believed the youths are the pillar of a new Rwanda, it was recommended that the education curriculum should include the right version of the history of Rwanda including what divided Rwandans and what needed to be done to restore unity.

Participants in the consultations concurred that Rwandans share a common culture that has important positive values that have been gradually disappearing under the pressure of foreign influence. It was therefore vital to restore Rwanda's culture and values which would help restore patriotism, nobility, integrity (to be *inyangamugayo*), respect, love and, consequently, unity.

It was further noted and recommended that the government of Rwanda should never at any time favour any religion over others. Instead religious leaders should help the government in its quest for national unity and reconciliation basing on common Rwandan traditional values.

Democracy and Governance

After lengthy debates on the establishment of democratic governance, the following conclusions and resolutions were made by the consultative gathering:

Participants resolved that the principle of suitable democratic governance be adopted in Rwanda, and that democracy should give the citizens the right to participate in issues concerning leadership and activities intended to develop them. It was stressed that participatory democracy would be adopted. The cabinet was given the responsibility of studying in detail the implementation and timetable of elections and other technical details for grassroots elections. It was also proposed that those elected should serve a two-year term in order to set the stage for national elections. It was agreed that the elections were to be piloted in local government structures and would be carried out up to the sector level.

It was in this connection that leadership in local government at all levels was to be exercised by elected committees instead of individuals. Local government elections would be based strictly on individual merit and not political party affiliation. To strengthen democracy in Rwanda, participants further agreed that in order to give people a visible role in governance, decentralisation would be adopted. This was aimed at bringing governance structures nearer to the people so that they could participate in decision-making, putting in place mechanisms for evaluating leaders, monitoring grass-root leadership and increasing accountability to the people.

Since bad leadership had totally destroyed the social fabric of Rwandans, it was resolved that Rwandans should elect their leaders, be empowered to remove leaders who do not deliver, participate in finding solutions to national problems and adopt a model of democracy for Rwanda that responds to Rwandan realities. It should not be a mere imitation of other democracies elsewhere.

It was further recommended that the rights of Rwandans must be respected by all, and that equality before the law must be the norm rather than the exception. There was also a communication that all forms of injustice and impunity must be eliminated and that people who committed genocide must face justice. Equally, new national symbols namely: the national anthem, the national flag and the coat of arms should be designed to reflect the unity of Rwandans.

Economy

Despite these economic challenges, it was agreed that since 1994 when the Government of National Unity led by the RPF came into power, some semblance of economic recovery was recognisable. The country's Gross Domestic Product (GDP) had picked up and it stood at 11% due to the sound economic management that had been initiated and inflation was at 4%. In general terms, the economy had gone back to 94% of where it was before the 1994 genocide. Rwanda's relationship with international financial institutions like the World Bank and IMF had also greatly improved. However, other donors hadn't yet picked great interest in supporting Rwanda at that time. Participants at the Urugwiro Consultations therefore resolved to lay down strategies that would see Rwanda's economy make a serious and quick recovery.

Among them were quick and far-reaching reforms in the agricultural sector since this was the backbone of Rwanda's economy. To fast track economic recovery, it was recommended that the Information and Communications Technology (ICT) sector be focused on for Rwanda to quickly develop. It was recommended that Rwandans be trained and mobilised to improve on their work ethic since it was through various economic activities, not the government, that the economy would grow.

Great focus also needed to be put on developing a strong national human resource that would see the economy boosted quickly and in a sustainable manner. The government was advised to lay down strategies to support private sector development. It was further resolved that Rwanda needed to lay down strategies that would see her become aid-free rather than always depending on foreign aid for her development. To cement it all, it was recommended that Rwanda strive for regional integration and find means of easily accessing the sea to ease foreign trade.

For Rwandans to regain their dignity or self-worth, it was observed and recommended that everything possible be done to reduce poverty among the population by creating jobs because it was generally accepted that poverty can create a conducive environment for disunity.

Justice

Following lengthy deliberations, the delegates recommended two categories of recommendations. The first category concerned crimes of genocide while the second addressed issues of ordinary justice.

Resolutions on the Crime of Genocide against the Tutsi

Firstly, concerning the genocide, the delegates agreed that the genocide against the Tutsi actually begun in 1959, and recurred in 1963, 1964, 1973, 1990, 1992 and 1993, reaching its climax in 1994. It came to be called the 1994 genocide against the Tutsi simply because that is the time when UN Security Council recognised it. Divisive politics from colonial times through the First and Second Republics, selfish and narrow interests of the few in power and exclusion led to the genocide against the Tutsi and due to the large number of genocide suspects, the classical justice system couldn't handle all the genocide cases in the Rwandan situation and bring them to a conclusion. Additionally, since the genocide against the Tutsi had been carried out by their fellow Rwandans, classical justice was unlikely to foster unity and reconciliation.

It was therefore recommended that a new justice system based on Rwandan traditional values be put in place. This system, called Gacaca, would involve ordinary citizens in order to get rid of the culture of impunity forever; inculcate the culture of honesty, and foster national unity, reconciliation and cohesion. The new justice system was to focus on crimes committed between 1 October 1990 and 31 December 1994. The participants at the Urugwiro Consultations insisted that the new Gacaca courts were not just reverting to the old traditional Gacaca but would dispense justice that reconciled Rwandans.

Recommendations on Ordinary Justice Challenges

It was further recommended that serious attention was needed in reforming the Justice system. Despite the semblance of the rule of law in place, some officials in the Justice system were still corrupt, divisive, and based their legal decisions on divisive lines, which impacted negatively on reconciliation efforts.

To fight corruption and related malpractices in the justice sector and other institutions of government, the Urugwiro consultations recommended the following: educating Rwandans on what corruption is and its manifestations; establishing a law that would oblige all politicians, judges as well as any other person in a position of influence in government to declare their assets before commencing their official duties and to do so annually; establishing the office of the ombudsman to inspect the working of the government institutions, including local government; establishing a mechanism to inspect the functioning of courts of law with a view to prosecuting and sanctioning corrupt judicial officials; setting term limits for judges and reformation of the supreme court and other courts of law.

Peace and Security

Finally, participants recommended that leaders at different levels be nearer to the people and assist them in solving their problems, thus rebuilding the trust between the government and the population. It was also recommended that citizens be mobilised to feel that they had a role to play in maintaining their own security, despite the efforts by security agencies. On poverty reduction, it was recommended that leaders continue to mobilise people to work harder and work together thus building trust.

In conclusion, the Urugwiro Consultations were and continue to be the benchmark of the foundation on which a new united, democratic and prosperous Rwanda that RPF struggled for is built. Many national programmes aimed at Rwanda's sustainable development are hinged on the outcomes of these consultations. The implementation of the Urugwiro recommendations is to be extensively discussed in the following chapter, which paves the way for a new Rwanda.

10

Setting the Transformational Agenda

Rwandans can never forget their tragic past but do not want to be defined by it.
Tony Blair

New national direction

Having concluded the Urugwiro Consultations which aimed at establishing a sustainable transformation agenda for Rwanda by early 1999, the Broad Based Transitional Government took into account the need to address the most pressing issues of Rwanda at the time. It therefore adopted a new transformation agenda which was to focus on key strategic issues starting with unity and reconciliation of the Rwandan people. This agenda for the transformation of Rwanda also integrated a set of new directions the country desired to take for a sustainable socio-economic development.

Prioritising Unity and Reconciliation

Forging national unity and reconciliation remains point number one on RPF's Nine-Point Programme. It would be impossible to institute a strong legal framework with a home-grown feel, or build strong national institutions in a country like Rwanda that had been characterised by deep divisions and suspicion, without national unity and reconciliation.

Indeed, even during the armed struggle and the Arusha peace talks, national unity and reconciliation had been viewed as a pre-requisite for the establishment and consolidation of democracy, peace and security, the rule of law, social cohesion and development.

To achieve this, the National Unity and Reconciliation Commission (NURC) was established in 1999 with the core mission of promoting peace, unity and prosperity in Rwanda, through the preparation and coordination of various national programmes aimed at building national unity and reconciliation among all Rwandans.

The Unity and Reconciliation Commission engaged in educating and mobilising the population on matters relating to national unity and reconciliation. It also made proposals on measures that could eradicate divisions among Rwandans and reinforce national unity and reconciliation. Another responsibility of the NURC, was to denounce and fight against acts, writings and utterances which were intended to promote any kind of discrimination, intolerance or even xenophobia.

In sustaining its activities and making sure that its objectives are met effectively, the Commission also organised summits which brought together all the stakeholders of unity and reconciliation for dialogues meant to discuss and promote unity and reconciliation.

Good progress towards achieving national unity and reconciliation, thanks to total commitment from the government, has been made through various initiatives by NURC. The initiatives which are mainly home-grown include, among others, *Ingando* (solidarity camps) that bring together diverse groups of people like students, farmers and civil servants to deliberate on issues like the history of Rwanda, the nation and citizenship, good governance, human rights, economy and social affairs.

The National Unity and Reconciliation Commission, along with institutions like Gacaca courts and others, have transformed Rwandan society into what it is today. Previously, some people thought it would not be possible for perpetrators of genocide and survivors to live together again and the fact that this has happened successfully is a great indication that the RPF-led government is making history and building a new unified nation.

Catalysing Long-Term Development: Vision 2020

Having established the various institutions to address the most pressing issues as discussed during the 1998-99 Urugwiro consultations, the transitional government was now in a position to lay down strategies and programmes to rebuild a new prosperous and unified Rwanda. These new strategies were to be implemented under a broad projection of the government; the Vision 2020.

In the year 2000, the government laid a strong and focused foundation for a new Rwanda. The Vision 2020 document was designed and adopted, setting national development targets and priorities for the next 20 years. The main objective of Vision 2020 is to transform Rwanda into a knowledge-based middle income country, thereby reducing poverty, health problems and making the country united and democratic. This vision has nine pillars that inform all efforts and activities, which is a departure from the methods used by all the previous regimes in the country. The nine pillars on which Vision 2020 sits are good governance and a capable state; a well governed country at all levels so as to be able to deliver the set objectives; human resource development and a knowledge-based economy; a private sector-led economy; infrastructure development; productive and market-oriented agriculture; gender equality; protection of the environment and sustainable natural resource management; science and technology, including ICT and regional and international economic integration.

The Vision was implemented immediately through the medium-term planning framework that began in 2002, with the first Poverty Reduction Strategic Plan (PRSP I). The six broad areas of priority under PRSP I where action was needed immediately and ranked by importance were rural development and agricultural transformation; human development; economic infrastructure; governance; private sector development and institutional capacity-building.

Since the initiation of Vision 2020, Rwanda has made much progress towards attaining these objectives and this is greatly attributed to economic planning with quick wins to make sure that people had food on their table, children went to school and the sick got treatment.

Agriculture

The first step towards economic recovery was to focus on Rwanda's exploitation of her agricultural potential. Production of enough food to feed the people, with surplus left over for sale was prioritised. Particular attention was paid to agriculture in areas that had historically been characterised by hunger and starvation — in parts of current Southern Province such as Gikongoro and in Eastern Province, for example in Bugesera. Mass mobilisation for production was made to produce whatever was suitable in particular areas. Cooperatives and associations in agro production were formed and assisted, especially with proper seeds and inputs to boost production, as well as linking producers to markets.

Marshland was reclaimed and used for rice growing and plenty of investments were put in both crop and land husbandry to improve unit production. This resulted in visible dividends in the short run and the country's yields surged. On the other hand, a lot of attention was paid to export crops, especially tea and coffee, to boost the nation's export base. Plenty of incentives were put in place including making it easy to access seedlings, fertilisers and loans. Strategies to restock the entire country with cattle, goats, pigs and poultry were put in place, including buying cows from areas that were well stocked and distributing them to other areas. Several exotic cattle and goats were imported to enhance productivity, some from overseas and others from neighbouring countries.

The next step in boosting Rwanda's economic potential was to tap into the tourism industry, which quickly became one of the country's main foreign currency earners.

Healthcare and Social Protection

The challenges faced by health services in the post-genocide period were highlighted earlier. They included the destruction and looting of health infrastructure during the war; chronic shortage of qualified health workers to run the services and lack of basic infrastructure such as roads and hospitals in some of the areas which had been neglected by the previous regimes. Despite the prevailing uphill task to provide at least basic health services to the sick and the injured after the devastating 1994 genocide against the Tutsi, the transitional government embarked on rehabilitation and re-equipping of the existing facilities with assistance from international friends who also provided health personnel to supplement those that were available. The government also embarked on construction of other facilities in previously neglected parts of the country. The government, with its meagre resources, concurrently embarked on both curative and preventive healthcare in all parts of the country and sometimes applied unconventional methods for survival.

In preventive healthcare delivery, a number of innovations that have had a vast impact on the population include public health mobilisers (*Abakangurambaga b' ubuzima*) who were trained in hygiene in every province.

These were volunteers who received training in simple but effective methods of disease prevention such as drinking boiled water, digging latrines, mobilising for vaccination of children and pregnant mothers and use of mosquito nets to prevent malaria. These volunteers were facilitated by the government to educate the population on disease prevention, and this has had a huge impact because over 78% of the diseases in Rwanda are preventable. This home-grown initiative has continued to work and save many lives.

One of the major challenges Rwanda faced in the post-genocide era was the low financial and geographical access to health facilities. The government introduced a system of health insurance across the whole country in 1998 to guarantee equitable access to health services. By June 2015, this home grown solution of Mutual Health Insurance (Mutuelle de Santé) covered 76% of the entire Rwandan population. This contributed to a decrease in maternal mortality per 100,000 births from 2,300 in 1994 to 210 in 2015. Under-five mortality rate per 1,000 births also reduced from 196 in 1994 to 50 in 2014. (The National Institute of Statistics of Rwanda 2014). With recent interventions, these rates are expected to reduce further.

A combination of good health policies and home-grown solutions has made Rwanda one of the African countries with very impressive health statistics. For instance dysentery (*Macinya*) that had characterised the country especially in the North, reduced so drastically that it is no longer a feared killer. Malaria prevalence has also reduced by 70%. Tremendous progress has been made in the prevention, treatment and care of HIV/AIDS.

A fund to support the vulnerable survivors of genocide was put in place in 1998. The fund has supported more than 400,000 students in secondary schools and 14,000 in universities since its formation. Hundreds of them have also been financed to access medical care even abroad.

The *Ubudehe* programme was launched in 2001 as part of a partnership between the Ministry of Finance and Economic Planning and the Ministry of Local Government in a bid to draft the Poverty Reduction Strategy Paper (PRSP)(Government of Rwanda (2001)). This process was named *Ubudehe* with reference to the Rwandan culture of mutual assistance whereby people would come together to address problems facing them.

In the past, Rwandans resorted to *Ubudehe* mainly in agriculture and house construction. Nowadays, Rwandans are faced with various problems such as construction of roads, ensuring child education, health facilities, security etc, which require collective efforts.

Due to the urgent need to quickly re-absorb the half a million unemployed and the underemployed people in the rural areas, a labour intensive programme known as HIMO was launched in 2002 and saw hundreds of thousands of rural people getting engaged in activities like road construction and terrace making in hilly parts of the country which enabled them to earn some money at the end of the day, thus fighting poverty.

Education

Like any other sector in Rwanda after the 1994 genocide against the Tutsi, education had greatly suffered from long-term neglect and the little that was in place was destroyed during the genocide. Infrastructure had been destroyed and teachers as well as students killed. That is why the transitional government embarked on rejuvenating the sector. The task proved to be daunting for the government to address alone. Because of this, the private sector was encouraged to build more schools and higher institutions of learning. This saw the birth of such institutions as Kigali Independent University (ULK), which was established in 1996, Independent Institute of Lay Adventists of Kigali (INILAK) in 1997, Kigali Institute of Management (KIM) in 2003 and others.

Some teacher training colleges were established such as Rukara College of Education and Kigali Institute of Education to increase the number of qualified teachers in primary and secondary schools. Other higher institutions of learning were established such as Kigali Institute of Science and Technology, Kigali Health Institute, as well as the expansion of the National University of Rwanda.

Since the pre-1994 education system in Rwanda was characterised by institutionalised hatred and many other forms of discrimination, a national examination council was established to ensure meritocracy and transparency in examinations, which has become the norm in Rwanda today. The classification of teachers and students by assumed ethnic affiliation was abolished and a new system that promotes national unity and reconciliation as well as equity of access to education was put in place. Many Rwandans were sent to study abroad mainly in India, the United States of America, UK and other places and this has had a positive impact on the economy as a result of a knowledgeable workforce.

Tertiary education in Rwanda had stagnated since the formation of the National University of Rwanda (NUR) which had only produced 2,160 graduates from its inception in 1963 up to 1993. From 1995 to 2000, a period of just five years, there were over 2,000 university graduates. Since 1994, the number higher institutions of learning has increased from one to 23. The total number of students receiving higher education rose from 2,000 to more than 70,000 todate. All these education reforms have produced qualified human resource in all domains.

Empowering Citizens

Rwanda experienced bad governance from colonial times up to 1994. The RPF believed that if Rwanda was to be democratic, power had to be given back to the people to decide on all major national issues. The avenue through which power would be taken back to the people was decentralisation which is why this was one of the pillars of Vision 2020.

In 2000, the transitional government adopted the decentralisation policy and strategy as one of the pillars of Vision 2020, with a commitment to empowering local communities to determine their own future, to achieve good governance, pro-poor service delivery and sustainable development. As a pilot project to test how Rwandans would behave in elections, just five years after the 1994 genocide against the Tutsi, the first local government elections were held in 1999, a year before the decentralisation policy was adopted. The elections, which turned out to be peaceful and transparent, were organised cautiously and held at cell level, but candidates were campaigning on merit, not on political party affiliation. This marked a fundamental shift in the way local leaders occupied their offices.

This was followed by the election of leaders at district level in 2001, making the first steps along the democratic path that Rwanda was embarking on. Prior to these elections, leadership from the lowest to the highest level was appointed and therefore accountable to the appointing authority and not to the people they served. In strengthening this democratic path that Rwanda was taking, an independent National Electoral Commission (NEC) was created in 2000 to oversee all elections in the country.

Despite the challenges that still faced the Broad Based Transitional Government (BBTG) due to the legacy of the genocide, a lot had already been done and it was time to embark on a fully-fledged democratic path guided by a constitution. The RPF strongly believed that this had to be a people-centered constitution which mirrored the aspirations of all Rwandans. The outcome of the constitution making process was to pave the way for both presidential and parliamentary elections. However, some Rwandans and even foreigners thought that it was not yet time for elections based on multi-party politics, considering the mistrust and suspicion that still lingered in the minds of many. But since RPF had fought for democracy, it was ready to stretch as far as possible and give Rwandans a say in the management of their country.

Constitution Making Process

Throughout its constitutional history, Rwanda had never had a constitution that responded to the expectations and aspirations of Rwandans. All prior constitutions were made with the help of foreign experts and most of the ideas were not related to the expectations of Rwanda as a nation.

The transitional government created a National Constitution Commission composed of 13 other commissioners. All members of the Commission, including its Chairman, were elected by the Transitional National Assembly. The composition of the Commission mirrored the political makeup of the Transitional National Assembly, which was representative of all political parties that made up the transitional government, an ideal that the RPF had maintained throughout the transitional period.

Driven by the spirit of having a constitution that reflected the people's wishes, the Commission's method of work included broad-based inclusive participation in order to solicit citizens' views. The Commission members travelled to all corners of the country and even visited Rwandans in the diaspora and sought experience from other countries worldwide. This way, the Commission sought to ensure that the draft Constitution was "home-grown", relevant to Rwanda's specific needs and reflected the views of the entire population. In addition to holding consultative meetings in many parts of the country to get people's views, they sent questionnaires to civil groups across the country.

Following these elaborate and extensive consultations, the draft constitution was published in 2003 and approved by the Parliament. It was then put to a referendum in May 2003. The turnout on voting day was overwhelming at 87% and the constitution was accepted, with 93% voting in favour. This process paved the way for both presidential and parliamentary elections, which would usher in a democratic dispensation. This was what RPF had fought for since its inception in 1987.

Following the promulgation of the new constitution, Rwanda's first democratically contested multiparty presidential and parliamentary elections were held in August 2003. The RPF's flag bearer, President Paul Kagame, attained 95% of the votes. The RPF's resounding victory paved the way for total transformation of the lives of Rwandans based on her 2003 manifesto.

The manifesto which endeared the RPF to voters is summarised in four pillars: good governance, justice, economic development and social welfare.

Part 4

Deepening Socio-Economic Transformation

11

Good Governance

The foundation of all our efforts is good governance, which means a relentless focus on delivering the results that citizens want.

President Paul Kagame

Where Rwanda has come from

There is no single universally accepted and applicable definition of good governance. However, it is generally agreed that good governance includes elements such as respect for human rights, the rule of law, effective citizen participation, transparent and accountable processes and institutions, an efficient and effective public sector, equal opportunities and values that foster responsibility, solidarity and tolerance. Governance is always conceived within a given context, and its definition is always based on one or more perspectives relevant to its application. Different countries and international organisations have various definitions of good governance. The World Bank, UNDP, European Commission, USAID, UK and Sweden have their own definitions of governance which they use globally (The World Bank, 2007; UNDP, 2006; European Commission, 2003; DFID, 2007; JGA, 2008).

In the Rwandan context, the Joint Governance Assessment (JGA) has defined governance as "the exercise of economic, political and administrative authority to manage a country's affairs at all levels, comprising the mechanisms, processes, and institutions through which that authority is directed". Good governance refers to attributes that are most likely to promote development, human rights, justice and peace. And those attributes include: state capability, accountability, responsiveness, inclusiveness, fairness and legitimacy.

From the 1950s, as Rwandans struggled for self-determination from Belgian colonialists, all the way through to independence in 1962, Rwanda was scarred by political violence caused primarily by the politics of exclusion and segregation that saw tens of thousands of mainly Batutsi killed, and hundreds of thousands others become refugees in neighbouring countries. It is these same practices that later culminated in the 1994 genocide against the Tutsi.

The RPF – during the liberation struggle and even after assuming state power in 1994 – was therefore determined to change the country's governance trajectory through the formulation and implementation of policies and strategies that would see Rwandans have a say in the management of their country without fear or favour, as well as access services that would improve their livelihood.

This is well captured in the original Eight-point Political Programme of the RPF, which stresses the need for the restoration of unity among Rwandans, establishment of democratic governance, elimination of corruption, the promotion of social welfare, and international cooperation based on mutual respect, among others.

It is this vision that guided governance during the transition period (1994-2003), with the ultimate goal of rebuilding a new nation founded on the principles of good governance and democracy.

Consensual Democracy and Power-sharing

It is generally accepted that broadly, based on their nature and operations, political systems are divided into two major categories. In the first category political parties are "political enemies" and their operations vis-à-vis the other side are driven by confrontation. In the other category political parties are rather political partners, and consensus and coalitions are their main drive. The two categories are respectively called majoritarian and consensual models of democracy (Lijphart, 1999).

In the past, political parties' ideological dimensions were dominated by centrality of the identity (Hutu, Tutsi identities for that matter). As a result, democratisation was periodically associated with tension and violent conflicts which culminated in genocide in 1994.

During the liberation struggle, the RPF advocated for constitutional provisions based on power sharing as opposed to the "winner take all" model. It rejected the "ethinic majority model" which was used as an excuse to exclude some sections of the population of Rwanda from politics. The RPF-led government introduced a paradigm shift that considers political stakeholders as partners and not enemies; the rule of the game being that consensus is privileged over confrontation. This strategic choice not only saved Rwanda from the perverse effects of democratisation but also cemented national unity and economic progress.

The 2003 Constitution is crafted in such a manner that the most important political positions in the country are shared in line with the fundamental principle of power sharing. Article 58 of the Constitution provides that "the President of the Republic and the Speaker of the Chamber of Deputies shall belong to different political organisations". This means that if a given political organisation wins the Presidential election, it cannot contest the position of the Speaker of Chamber of Deputies. Another important proposition of the Constitution which jealously safeguards the fundamental principle of power sharing is Article 116 entitled "composition of cabinet". Article 116 (4) states: "The members of Cabinet are selected from political organisations on the basis of their seats in the Chamber of Deputies..." Article 116 (5) stipulates that: "... a political organisation holding the majority of seats in the Chamber of Deputies shall not exceed fifty (50)% of all members of the Cabinet". Furthermore, political organisations enjoy their political rights through participation in the Forum of Political parties. However, the adherence of political organisations to the Forum, which is used as a platform to discuss national political agenda, is voluntary (Republic of Rwanda, 2003).

Nearly 80% of Rwandans are satisfied with power sharing while 85% of Rwandans are satisfied with the state of democratic rights and freedom. (Republic of Rwanda, 2014).

Free, Transparent and Peaceful Elections

With a firm legal framework embedded in the constitution, and following the 2003 general elections, peaceful, transparent, free and fair elections across the whole spectrum of governance structure (presidential, legislative and local government) have become the norm in Rwanda, thus consolidating a firm democratic system. That Rwandans can vote basing on a candidate's qualities, not their origin, religion or sex, is a complete departure from the past. By 2013, the National Electoral Commission (NEC) had successfully conducted two presidential, three legislative and three local government elections, where voter turnout exceeded 90%.

To many political observers, this turnout is a clear indication of the confidence and trust that Rwandans have developed in the democratic path that RPF ushered in. And this is not just a matter of perception; different studies have shown so. For example, the 2012 Legatum Prosperity Index, an independent non-partisan public policy organisation whose research, publications and programmes advance ideas and policies in support of free and prosperous societies around the world, shows that 85.7% of Rwandans surveyed have confidence in the honesty of elections compared to the global average, which is at 52% (Legatum, 2012).

A feature of Rwanda's journey towards a free and democratic society is that Rwandan communities abroad participate in presidential and legislative elections. According to NEC, in the 2003 presidential and legislative elections, 19,000 Rwandan voters in the Diaspora cast their votes at various polling stations that had been set up in Rwanda's diplomatic missions abroad.

Many local and international election observers have always given a clean bill of health to Rwanda's elections. This has increased confidence in the democratic path charted by the RPF leadership and as a result, new democratic and independent institutions have come into existence. For example, Rwanda's parliament is made up of two chambers – the Chamber of Deputies and the Senate. These two chambers are complementary in nature, but independent of each other. The Executive is overseen by Parliament, according to the constitution, while the judiciary is also independent from the Executive and the Legislature.

Establishing Core Institutions

To further the cause of good governance in Rwanda, anti-corruption and public accountability institutions were created by the RPF. Their operational capacity continued to be strengthened so as to achieve greater accountability. They include:

- Office of the Ombudsman,
- Office of the Auditor General for State Finances
- Rwanda Public Procurement Authority
- Rwanda Revenue Authority, and
- Rwanda Governance Board.

These institutions are mandated to fight injustice, corruption, and abuse of public office by public officials and related offences in both public and private administration and to promote the principles of good governance. They are the first of their kind in the history of Rwanda and are geared towards the promotion of good governance based on the principles of accountability and transparency. Rwanda has also signed and ratified the United Nations Convention against Corruption (UNCAC), the African Union anti-Corruption Convention (AUCC) and the UN Convention against Transnational Organised Crime (UNTOC).

Senior public servants, including the Head of State and other government employees in Rwanda, are required by law to declare their assets every year to the Ombudsman's Office. In 2004, President Paul Kagame set a national precedent by becoming the first senior government official to declare his personal and family assets to the state Ombudsman as part of efforts to promote transparency and curb corruption. Since then, this has become an annual exercise and those who have not declared their assets have been sanctioned accordingly, whatever rank they hold in government. Consequently, in recent years, the World Bank has on several occasions recognised Rwanda for its policy of zero tolerance to corruption. The 2013 Global Corruption Barometer by Transparency International also ranked Rwanda as the least corrupt country in Africa.

Furthermore, in 2011, the Government of Rwanda established the Rwanda Governance Board (RGB) to serve as a one-stop centre for governance related services to generate greater public policy impact. RGB was given the mandate to promote the principles of good governance and decentralisation, monitor the practices of good governance in public and private institutions and conduct research related to governance for achieving good service delivery, sustainable development and prosperity.

As shown above, every year, the Rwanda Governance Board produces the Rwanda Governance Scorecard (RGS) and the Citizen Report Card (CRC) in order to generate evidence to inform public policy formulation and implementation. Findings from CRC and CSC are used in evaluation of leaders' performance to promote citizen-centred governance.

Promotion of National Unity and Reconciliation

Forging national unity and reconciliation remains point number one on the RPF's Nine-point Programme. Without this, it would be impossible to establish a strong home-grown institution that takes account of local conditions in a country that had been characterised by deep divisions and suspicion.

Indeed even during the armed struggle and the Arusha peace talks, national unity and reconciliation had been viewed as a prerequisite for the establishment and consolidation of democracy, peace and security, the rule of law, social cohesion and development. To achieve this, the National Unity and Reconciliation Commission (NURC) was established.

Good progress towards achieving this goal has been made through various initiatives. These initiatives, which are mainly home-grown include, *ingando* (solidarity camps) that bring together diverse groups of people like students, farmers and civil servants to deliberate on issues like the history of Rwanda, the nation and citizenship, good governance, human rights, economy and social affairs.

Ingando was and remains part of the civic education that Rwandans from all walks of life should undergo and it is a means of imparting democratic values and patriotism.

Citizen participation in a democratic society must be based on informed, critical reflection, and on understanding and acceptance of the rights and responsibilities expected of a citizen. Thus the RPF believes that if Rwanda is to be self-reliant, her citizens must understand the political dynamics within the country and even on the world stage, so as to participate in the governance of their country from an informed point of view, hence underscoring the importance of *Ingando*.

On 16 November 2007 *Ingando* was transformed into *Itorero ry'Igihugu* (traditional civic education institution). While officially launching *Itorero ry'Igihugu*, President Paul Kagame said: "We have again gone back to our traditional culture to seek solutions to some of the problems we face... this shows how rich good our traditional culture was."

With civic education imparted to various groups of citizens, important milestones along the way to national unity and reconciliation continue to be reached. This is evidenced by the Rwanda Reconciliation Barometer (RRB), a national public opinion survey whose objective is to track progress on the road to reconciliation in Rwanda.

The RRB of 2012 indicates that 90% of the population feel proud to be citizens of Rwanda (*Ubunyarwanda*) and 94% feel that common national values leading to national reconciliation are being promoted. Further still, more than 82% believe that the country's leadership cares about all people in Rwanda equally. Regarding good governance issues, Rwanda's good performance has not only been captured by local surveys, but even international ones. According to the 2012 Legatum Prosperity Index, Rwanda is ranked 55th out of 142 countries surveyed worldwide in the governance index.

Implementing Decentralisation

The RPF-led government continued to devise means of giving Rwandans a voice in the governance of their country. The initial National Decentralisation Policy was adopted and approved in 2000. Political decentralisation aims to give citizens or their elected representatives more power. It also gives citizens or their representatives more influence in the formulation and implementation of laws and policies. The revised National Decentralisation Policy of the Government of Rwanda (June 2012) defines decentralisation as a means of transferring responsibilities, authority, functions, as well as power and appropriate resources, to district and sub-district levels.

Prior to decentralisation, leaders from the lowest to the highest level were appointed and therefore accountable to the appointing authority and not to the people they governed. The RPF believes that decentralisation is the main mechanism to promote good governance through local people's improved participation, promotion of transparency and accountability.

In 2003 after the promulgation of the new constitution, all local leaders from cell to district level were elected. Local Government elections were first piloted in 1999 and since 2003, free and fair elections at all levels have been a regular occurrence and are becoming a culture that Rwandans associate with national unity, poverty elimination and community development.

This is evidenced by statistics from the National Electoral Commission (NEC) in 2010, where voter turnout in Presidential elections was at 97%, while turnout for local government elections in early 2011 was 93%. This is an indication that Rwandans under RPF leadership are exercising their civil rights and have a voice in the leadership and management of their country.

Rwandans are satisfied with the political trend that the country has taken as shown in the 2012 Rwanda Reconciliation Barometer (RRB), a scientific survey carried out by the National Unity and Reconciliation Commission, in which 82.6% of Rwandans strongly agreed on the need to vote in an election. The same survey indicates that 71.4% of Rwandans willingly attend community meetings so as to participate in decision-making processes.

One of the key tools introduced by the RPF-led government since 2006 to reinforce participation and accountability of local government is the performance-based contracting, locally known as *Imihigo*. *Imihigo* is an old Rwandan cultural practice in which an individual would set him/herself targets to be achieved within a specific period of time.

This home-grown initiative has brought about radical development in districts, sectors, cells and villages, especially improved healthcare, infrastructure like schools, health centres, roads, modern markets and improved service delivery.

Given Rwanda's long history of highly centralised and dictatorial rule prior to 1994, it is laudable that since 2000 the country has developed a fairly strong local governance system with capable local leadership voted in through regular elections, functioning District Councils and well-equipped administrative structures.

The decentralisation policy, therefore, has allowed communities to assume responsibility for planning, service provision and holding their leaders accountable.

In Rwanda's context, these ideals would not have been achieved had Rwandan society remained divided along petty lines such as people's origin, region, religion and other divisive social-political categorisations that had come to define Rwandans.

Gender Equality

Before 1994, women had limited rights not only to political power but also property. Previously a married woman received land from her husband only to provide for the needs of the family. If her husband died and the marital union had produced no male children, a widow could stay on her husband's land only with the agreement of her husband's relatives. Since wife-inheritance was still in practice, a widow was sometimes obliged to marry the brother of her deceased husband in order to stay on her late husband's land. Daughters did not automatically inherit from their fathers, although sometimes they could obtain land as a gift or inherit it when they had no brothers.

These discriminatory practices were exacerbated by the Genocide. In addition to trauma from the Genocide, many widows and other single women found themselves without property or land because their sons had also been killed. This changed when the government of Rwanda established the National Land Reform in 1999 which states that "women, married or not, should not be excluded from the process of land access, land acquisition and land control, and female descendants should not be excluded from the process of family land inheritance." This was remarkable in an environment where previously, a woman would not even open a bank account without the permission of her husband.

The RPF has made women's empowerment and inclusion in all sectors of national life a foundation stone for the country's reconstruction. This goes a long way back to the history of the RPF's liberation struggle, when women were found in all key structures of the Front, including on the frontline as commanders.

In its structure, the RPF also has a Women's League that has leadership structures from the grassroots to the national level. Later the RPF ensured this was well enshrined in Rwanda's constitution, which requires a minimum of 30% women representation in decision-making organs.

Following the 2013 legislative elections, Rwanda has the highest women representation (64%) in parliament in the world.

On 5 July 2013, while addressing thousands of women at a 'Meet the President' event, President Kagame said: "Gender equality in every sector is not a favour; it is your right. It is the way it should be. The right to equality is not something that can be given or taken. It begins with each of you believing in your equal ability to achieve."

Access to family planning and economic prospects through women's credit funds has also been greatly enhanced, making women more self-reliant, especially in a situation with many female headed households.

The government has also made girls' education a priority to enhance women's participation in various sectors of the nation. To safeguard education opportunities for girls, the Rwandan government has enacted a range of policies geared towards achieving the MDGs of universal primary education, gender equality and women's empowerment.

These policies are consistent with Rwanda's international obligations under the Convention for the Elimination of Discrimination against Women, the Convention on the Rights of the Child, and the International Covenant on Economic, Social and Cultural Rights. They also contribute to meeting Rwanda's obligations under the Beijing Platform for Action and the Dakar Goals on Education for All.

Already the benefits of these policies are beginning to show. According to UNICEF, Rwanda has the highest primary school enrolment in Africa. Gender parity at primary level has been achieved with girls' net enrolment rate standing at 98% in 2012, which is higher than that of boys at 95%. The girls' completion rate is at 77.7%, yet the overall completion rate at primary level is 72.7% (UNICEF, 2012).

Efforts are now underway to encourage girls to do well at school and achieve higher results and special emphasis has been placed on encouraging them to enrol in science subjects. The First Lady, Mrs Jeannette Kagame, through her Imbuto Foundation gives awards and prizes to girls who score top marks in national exams. This has strongly boosted girls' desire to perform better at school.

For the above successes not to be lost in various national programmes, a Gender Monitoring Office (GMO) was established. Its main responsibility is to monitor and carry out evaluation on a permanent basis of compliance with gender indicators intended to respect gender in the context of the vision of sustainable national development and to serve as a reference point on matters relating to gender equality and equity.

In recognition of his leadership's success in gender parity, President Paul Kagame received the African Gender Award in Dakar, Senegal, in 2007 and the Global UNICEF Children Champion Award in 2009 for promoting children's rights, particularly in education.

Empowering Youth

With 70% of the population made up of young people below 30 years of age, the government of Rwanda under the RPF leadership recognises not only the challenge but also the opportunity this presents.

Speaking at Youth Connekt Dialogue 2013 in Kigali, where thousands of youth had gathered, President Kagame said: "The youth are Rwanda's future, its *agaciro* (self-worth) in all ways, in terms of strength and leadership, and they are the value and foundation of what every country wants to achieve. This is what youth means." Indeed this is what the RPF believes in since it has a Youth League that has structures from the village - *umudugudu* - to the national level. In this regard, the RPF has revised its constitution in order to have a youth representative on its National Executive Council.

Since 2008, the Government has made sure that there is always an independent ministry in charge of youth to champion their interests and plan for their development. The Ministry is tasked with putting in place a policy framework so that the youth can contribute to the economic and social development of Rwanda.

There is also the National Youth Council (NYC) which has got administrative structures from the village to national level. The NYC encourages young people to pool their knowledge and efforts through cooperatives to boost their participation in the social-economic development of the country.

To have access to financial credit, the Government has helped the youth to establish the Youth Savings and Credit Cooperative for Self Employment and Development (COOJAD). Through COOJAD the youth are now able to access loans.

Through this initiative, the youth have formed cooperatives in various fields like buying motorcycles to get into the transport business. This has boosted their self-esteem since they are able to financially solve their own problems.

An example of such cooperatives is STAMORWA Cooperative which boasts of a membership of about 200. Out of 200, more than 140 members have so far acquired their own motorbikes, which they use in transporting people countrywide.

The youth's increased access to credit has changed the lives of thousands of them and some have been able to build houses, buy cows and plots of land. Since its inception, COOJAD has extended more than US$1 million in credit to the youth.

As a result, in April 2009 COOJAD was recognised for its outstanding contribution to poverty reduction by the International Labour Organisation at the Youth Employment Summit in Kampala, Uganda. Thus, although a private youth initiative, COOJAD has received Rwf 70,000,000 (US$ 119,000) from the government to help with staff costs and overheads.

Due to challenges like drug and alcohol abuse by a significant proportion of the youth, the Government has set up the Iwawa Rehabilitation and Vocational Training Centre. The centre's main mission is to offer vocational and technical training as well as psycho-social counselling for young drug addicts. The ultimate aim is to saving such categories of youth from a life of drug abuse and unemployment which would lead to crime.

Since its inception, thousands of youth have been given basic vocational training in carpentry, plumbing, tailoring, hair dressing and commercial agriculture and in the process turned into useful citizens.

To give the youth avenues through which their issues can be addressed, the RPF government adopted a policy whereby two youths, one male and one female, are elected through the National Youth Council structures, to the National Parliament and a third youth is elected to the East African Legislative Assembly (EALA).

Rwanda was the first country in Africa to ratify the African Youth Charter in 2006. Due to the government's commitment to youth promotion, Rwanda hosted the Annual Commonwealth Youth Conference in 2010, the second African country after Ghana to do so.

Due to his tireless efforts to uplift the youth and give them a genuine voice in the running of their country, President Kagame has been decorated with various international awards, among them the Global Leadership Award by the Young Presidents' Organisation in 2003.

Empowering Civil Society Organisations

In Rwanda, the existence of civil society organisations (CSOs) dates from the arrival of Christian churches, mainly the Catholic Church through its mission in 1956. These CSOs were largely agriculturally oriented and answerable to the Catholic Church. Since 1980, CSOs, mainly developmental NGOs and peasant associations, benefited from international support primarily from the World Bank and this has contributed to their expansion to the extent that in 1991 the number of CSOs was approximately 170 (Uvin, 1998).

During the early 1990s, a number of organisations emerged in the area of human rights. From the beginning, these organisations have always fought for civil liberties and social justice. A third group of CSO umbrella organisations emerged after the Genocide, made up of associations and organisations created after 1994 to address the consequences of the Genocide. These, including Ibuka and AVEGA-Agahozo, are dedicated to protecting civil rights and assisting survivors of genocide (Mukamunana and Brynard, 2005). This period also witnessed the establishment of various women organisations and other organisations working in areas such HIV and AIDS and environmental protection.

The RPF is in no doubt that in established and emerging democracies, weighed down by weak democratic institutions, civil society organisations (CSOs) must take a leading role in preventing democracy from backsliding. This is so because CSOs promote public participation in decision-making processes, advocate for transparency and accountability by those in public offices and defend human rights.

It is against that political background that the RPF government has strongly supported the establishment and proper functioning of CSOs in the country. This is aimed at laying down a very strong cornerstone for people's participation in the running of the country and holding public officials to account.

It is for this reason that the government supported the creation of Rwanda Civil Society Platform (RCSP) in July 2004 which brings together all local civil society organisations operating in the country.

The government has also strived to forge a close collaboration between CSOs and government departments. This is why an engagement forum has been created by the Ministry of Finance and Economic Planning that brings together ministry officials and members of CSOs to discuss national budget priorities and how the national budget is implemented.

CSOs are also represented in the Rwanda Economic and Social Council (RESC), charged with overseeing the economic and social welfare challenges encountered by Rwandans and how they can be overcome.

The Civil Society Development Barometer of 2012 revealed that CSOs are generally regarded by Rwandans as effective in empowering people and advancing social interests. The recent enactment of the Access to Information law is likely to enhance CSOs' policy advocacy capacity and engagement.

Reforming the Media Sector

The media is an important sector for governance and development of every nation. Unfortunately, state and private media outlets participated in the preparation and actual execution of the 1994 Genocide against the Tutsi. Despite this dark past, a vibrant and responsive media sector is needed for Rwanda's reconstruction and development. And indeed, the RPF considers that a free, independent and responsible media is an important partner in nation building. A vibrant media sector spurs informed citizens, and these constitute a foundation for a more healthy, democratic and progressive nation. In addition, the media is paramount in helping the public check their elected representatives as they carry out their official duties.

It is because of this strong political conviction that the RPF government has created an enabling environment for a free, independent and responsible media to thrive. Unlike the situation in 1960s where there was only one state radio station with a handful of newspapers mainly controlled by the government and the Catholic Church, Rwandans are now able to access more than 20 privately-owned FM radio stations and a good number of daily, weekly and monthly publications with numerous online news outlets.

International broadcasters like the British Broadcasting Corporation (BBC), the Voice of America (VOA), Deutsche Welle Radio and Radio France International (RFI) are accessible in Rwanda on FM frequencies, thanks to a strong media infrastructure that has been established by the government.

The former State broadcaster (ORINFOR) has now undergone reforms and under the new 2013 law it was transformed into a public broadcaster – Rwanda Broadcasting Agency (RBA). The major mission of RBA is to act as a bridge between the government and the citizens, instead of being a one-way channel for leaders to convey their messages to the people.

The government has invested more than Rwf 11.9 billion in the construction of state-of-the-art studios for both Rwanda Television and Radio Rwanda. According to many electronic media specialists, when complete, these studios are going to be some of the best on the African continent.

The government has left media regulation to the media practitioners. Thus the Rwanda Media Commission, a self-regulatory body, has been established with the support of the government to handle media related complaints from the public and is run by media professionals themselves.

The government has made another important milestone in its quest to have a free media by enacting the Access to Information law (2013), making Rwanda one of the 11 African countries to enact such a law that is widely recognised as a cornerstone of good governance and an important anti-corruption tool.

To cement it all, President Paul Kagame holds a regular monthly press conference that is broadcast live in a question-answer session.

Security for Stability and Sustainable Development

Security is point number two on the RPF Nine-point Programme, which articulates that RPF shall defend the sovereignty of Rwanda and ensure the security of the people and their property.

When the Government of National Unity took office in 1994, it immediately set out to establish peace and security inside Rwanda and along her borders.

Since then, far-reaching reforms and capacity building within various security organs like the Rwanda National Police (RNP) and the Rwanda Defence Force (RDF) have been prioritised.

It was on 16 June 2000 that the new Rwanda National Police (RNP) was established by law. It came out of a merger of three forces that had existed before 1994: the Gendarmerie Nationale, which was under the Ministry of Defence; the Communal Police under the Ministry of Internal Affairs; and the Judicial Police that was under the Ministry of Justice.

The reforms and capacity building initiatives made the RNP a modern and effective people-friendly policing force to the extent that today it is often called on to participate in UN peacekeeping operations worldwide.

Today the RNP is an active member of regional and international police bodies like the Eastern Africa Police Chiefs Cooperation Organisation (EAPCCO) and the International Criminal Police Organisation or INTERPOL.

In 2007, the RNP introduced Community Policing Committees (CPCs) countrywide to involve citizens in maintaining security. The committees, to which community members are proud to belong, are run at village, cell, sector and provincial levels. Community representatives manage the committees and they are responsible for setting priorities in collaboration with a designated police officer.

This initiative has seen easy flow of information between the police and the communities, thus playing a pivotal role in reducing crime rates which is why Rwanda has one of the lowest crime rates globally.

Similarly, the army has been transformed into a professional institution. The new army which was previously a liberation force known as Rwanda Patriotic Army (RPA) was established by law on 17 May 2002 and renamed Rwanda Defence Force (RDF).

With internal restructuring and capacity building within the army, Rwanda now has a professional and effective defence force that is pro-people. This has earned the RDF national, regional and international respect.

As a sign of confidence in Rwanda's Army, the RDF men and women are currently serving in UN and AU Peacekeeping operations both on the African continent and in other parts of the world.

Back at home, the RDF has introduced what is called 'Army Week' a community outreach programme to help the vulnerable in the communities. Though dubbed Army Week, it sometimes runs for weeks and has seen the rank and file of the RDF play a major role in activities aimed at national development.

To increase people's access to specialised medical services, the medical staff of the RDF treat a variety of illnesses countrywide, which otherwise would have required patients to travel to referral hospitals in the capital, Kigali.

In fulfilling its mission of playing a role in the development of Rwanda, the RDF has constructed thousands of houses for needy citizens during many phases of Army Week. It has also participated in *Umuganda* activities and has become one of the cornerstones of Rwanda's transformation.

The Rwanda Defence Force and National Police have ensured that citizens feel safe walking alone at night. According to the 2012 report released by Gallup Inc (Gallup, 2012). Ninety two percent of those surveyed confirm this.

The Legatum report of 2012 has a similar figure of 92.20%. The global average is 61.90%.

Also in the Legatum report, 98.30% of Rwandans surveyed have total confidence in the military. The global average is at 73.20%.

International Relations and Cooperation

In contrast, the image of Rwanda in the immediate aftermath of the 1994 Genocide, today the country stands as a credible partner to many because of its international standing and active participation on the global stage.

All this hinges on the RPF's political programme, which stipulates very clearly that her foreign policy would be based on equality, peaceful co-existence and mutual benefit between Rwanda and other countries.

Indeed since 2003, Rwanda has embarked on a strong diplomatic course aimed at productive engagement with state and non-state actors globally. This approach has seen Rwanda maintaining ties with regional neighbours and entering into new regional and international partnerships. Rwanda has opened new diplomatic missions in various parts of the world and strengthened the already existing ones. Rwanda has today 26 diplomatic missions abroad, including nine in Africa, eight in Europe, six in Asia and three in America. Nearly half of the missions were opened after 1994. The new diplomatic missions include those in Sweden, Singapore, the Netherlands, Nigeria, Senegal, South Africa, Turkey, South Korea, the UK, Egypt, Zambia and Israel.

In a similar manner, many countries and international organisations have strengthened ties with Rwanda while others have entered into new diplomatic relationships and established diplomatic representations in Kigali.

Regionally, Rwanda is now an active member of the East African Community (EAC). November 29, 2009 marked a historical day in Rwanda's diplomatic relations as it became the 54th member of the Commonwealth of Nations. Rwanda's admission was based on four main grounds: democracy and democratic processes such as free and fair elections, the rule of law, the independence of the judiciary and good governance.

Other positive aspects considered include protection of human rights, freedom of expression and provision of equal opportunity to all Rwandans. This enabled Rwanda to become the second country after Mozambique to be admitted into the Commonwealth without any direct colonial link or constitutional connection to Great Britain.

In the spirit of a foreign policy based on mutual benefit between Rwanda and other countries, Rwanda's admission to the Commonwealth has given her access to a market of over two billion people and with a volume of trade exceeding US$2.8 trillion annually (Commonwealth Network,

2008). Due to Rwanda's commitment to her international obligations, President Paul Kagame has on many occasions been called upon to chair high level International Committees for the benefit of the global community and Rwanda as well.

Other senior members of the new Rwandan leadership have also been at the helm of various regional, continental and international organisations, occurring for the first time in the history of Rwanda. Such organisations include the East African Community (EAC), African Union Commission (AU), the African Development Bank (AfDB) and World Trade Organisation (WTO), among others.

Since 2003, the Rwandan leader, President Kagame, has been on many state visits to different countries and several heads of state and other leaders from the Region, Africa, Europe, North America, and Asia have officially visited Rwanda to strengthen diplomatic ties with their respective countries.

Peacekeeping

The RPF's commitment to the respect and protection of human rights and protecting those in danger is not limited to Rwanda's national borders. Following security and peace consolidation at home after the 1994 genocide against the Tutsi, the RPF-led government has stood up to its international responsibility of maintaining peace and security and suppressing any act of aggression or breach of peace.

In 2004, Rwanda became the first country to volunteer a peace-keeping force to the war-torn Darfur region of Sudan. Rwanda is the sixth largest troop and police contributing country to UN peacekeeping operations across the world. It is also the second biggest contributor of female police peacekeepers globally, with over 4,000 troops, 400 police and 13 military observers in different countries. These include South Sudan, Sudan, Haiti, Liberia, Guinea-Bissau and Ivory Coast.

Rwanda's role in peacekeeping has been vital, including providing leaders for the most challenging UN Missions, such as the African-United Nations Hybrid Operation in Darfur (UNAMID) and the United Nations Multidimensional Integrated Stabilisation Mission in Mali (MINUSMA).

For the first time in the history of peacekeeping missions, Rwanda has championed women peacekeeping especially in operations involving vulnerable women and girls in situations of conflict. They have also been engaged in activities to promote conflict resolution mechanisms such as community work (*Umuganda*). Further more, they have contributed to the construction of much needed infrastructure like markets, schools and roads and introduced energy saving stoves in mission areas.

These activities have greatly endeared Rwandan peacekeepers to people in their mission areas. On many occasions, Rwandan peacekeepers have been decorated with medals for their zeal and professionalism while executing their responsibilities.

Home-grown Solutions in Governance

Performance contract (Imihigo)

As earlier mentioned, traditionally, *imihigo* were contracts or agreements between warriors and the king to bring success in terms of conquests and spoils of war. As the declarations were made public in the presence of peers, the warriors had to do everything possible to bring success home in order not to lose respect and to escape possible punishment from the king. As such, success was met with rewards and conquering heroes were praised in songs and poems.

Today's *imihigo* is a public commitment to achieve particular targets in any public office and this has been institutionalised in particular at district level. Thus leaders at various levels annually commit themselves to achieving development goals. For District Mayors and Ministers, the performance contract is signed between them and the President of the Republic.

When they sign *Imihigo*, the Mayors commit themselves to such activities as construction of health centres and roads, provision of electricity to local people, safe water and better performance in schools.

Imihigo Day has become an accountability forum, where public officials are held accountable to the public in terms of service delivery and the best performing mayors are recognised and rewarded. Thus *Imihigo* is a yardstick for good governance.

Joint Action Development Forum

The Joint Action Development Forum (JADF) is a multi-stakeholder platform that was put in place to facilitate and promote full participation of citizens in the decentralised and participatory governance and to improve service provision processes. It has representatives from the public sector, private sector and civil society.

The JADF builds on the traditional values of solidarity and mutual support towards a common agenda of ensuring social welfare. It applies the tradition of providing assistance in any activity or pressing duty that cannot be handled without community participation.

The JADF exploits positive aspects of cultural heritage which have proven their worth in community development. Traditional practices that were used to engage people individually in the past are replicated at institution level today by the JADF after combining them with modern participatory concepts, such as creating space for inclusive dialogue, synergy and accountability, establishing a shared agenda of development in the district and determining outcomes for monitoring and peer-review.

The JADF was recognised by the International Republican Institute among the best governance innovations in Africa in its 2013 Africa Regional Governance and Best Practices Report.

National Dialogue (NDC) Umushyikirano

The National Dialogue Council (NDC), known as *Umushyikirano*, was established by the 2003 Rwanda Constitution in its Article 168. It is a home-grown annual event chaired by the President of the Republic. It brings together representatives of Local Councils, Civil Society and other members of the Rwandan community to debate on issues relating to the state of the nation, the state of local government and national unity.

Twenty years after the 1994 Genocide against the Tutsi, Rwanda has deployed considerable efforts in building the nation in all aspects. These efforts have by and large borne fruit and Rwanda has made significant progress towards achieving its Vision 2020. However, there still exist challenges that hinder progress towards achieving the desired development goals. The National Dialogue Council meeting serves as a platform for the entire nation to share ideas that will contribute to finding solutions to the existing challenges through the direct participation of citizens. It is broadcast live to encourage direct participation by all citizens at home and abroad.

The 12th National Dialogue Council (December 2014) provided an opportunity and platform to discuss emerging issues facing families and, together, agreed on solutions and sustainable strategies to address them.

National Leadership Retreat (NLR) Umwiherero

The National Leadership Retreat is an annual meeting that brings together senior leaders from government and the private sector. It is intended to review progress in specific areas in governance and economy, highlighted in the previous retreat and to set the agenda for the forthcoming year. This is an occasion that is regarded as a performance audit where leaders are held accountable to their peers and the citizens. This year marks the 12th annual National Leadership Retreat.

Itorero

Itorero is a traditional leadership development institution. In pre-colonial Rwanda males in *Itorero* would be taught values like nationalism, patriotism, hard work and honesty and integrity for a unified Rwanda. All this made young Rwandans understand and appreciate their society and be ready to serve it in any capacity and at any time as the need arose. Today *Itorero* is open to all Rwandans irrespective of gender

Due to the bad legacy left behind by bad politics since the 1950s, the RPF-led government saw it fit to revive the traditional institution of *Itorero* if Rwandans were to again live harmoniously and peacefully. Thus in 2007 the tradition of *Itorero* was revived to train citizens, especially leaders, in what it means to be Rwandan and to equip them to lead others.

Since its re-introduction, men and women have gone through this new training that goes down up to village *Umudugudu* level.

As part of their national service, senior six leavers do community work while waiting for admission into tertiary institutions.

These home-grown initiatives have strongly cemented people's participation in the management, reconstruction and development of their country. To many observers, Rwanda is an example of how traditional culture can be a source of inspiration in finding solutions to modern day challenges.

Top: Beneficiaries of the Girinka programme receive cattle

Bottom: Umuganda: Rwandans gather on the last Saturday of the month to do community work and general cleaning

12

Justice

> *Rwanda prospers because it chose to forgive.*
> Pastor Rick Warren

Rebuilding the Justice System

An effective and efficient judicial system is the foundation for any democratic society. Rwanda, perhaps more than any other country in the world, needed an effective judiciary in the aftermath of the 1994 Genocide that had left more than one million people dead and many more living in desperate conditions.

Like many other sectors in Rwanda after 1994, the judiciary needed to be rebuilt to meet the challenges created by the Genocide. For instance, thousands of genocide suspects in prison awaited trial while thousands of genocide survivors yearned for justice.

To address this dire situation, the RPF-led Government resorted to one of the pillars of governance it had committed itself to: the rule of law that supports and protects all its citizens without discrimination. That is why in 2004, extensive reforms within the judicial system were introduced to create a strong, responsive, professional and independent judiciary that Rwandans could trust and respect.

Separation of Powers within the Judiciary

The justice system that the RPF government inherited was driven by political influence. This system was fused in one supervisory body, the Ministry of Justice, which oversaw the functioning of the judicial police, the criminal investigation, the prosecution and the prison services.

To revitalise the public's trust and respect for these institutions, it was necessary to have them separated. Consequently, in 2003, they were split into three distinct entities, with full financial and administrative independence. The entities are the Ministry of Justice, the Supreme Court and the National Prosecution Authority. These reforms significantly reduced the powers and reach of the Minister of Justice and made the new departments more transparent and professional. The new judicial institutions were also given innovative legal frameworks to deal with human rights. For example, a suspect cannot be held in custody for more than 72 hours without charge and must appear in a court within a further four days.

National Prosecution Authority

In order to give the National Prosecution Authority autonomy, a High Council of the Public Prosecution, which is the supreme organ responsible for the smooth functioning of the public prosecution in the country, was established.

The Council is responsible for taking decisions, recruitment and appointment of staff which is done through an open and competitive process as well as the promotion of staff. The High Council of the Public Prosecution is composed of persons from different organs with experience and expertise and this enables it to provide general policy guidance to the prosecution for it to operate professionally.

The National Prosecution Authority has branches across the country and is headed by the Prosecutor General. This was done in the spirit of decentralising justice and bringing it nearer to the people. This new structure facilitated the professional coordination of prosecution activities, and management of prosecutors and other prosecution personnel.

The National Prosecution Authority has several special units such as the Economic and Financial Crimes Unit, the Genocide Fugitive Tracking Unit (GFTU), Sexual and Domestic Violence Unit, Genocide Ideology and related Crimes Unit, Witness and Victims Protection Unit, all of which have helped in delivering justice.

Similarly, the Inspectorate General of the Prosecution was created to oversee the functioning of prosecutors. It has a mechanism of evaluating prosecutors, and sanctioning or rewarding them according to their performance.

Prosecutors in managerial and administrative positions have a limited term of office to ensure transparency, efficiency and accountability. All these initiatives have enabled the Prosecutor's Office to handle more cases in courts of law than ever before.

Restructuring of the Court System

Following the reforms of 2003, a total overhaul of the court system was implemented with the aim of making the courts more efficient and effective. Accordingly, the structure of the Supreme Court was reduced from six separate chambers, each with its own president, to a single unit under the leadership of the Chief Justice. This helped to avoid conflicts between various chambers of the court and enabled them to use available resources more efficiently.

A new High Court of the Republic was created and replaced the former four chambers of the Supreme Court, and has significantly improved coordination. The High Court of the Republic has two lower levels, namely the Intermediate Court and the Primary Court (District), spread across the country to facilitate access to justice by the population.

It is clear that the management and operation of this single court with a centralised management enjoys a comparative advantage over the previous different courts, which would sometimes take different and conflicting decisions. The new structure has had a positive effect on the efficiency of the High Court because it facilitates harmonisation of jurisprudence.

Since the proper functioning of the courts is vital in any law abiding society, an Inspectorate General of Courts was established to oversee the functioning of courts on a daily basis. This aims at identifying best performing court judges and personnel who are in turn rewarded while poor performers are sanctioned accordingly. In addition, judges are evaluated and any judge who is rated poorly is subject to suspension. Heads of courts, on the other hand, have a fixed term of office. This has seen judges perform to their best.

For the first time in the history of Rwanda, Commercial Courts were established to speed up the resolution of commercial disputes. This was crucial to the RPF-led government that is committed to making Rwanda a business-friendly country.

The reforms have introduced 'single judge seating' at all levels with the exception of the Supreme Court. In return, this initiative has seen sharp reduction of delays and baclogs, which had previously characterised Rwanda's judiciary, in the disposal of cases.

The graph depicts the number of cases filed, disposed and pending in all courts.

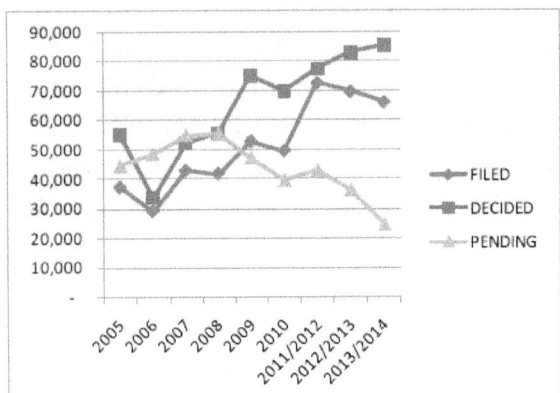

YEAR	FILED	DECIDED	PENDING
2005	37,136	54,869	44,414
2006	28,975	33,605	48,304
2007	42,739	52,282	54,712
2008	41,684	55,718	55,450
2009	52,754	75,096	46,988
2010	49,537	69,834	39,205
2011/2012	72,509	77,187	42,670
2012/2013	69,537	82,707	35,091
2013/2014	65,885	85,124	24,338

Source: *Supreme Court Annual Report 2013-14*

Capacity Building for Public Trust

Before 2004, due to low levels of education, coupled with poor remuneration and a bad political climate, judges were incompetent and discriminatory in their day to-day work.

The reforms set up a minimum education requirement of at least a bachelor's degree in law for one to practise law in Rwanda. As a result, since 2007, all the 281 judges possess at least a first degree in law, while others have already acquired master's degrees. This has led to improvement in the quality of judgments.

In addition to academic qualification, judges have received technical training in fields like case processing and judgment drafting. The Ministry of Justice has also established the Institute of Legal Practice and Development (ILPD), the first of its kind in Rwanda, to coordinate professional training for the judicial officials.

Private legal practitioners agree that the reforms that were implemented since 2003 have resulted in a better, more organised court system and a faster process of dispute resolution.

Infrastructure

Physical infrastructure have been put in place to accommodate court premises and create a conducive working environment. Dozens of modern buildings such as the Supreme Court and the High Court Headquarters in Kigali have been constructed and others renovated.

All court premises within range of GSM networks are connected to the Internet. To facilitate easy exchange of information between different courts, Local Area Networks (LAN) have been installed at all intermediate courts, the High Court and its chambers as well as the Supreme Court. The introduction of ICT in the courts is one way of contributing to a speedy delivery of justice.

Strengthening the Human Rights Commission

From the 1950s, Rwanda experienced grave violation of human rights that later culminated in the 1994 Genocide against the Tutsi. That is why the RPF envisaged a nation that would respect the rule of law to the letter.

Indeed, the National Human Rights Commission (NHRC) was established in 1999, as had been agreed under the Arusha Peace Agreement signed between the Habyarimana regime and the RPF in 1993.

For the NHRC to carry out its mandate without any political influence, an amendment to the law establishing the commission was made in 2007 clearly stating that it is an independent institution – both financially and administratively – that cannot take any instructions from anybody.

Its mission is to foster respect for human rights in Rwanda, where every individual lives in peace, harmony and prosperity and fully enjoys his/her rights.

To achieve this, the National Human Rights Commission has developed various strategies. They include:
- Educating and mobilising the population on matters relating to human rights;

- Examining human rights violations committed within the territory of the Republic of Rwanda by state organs, public officials (using their duties as a cover), corporate and non-corporate organisations, as well as individuals;
- Carrying out investigations on human rights abuses in Rwanda and filing complaints with competent courts;
- Collaborating with other organs in designing strategies to prevent violations of human rights;
- Preparing and disseminating reports on the human rights situation in Rwanda on a yearly basis and at any time as deemed necessary;
- Providing views on bills relating to human rights upon request or at its own initiative;
- Sensitising relevant government institutions on the ratification of international human rights conventions, their integration in existing internal law; and
- Carrying out visits to places of detention to check whether the rights of detainees are being respected, among others.
- Rwanda has signed and ratified various human rights conventions.

The establishment of an independent institution mainly focusing on the respect of human rights in Rwanda has resulted in a society that abides by the rule of law despite various challenges.

As a result of these reforms, confidence in Rwanda's justice system has been restored and this has led to the eradication of the culture of impunity while at the same time, building unity and reconciliation. The reforms have also made it possible for countries in Africa, Europe and North America to extradite Rwandan genocide suspects to be tried in Rwanda's courts.

Additionally, the International Criminal Tribunal for Rwanda has sent a dozen genocide suspects to be tried by Rwanda's judicial system, following the abolition of the death sentence in Rwanda in 2007.

These efforts to reform the justice system have been recognised in both local and international surveys. For instance, in 2012 the Legatum Prosperity Index reported that 83.90% of Rwandans surveyed indicated strong confidence in the judicial system compared to the 52.50% global average.

Fighting Genocide and its Ideology

The 1994 Genocide against the Tutsi left the country's population traumatised and its infrastructure decimated. Since then, Rwanda has embarked on an ambitious justice and reconciliation process with the ultimate aim of enabling all Rwandans to once again live side by side in peace.

Besides, and as expressed in point nine of the Nine-point Programme, the RPF is committed to fighting genocide and genocide ideology.

It was therefore high on the RPF government's agenda to deal with severe consequences of the genocide, prevent the spread of the genocide ideology and preserve the memory of genocide so as to have a society that would never experience genocide again in the future.

This saw the creation of the National Commission for the Fight against Genocide (CNLG), which is a government institution dedicated to achieving this noble cause.

National Commission for the Fight against Genocide (CNLG)

In 2007, the National Commission for the Fight against Genocide (CNLG) was formed with a mandate to prevent genocide and the spread of its ideology and to mobilise resources to assist the survivors of the genocide.

It is also charged with developing initiatives aimed at responding to the consequences of genocide such as trauma and other diseases suffered by the survivors due to genocide.

Another important responsibility of CNLG is to preserve the evidence of genocide for generations to come. This includes building and maintaining genocide memorial sites, and digitisation of genocide archives.

The Commission plays the important role of coordinating all commemorative activities for the 1994 Genocide against the Tutsi in Rwanda and generating strategies for fighting attempts at revisionism, denial and trivialisation of the genocide.

An annual national commemoration day to remember the victims of the genocide is marked every year on 7 April in Rwanda and across the world.

Through its commitment to fight genocide by preserving the memory, the Rwandan government has through advocacy seen the United Nations dedicate that date as the Day of Remembrance of the Victims of Genocide in Rwanda.

Preserving Memory

The RPF strongly believes that the preservation of the memory of genocide is of paramount value. Since 1994, and especially after the creation of CNLG in 2007, various initiatives have been put in place to communicate the importance of preserving the memory of genocide for Rwandans as well as the international community.

Every year, as mentioned above, Rwandans engage in an official 'Week of mourning' from 7 to 13 April. Throughout this week, Rwandans and friends of Rwanda are given an official opportunity to come together and share their grief and remember those who were brutally killed in 1994.

The new arrangement is such that the week is marked at the lowest level of administration (*Umudugudu*) in the whole country with activities such as vigils, thus bringing together all Rwandans with a view to fostering unity and reconciliation and preserving memory.

Home-grown Solutions

The post-transition period in Rwanda has been marked by innovations to make sure that all systems put in place address people's needs efficiently and effectively to reconstruct and rehabilitate a country that was brought to the brink of destruction by the 1994 genocide. Such innovations have not only seen unity and reconciliation strengthened, but they have also helped to deliver justice.

Gacaca Courts

It should be recalled that more than 120,000 individuals had been arrested and provisionally detained for the crime of genocide. It would have taken more than 100 years to try them in the ordinary courts. (Republic of Rwanda 2012).

To address this issue and to bring about justice and reconciliation the RPF-led government in 2005 adapted and adopted the traditional community court system called Gacaca.

Under the system, people at the local level elected persons of integrity from their community as judges to preside over trials of genocide suspects accused of all genocide crimes except those accused of planning genocide. The courts gave lower sentences if the accused was repentant and sought forgiveness from the victims. Often, the accused who confessed to their crimes were either acquitted or received the lesser penalty of community service.

More than 12,000 community-based courts tried over 1.9 million cases throughout the country in a period of 10 years (www.rwandapedia.com). The Gacaca trials also served to promote reconciliation by providing a means for victims to learn the truth about the death of their family members and relatives. They also gave perpetrators the opportunity to confess their crimes, show remorse and ask for forgiveness in front of their community.

The Gacaca courts officially closed on 4 May 2012. Many legal scholars have visited Rwanda to learn and research on the functioning of Gacaca courts and to see if a similar court system can be applied in other countries where there is conflict.

Community Mediators (Abunzi)

As part of government efforts to increase access to justice, the *Abunzi* were introduced in 2009 and incorporated into the formal justice system. This system of dispute resolution originates from traditional Rwandan culture, where *Abunzi* (mediators) would arbitrate conflicts in the community.

Disputes resolved by these "mediation committees" involve people living in the same community or from the same family.

Among the civil cases, mediators resolve disputes related to land and other immovable assets; cattle and other movable assets; breach of contractual obligations in case the subjects do not involve central government, insurance and commercial contractual obligations, family cases related to civil status; and successions, among others.

In all the above cases, the matter at issue should not exceed three million Rwandan francs, except for the cattle and other movable assets, whose value should not exceed one million francs. It is worth noting, however, that complainants still have the right to appeal to the formal courts if not satisfied with the *Abunzi* verdict in resolving the dispute.

According to the 2010 Citizen Report Card (CRC) survey conducted by the RGAC (Rwanda Governance Advisory Council) which later became Rwanda Governance Board (RGB), in all districts, the 'mediation committees' rated as the best appreciated dispute resolution instrument in comparison with other mechanisms put in place to allow easy access to justice. According to the survey, 81.6% of respondents declared that they were satisfied with the service delivery of the 'mediation committees' in resolving their disputes, 63.4% for ordinary court, and 48.1% for the Prosecution.

Taking Justice to the People

Rwanda's main strategy for decentralising justice has been the establishment of a Maison d'Accès à la Justice (MAJ) or Access to Justice Bureau in every district.

Conceived as a central authority for the poor and less privileged to assert their legal rights especially in rural areas, the MAJs are run by lawyers employed by government. The MAJs primarily take care of civil and commercial cases. However, they are only limited to offering free legal advice without actual representation in criminal courts.

With the introduction of MAJs, women, children and other vulnerable people, who in the past have had to walk long distances to file cases, will easily access legal advice in their locality.

Travail d'Intérêt Général (TIG)

As the government grappled with the challenges left by the 1994 Genocide, it became necessary to find new ways of addressing them. This is how TIG, a French acronym loosely translated as 'community service' as an alternative to custodial sentence, was conceived.

Under TIG, convicts who confessed their involvement in the 1994 Genocide against the Tutsi were given the chance to serve half their sentences outside prison, doing community work. Their work included construction of houses for genocide survivors and other people without shelter, building of roads, farming and other development activities.

In this way, TIG reinforced the national unity and reconciliation process and also contributed to national economic development. It also enabled the convicts to acquire new professional skills to facilitate reintegration in society, in addition to the training in human rights.

13

Economic Development

Rwanda is a success story and investing in it continues to be the right thing to do.
David Cameron

Reviving the Economy

Point four of the RPF's Nine-point Political Programme states that it will make every effort to promote Rwanda's economy based on her natural resources.

With the security and economic stability largely achieved during the transition period (1994-2003), the RPF government after 2003 focused on growing the economy to the next level. Specifically, this would involve transforming the agricultural sector, building a better and modern network of infrastructure, improving the industrial sector, supporting the growth of the private sector and protecting the environment for sustainable development.

Agriculture for Sustainable Development

Agriculture is important as an economic activity, as a livelihood, and as a provider of environmental services. This makes the sector a key instrument for increasing incomes, alleviation of poverty, improving food security, combating malnutrition and driving overall economic growth.

The sector currently accounts for 35% of GDP, generates 70% of export revenues and employs close to 80% of the population (MINAGRI, 2012). Over the last decade, agriculture grew at an average of 5.2%; and as a result, the share of the population likely to have insufficient food fell from 75% before 1994 to 21% by 2012, while the share of women households with insufficient food access fell by 50%. More recently, a poverty reduction score of 12 points has been recorded and the agricultural sector also directly accounted for 45% of the 12 points in poverty reduction registered from 2005 to 2011 (REU, World bank, 2013).

This success is a result of a concerted government-led programme of sector transformation.

Agricultural Baseline in 1990

In 1990, up to 95% of the Rwandan population was engaged in agriculture, which was subsistence based with relatively low levels of productivity (MINAGRI, 2013). Coffee and tea dominated exports. Only 2% of the national budget was assigned to agriculture. As a result, the use of fertilisers and pesticides was very low, which negatively effected overall productivity.

There was also no comprehensive approach to land husbandry or soil conservation, which led to loss of fertile soil and low use of land in areas with unsuitable topography.

In general, the sector was characterised by low yields and chronic food insecurity. For example, Rwanda's Global Hunger Index Score (GHI) in 1990 was rated at 30.8, classified as 'Extremely Alarming' on a global scale (IFPRI, 2013). This score rose to 35, an unacceptable human hunger index. The dominance of subsistence farming and low productivity in a country where more than 90% of the population relied on agriculture for their livelihood, meant that 47.5% of the population lived in poverty (IPAR, 2012) and this rose to 77% in 1994.

The livestock sector was also relatively undeveloped. In 1990, there were 615,000 heads of cattle, dominated by the traditional Ankole cattle. Even then, 80% of the cattle were lost between 1990 and 1993 (MINAGRI, 2013).

Agriculture Today

Rwanda is now widely regarded as a development success story, with high GDP growth and decreasing poverty. Agriculture was one of the key drivers of this success. As the primary source of employment, progress in the sector has contributed to reducing poverty from 58.9% in 2000, to 44.9% in the last decade (EICV III, NISR 2011). The goal is to reduce it further, to 30% by 2017. The Global Hunger Index 2013 reports that Rwanda has reduced its hunger score by 50%, down from 37.3 in 1995 to 15.3 in 2013. Rwanda is one of the three countries in Africa that have been able to achieve this level of hunger reduction in the last 20 years. (IFPRI, 2013).

The remarkable achievement in poverty reduction and food security was supported by government investment in rural development directed at raising productivity and increasing domestic food and nutritional security.

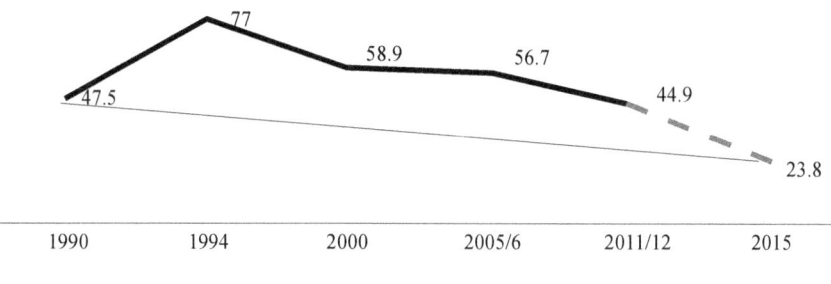

Figure 1: Poverty trend from 1990 to 2012, with estimated continued reduction to 2015 (NISR, 2012)

Ensuring Food Security

Food security has been the major concern of the agricultural sector and both government and development partners have heavily invested in areas that can ensure it is achieved.

As a result of these investments, between 2000 and 2012, infant mortality reduced from 11% to 5%. The primary driver in this achievement was an increase in production of key staple crops which led to improved nutrition for the population. The increase in production and nutrient availability has recently been rising faster than population growth generating a surplus in the availability of calories. There was a substantial increase in the availability of Kcal per day per capita from 1,773Kcal in 1990, to 2,642 Kcal in 2011 and 3,205 Kcal in 2013.

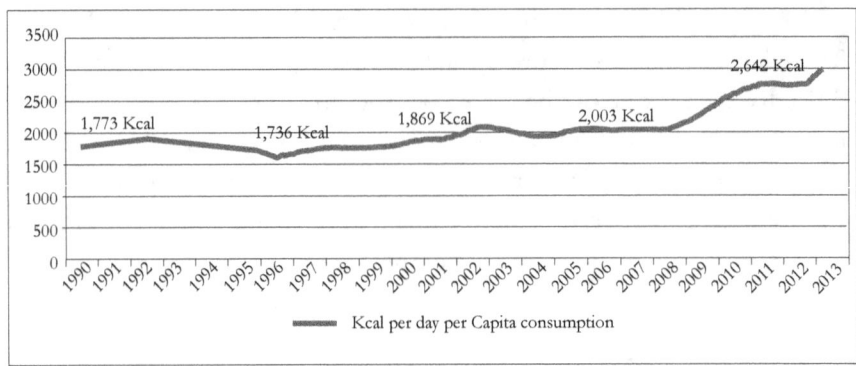

Figure 2: Increase in Kcal per capita consumption from 1990 to 2013

As shown in figure 2 above, during the period from 1990 to 2013, availability of calories increased by 80% to 3,205 Kcal per capita exceeding by far the 2,100 Kcal daily calorie consumption for an adult recommended by the Food and Agriculture Organisation (FAO, 2003). From 1990 to 2000, food availability per capita was far below recommended levels. Actual Kcal availability in Rwanda is now 153% grater than average recommendations as shown in Figure 3 (MINAGRI, 2013).

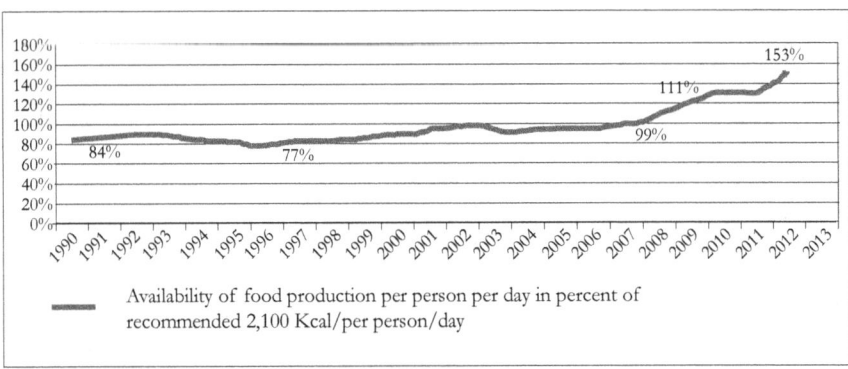

Figure 3: Availability of energy as a percentage of the recommended adult consumption of 2,100 Kcal

The increase to over 100% since 2000 is a reflection of domestic food security. Now, only 17% of the population is classified as borderline food insecure, a reduction from over 70% before 1994 (MINAGRI, 2012). This is due to better production and also management of harvests due to improved market infrastructure. Food security at the national level is also ensured by the national strategic reserve which stores selected crops of maize and beans, to ensure a buffer reserve in times of drought.

The major interventions to drive this increase include the Crop Intensification Programme, the One Cow per Poor Family, advances in irrigation and the land husbandry programme to mention but a few, which are discussed below in detail.

Crop Intensification Programme (CIP)

One of the most important programmes in the drive to achieve domestic food security was the Crop Intensification Programme (CIP) by which farmers with contiguous plots grow the same crop in order to create economies of scale and a surplus that can be sold at the market. It was launched in 2007 with three key pillars: land consolidation to deal with fragmentation of the agriculture landscape, input access to increase productivity and reduction of post-harvest losses. Land consolidation was a major innovation in the home-grown category,

As a result of CIP, production of staple crops increased; pulses by 30%, cereals by 30-60% and tubers by 5 to 10 fold in Figure 4. These results happened because under CIP, fertiliser application increased from 2-4kg/ha to 29 kg/ha and the number of farmers using improved seeds increased from 29% to 56%, both generating better yields (MINAGRI, 2012). This was followed by an aggressive programme to reduce post-harvest losses; and in grains (cereals and pulses that were most affected), post-harvest losses were reduced from 35% to 12%. Training in handling and proper storage after harvest, as well as construction of community harvest and storage facilities were critical to post-harvest loss reduction. (MINAGRI, 2012).

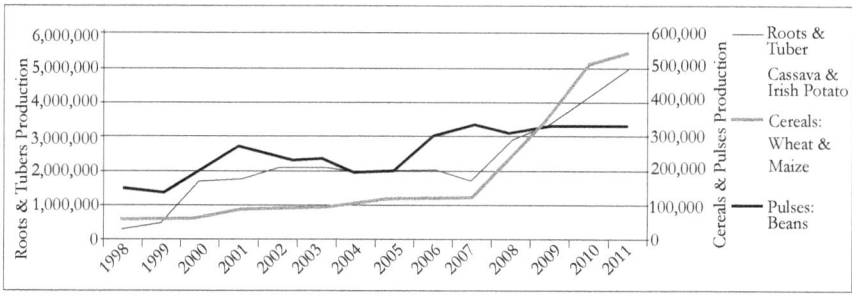

Figure 4: Increased staple crop production since 1998

The fertiliser and seed sectors are now being privatised to increase the efficiency of the input market, and it is expected that new models of farming such as contract and satellite farming will further help to commercialise the sector and improve domestic food security.

Irrigation

In addition to the CIP, investments to transform Rwanda's physical environment, particularly in irrigation, terracing and land husbandry, have also contributed to the increase in production. In 1994 only 3,600 ha of land were irrigated, mainly for rice production. Driven by the Irrigation Master Plan Study completed in 2010, recent investments have focused on increasing the area under irrigation which now stands at 24,000ha, an eight fold increase in only the last decade (MINAGRI, 2013).

Rice yields in developed marshlands are close to internationally acceptable standards at 6-7tonnes/ha up from 2 tonnes per ha (MINAGRI, 2013). The production of strategic crops like maize and beans has increased under irrigated agriculture from 1tonne/ha (maize) to 4-5tonnes/ha and 0.5tones/ha (beans) to 2.5 -3 tonnes/ha from 2006-2012 (MINAGRI, 2013).

To ensure sustainability and ownership of the irrigation schemes, water user organisations have been established. The increase in irrigation is shown below in Figure 5.

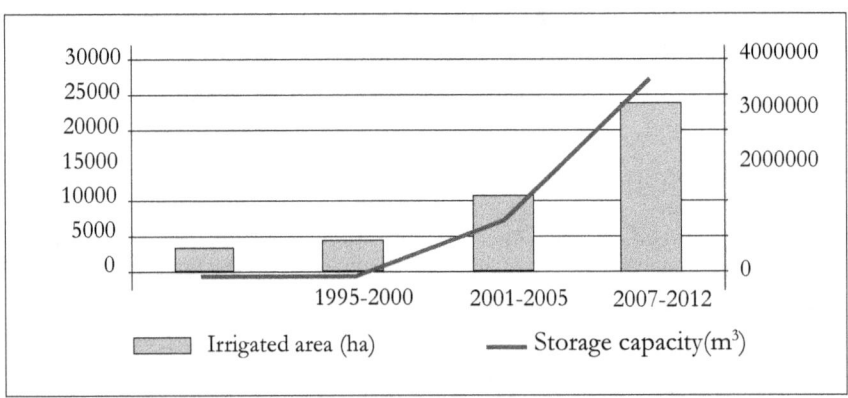

Figure 5: Irrigated area and water storage from 1994 to 2012

Land husbandry and Terracing

In 1988, only 37% of land was protected against erosion, mainly using progressive terraces. After 1994, a comprehensive land husbandry programme of terracing and agro-forestry was rolled out nationwide to reduce soil loss. Later in 2008, a more ambitious comprehensive land husbandry programme that combined terracing with water harvesting and increased productivity was introduced. This programme that has been nicknamed, 'unfold Rwanda' increased land available for cultivation by 47% (20% from previously eroded soils and 27% from land previously considered too marginal for agriculture). Alongside an aggressive compositing and liming programme, the resulting terraces are turning into major food baskets. On these terraces, erosion is reduced by 70-90% and water is harvested in reservoirs and used in irrigation. Production on terraced slopes has increased from an average of 469USD/ ha/year to 2,240 USD/ha/year. Figure 6 below illustrates the trend for areas protected against erosion.

Today the land effectively protected against soil erosion is over 70%. (Soil Erosion baseline Report, 2013).

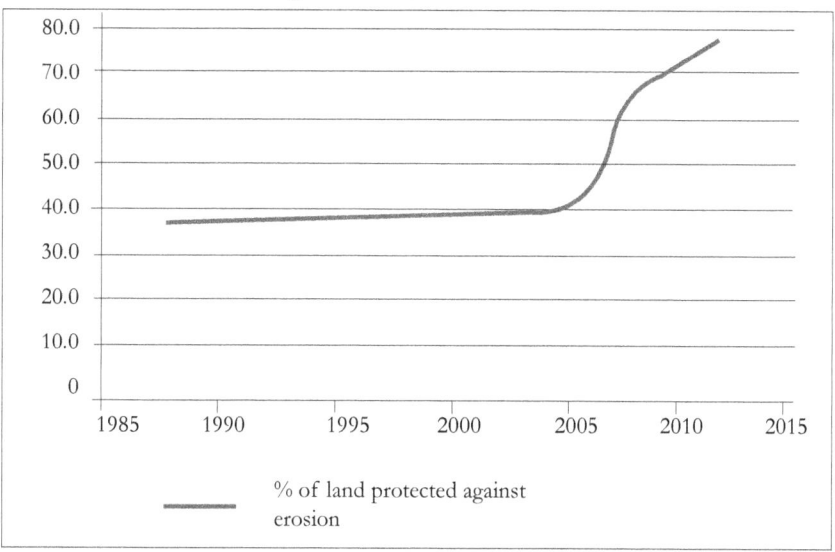

Figure 6: Proportion of land protected from soil erosion 1988-2012

Mechanised agriculture

An important enabling factor in addition to the physical environment of land and water is machinery to support planting and harvesting. In 1994, agriculture was mainly subsistence and non-mechanised. Since then, government has, in collaboration with the private sector, invested heavily in mechanisation.

At least 20% of land is now under modernised agriculture, an increase from 3% in 2000 (MINAGRI, 2012). In addition, a tractor assembly plant, which will allow domestic assembly of a minimum 2,000 units per year, is now nearing completion. Farmers have received training in operation, repair and maintenance of equipment, and this is now integrated into technical education (TVET) at the Institute of Agriculture and Animal Husbandry (ISAE) and Institute of Agriculture, Technology and Education of Kibungo (INATEK).

To ensure continued and sustainable mechanisation, the government is handing over responsibility to the private sector and there are currently eight major players in this sector. Figures 7 and 8 below illustrate the demand for mechanisation and trainings.

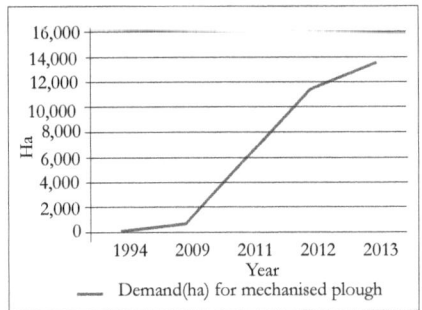
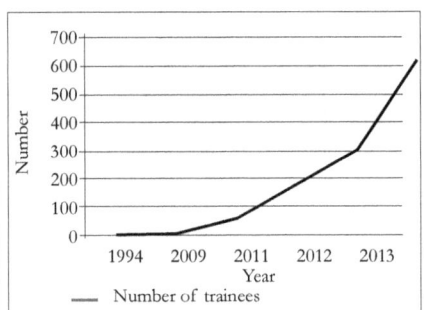

Figure 7: Area under mechanisation 1994-2013 (ha)

Figure 8: Training for mechanisation 1994-2013

Livestock

Livestock is an essential element of nutrition, and the sector has developed significantly since 1994, when 90% of animals were killed.

The headline livestock project to increase ownership and provide a productive asset is the 'Girinka', the One Cow per Poor Family Programme.

Started in 2006 as an initiative of President Paul Kagame to support poor families access nutrition, Girinka has since reached 196,000 poor and vulnerable families. It is rated by citizens as one of the most successful programmes of the RPF Government. It has also directly contributed to the reduction of poverty and rebuilding of the Rwandan society. It is by far one of the most successful Home-Grown Solutions that characterise the RPF Government.

Milk production increased several-fold from 92,628 tonnes in 1999 to 489,961 tonnes in 2013 and the country has been able to start a school milk programme, The One Cup of Milk per Child programme. Nutrition will continue to be a priority investment area for the government.

To support the development of the dairy value chain, government has, in collaboration with the private sector, established milk collection centres and processing plants. The dairy sector continues to show substantial potential domestically and regionally, and in 2013 Rwanda launched the Dairy seal of Quality to provide consumer reassurance about the milk products.

More generally, meat production has increased with investment in the livestock sector, including animal distribution, training in animal health and provision of vet services. By 2010, 68.2% of rural households had access to livestock with most rural households owning goats (53%), cattle (47.3%), chicken (45.5%), and pigs (24.1%) (EICV III, NISR, 2011). These animals provide nutrition, a productive asset and a savings vehicle for rural households. (Figure 10)

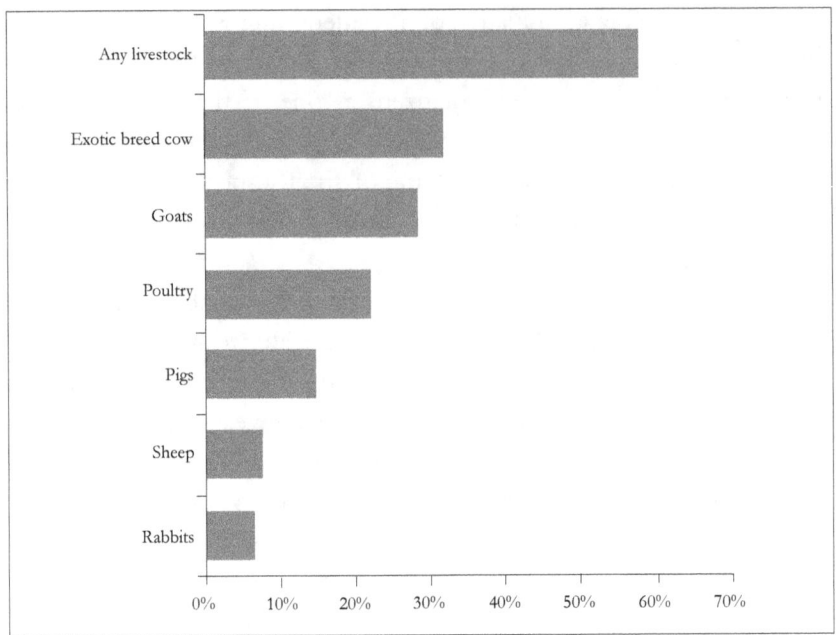

Figure 9: A graph showing ownership of livestock (NISR, 2012 Census)

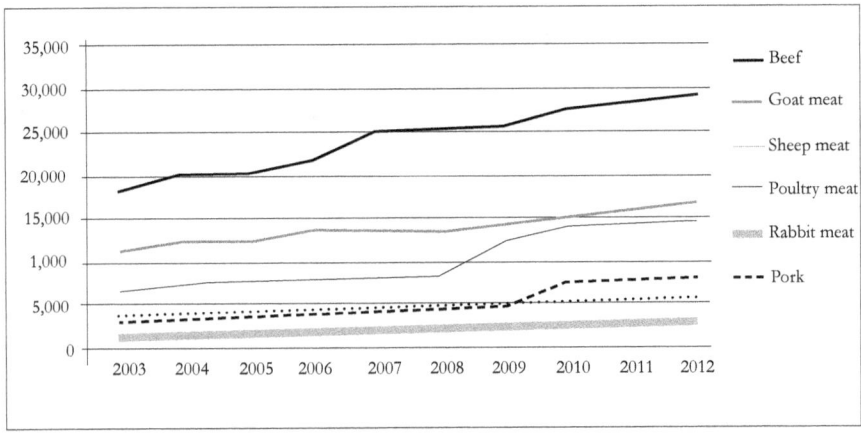

Figure 10: Rising trend in meat production (MINAGRI, 2013)

Exports

Exports stopped during the 1994 genocide, and Rwanda's primary export, coffee, was devastated, with many trees cut down or burned. The government and development partners launched a liberalisation programme in 1995 to revive the industry. As a result, private exporters increased from three in 1998 to five in 2002, and more than 20 by 2013. In order to boost coffee exports, Rwanda entered the Cup of Excellence competition in 2008, becoming the first African country to do so. Rwanda coffee was recognised as one of the best by world standards. Following this, renowned international buyers such as Starbucks, Rogers Family Co., Intelligentsia and others entered the Rwandan market and farmers obtained a premium price rising from US$0.20/kg in 1994 to US$3/kg in 2008 and as much as US$20/kg in 2013.

The figure below indicates the steady growth of coffee washing stations to ensure quality in the coffee export market. It is projected that the number of washing stations will grow to 349 by 2017.

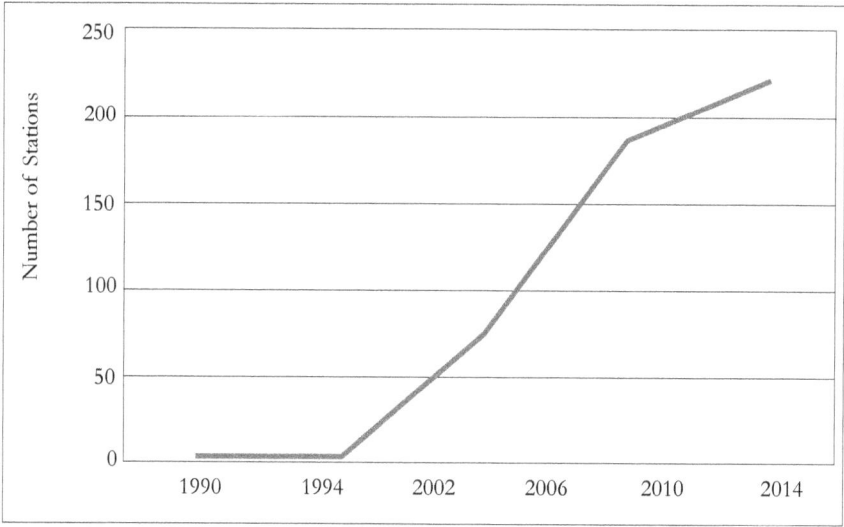

Figure 11: Coffee bean washing stations growth from 1990-2013

Tea is Rwanda's second export, and has been a remarkable success story since 1994. Until 2004, the industry was public, but since the privatisation, tea production and revenue have increased. Both the quantity of black tea exported and revenues accrued have been rising progressively, reaching 22,670 tonnes and US$ 51.8 million in 2014, compared to 10,657 tonnes and US$ 16.1 million in 1990, having fallen to a low of US$ 3.4 million. (BNR data 2014)

The quality of Rwandan tea is also recognised globally, generating good market prices at the Mombasa Tea Auction. Figures 12 and 13 show the increasing trend in both tea production and revenue generated from 1990 to 2012, with the 1994 drop indicated.

The comprehensive transformation of the tea and coffee industry, including new planting material, cultivation, privatisation, research, management and export to international markets is an example of the progress the sector has made since 1994. The development of these cash crops has both supported national growth and smallholder incomes, as both crops are mainly grown by smallholder farmers.

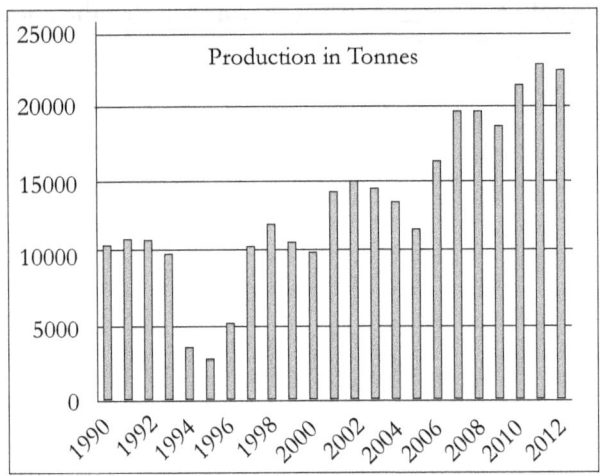

Figure 12: Increasing tea production 1990-2012

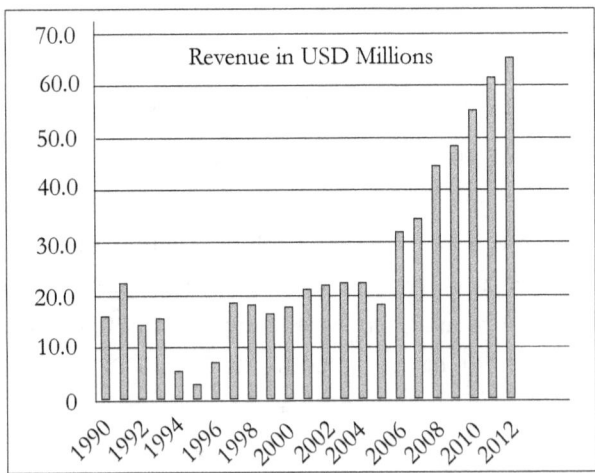

Figure 13: Increased tea revenues 1990-2012

Future Projection

Since 1990, and considering the losses of 1994, the agriculture sector has made major advances in the three key areas of food security, nutrition and growth, which have supported the overarching goal of poverty reduction and a better life for the people of Rwanda.

The strategic vision for the future prioritises further agricultural intensification and commercialisation and embraces the sector as a source of jobs and economic transformation. The main focus is increased production of staple crops and livestock products, and greater involvement of the private sector to increase agricultural exports, processing and value addition.

Investing in high-value crops while also exploiting the opportunities offered by staple crops will facilitate both domestic food security and higher rural incomes. In the short-term, continued increase in food production will ensure further reductions in rural poverty and malnutrition. In the medium-term, the goal is to move Rwandan agriculture from a largely subsistence sector to a more knowledge-intensive, market-oriented sector, sustaining growth and adding value to products.

Rwanda will also become an increasingly important player in international markets for both traditional commodities and new exports. Sector programmes will aim at realising the Economic Development and Poverty Reduction Strategy (EDPRS) II targets of 8.5% agricultural growth and 11.5% GDP growth, to reduce poverty to below 30% and to support the achievement of Vision 2020.

Investments in the agricultural sector by the public and private sectors, civil society engagement and committed and fruitful partnerships with farmers will continue to drive Rwanda's national development trajectory.

Top: Inyange staff in the pineapple juice making plant

Middle: Men and women picking tea

Bottom: Women drying and sorting coffee as part of the coffee quality excellence programme

Top: Terraced hills in Gicumbi District

Bottom: Girinka beneficiary feeding her cows

Infrastructure Development

Modern economies are built on an integrated network of infrastructure - roads, modern airports, water supply and sanitation services, and electricity power supply.

Road Transport

The development of a modern transport system is crucial for Rwanda as it seeks to increase trade and as part of the economic integration of East Africa. From 2003, the RPF-led government embarked on a campaign to rehabilitate the existing road network and build new ones internally and also those connecting Rwanda to the neighbouring countries of Uganda, Burundi, Tanzania and the Democratic Republic of Congo. For this reason and to give the sector clear policy diection, a Transport Sector Policy was developed in 2008.

Two yeas later, the Rwanda Transport Development Agency (RTDA) was created to manage all aspects of transport in the country.

According to data from RTDA, the total length of roads in Rwanda in 2013 was about 14,000km, part of which was paved. The newly built roads since 2003 include the Kigali-Bugesera-Kirundo road, which connects Rwanda to Burundi.

The tarmacked road network which also links Rwanda with neighbouring countries has led to the development of a vibrant transport industry, largely privately owned. Buses daily ply the roads radiating from Kigali to major towns like Huye in the south, Musanze in the north, Rubavu and Rusizi in the west and Nyagatare in the east. The main roads linking Rwanda to neighbouring countries have also witnessed an increase in traffic from Kigali to Kampala, Nairobi, Dar es Salaam, Bujumbura, and Juba in South Sudan, among others.

Air Transport

As Rwanda's economy continues to grow and international trade and travel increases, demand for quick, regular and efficient air transport has also grown. Since 2003 the government of Rwanda has put emphasis on connecting the country to the rest of the world by air. In order to meet this growing demand for air travel, three main airports have undergone significant expansion. These include terminal and runway expansions and new security, navigation and meteorological systems.

For instance, the Kigali International Airport has had its terminal and apron expanded, a new modern transit hall built and check-in desks improved and doubled from nine to 18 in order to handle the growing number of passengers. The luggage conveyor belts have also been increased from two to three.

Because of these renovations and the good business environment prevailing in Rwanda today, Kigali International Airport has turned into a busy transport hub, handling an increasing number of passengers annually. In 2013, for example, 559,531 passengers travelled through Kigali from a few hundred in 2003 (Statistical Year Book 2014).

Kamembe International Airport, situated in Rusizi, western Rwanda, just a few kilometres from DRC's Bukavu town, has also seen large scale renovation. The airport now has a new terminal, new control tower with new navigation and meteorological systems and fire trucks. The runway has been extended from 1,500m to 2,200m.

With a major focus on improving air transport in Rwanda, the RPF-led government revamped the national carrier which was originally flying under the name RwandAir Express. Thus in 2009, it changed its trade name to RwandAir. Since then the national airline has embarked on a fleet acquisition programme with a focus on the future. RwandAir's investment is guided by safety, technology and efficiency. The airline now boasts of a modern fleet of two Boeing 737-700NG, two Bombardier CRJ-900 NextGen, one brand new Bombardier Q-400 Next Gen, two Boeing 737-800NG and a Boeing 787 Dreamliner, to be delivered between December 2015 and early 2016.

RwandAir, officially registered with IATA, has spread its wings to the region, and beyond with daily routes to East African Community capital cities, Johannesburg and Dubai. New flights to Lagos in Nigeria, Libreville in Gabon and Brazzaville in the Republic of Congo, as well as to Accra (Ghana), Juba (South Sudan), and Douala (Cameroon) and Lusaka have also been introduced.

Rwanda is one of Africa's fastest growing air markets. This has attracted world class airlines to launch their flights at Kigali International Airport. Such airlines include KLM Royal Dutch Airlines, Turkish Airlines and Qatar

Airways in addition to others like Ethiopian and Kenya Airways which have had long-standing operations in Rwanda's skies.

In order to accommodate the increasing volume of passengers and a growing number of international airlines, and due to the limited space for expansion of Kigali International Airport, plans to build a bigger and modern international airport were made. The new international airport will be situated in Bugesera District, approximately 24km south of Kigali. Two runways will be built to rival the capacity of the world's largest airports.

Upon completion, the New Bugesera Airport will serve approximately 450 passengers per peak hour and over one million annually with eight flights per peak hour.

Rwanda is becoming a regional air traffic hub, following the signing of an agreement in 2011 between Rwanda and the Common Market for Eastern Africa and Southern Africa (COMESA) to host a regional Communication Navigation Surveillance/Air Traffic Management Centre (CNS/ATM). The Centre will centralise air traffic control for the entire COMESA region and allow a seamless flow of traffic in the airspace. For this purpose, a state-of-the-art communication tower on Mt Kalisimbi, which will host an advanced high-technology radar system to provide sky safety and surveillance to the region, is being built.

Rail Transport

One of Rwanda's largest infrastructural projects to facilitate transport and trade is the planned 494km regional railway connecting Kigali to Gitega and Musongati in Burundi and Isaka and Keza in Tanzania, which is along the Central Corridor linking the hinterland to the sea port of Dar es Salaam in Tanzania.

Another recent project that the government of Rwanda, under the RPF, is involved in is the Kampala-Kigali railway line, which is part of a regional project connecting Kenya, Uganda and Rwanda along the Northern Corridor, linking Kigali to the Indian Ocean sea port of Mombasa in Kenya. The Project is expected to be completed in 2018 at an estimated cost of US$13.5 billion and Rwanda, Uganda and Kenya will jointly mobilise funds for it.

According to some media reports quoting experts, once the Standard Gauge railway line, is operational, trains will be able to ferry cargo at speeds of up to 120km per hour, thus improving transport of goods on the Northern Corridor. These two projects will foster economic integration within the East African Community and reduce transport, time and costs, ultimately reducing the cost of goods in Rwanda.

Energy

The RPF has always recognised the fact that a reliable supply of energy is a basic prerequisite for economic development and improvement of living standards for all.

That is why it is committed to increasing energy in Rwanda and making it accessible to all including homes, schools, health facilities and industries.

For the country to achieve this, several hydro power projects are being undertaken. One of them, a 28MW plant on Nyabarongo River, came on stream just before the end of 2014. Another project is the World Bank-funded Rusumo Hydro-electricity Project, expected to generate 80MW on completion. This project will benefit the people of Rwanda, Burundi and Tanzania, thereby reducing electricity cost, promoting renewable energy and advancing regional cooperation and development. Rusizi III, which will generate 147MW to be shared by Burundi and DRC, was also launched.

In 2010, the government launched a programme – the Access Scale-up Roll-Out Programme – to make electricity available to more people. As a result, the number of people accessing electricity has increased from 9.5% in 2010 to 16% in 2012 compared to 2.4% in 1996. This programme that aims at increasing access to electricity in all sectors of the economy, but particularly homesteads, started from a very low base. Its performance has been a remarkable 296% between 2008 and 2012. This has led to various small-scale agro-processing plants and cottage industries being set up in many parts of the country, which has in turn led to improved livelihoods.

Good progress has been made in terms of quality supply since 2003 and the load shedding which was very common across the country and more particularly in Kigali City is becoming a thing of the past.

Installed electricity generation capacity stands at 160MW and the national electricity grid has been extended to over 3,400km of medium voltage and 396km of high voltage. The target is to reach 563MW by 2017. This power is expected to come from different domestic sources and shared sources including hydro (320MW), methane gas (300MW), peat (200MW), geothermal (310MW) as well as solar energy.

Additional electricity is expected to come from neighbouring countries. From regional sources, transmission lines are being built between Rwanda and countries in the region, namely Uganda, Burundi, DRC and Tanzania to support power trade between them. Rwanda has aready signed a MoU to purchase up to 400MW from Ethiopia by 2017, 50MW from Uganda and up to 200MW from Kenya.

Water and Sanitation Services

The importance of adequate water supply and sanitation services as drivers for social and economic development, poverty reduction and public health is fully acknowledged in Rwanda's Water Supply and Sanitation policy and related strategies. In this regard, the government of Rwanda has committed itself to reaching 100% water and sanitation services by 2020. The treatment and distribution of water has therefore been given high priority in fulfilling its mandate to supply clean water to the population.

The private sector also plays an important role in this network, where 74% of the 1024 water supply systems in the country are operated and managed by Small and Medium Enterprises that have formed cooperatives. (WASAC 2014)

In order to satisfy the growing demand for safe drinking water and in line with the increase in the population of Kigali, the government has initiated a short-medium term solution project – the Kigali Bulk Water Supply Project – to supply 400,000m3 per day to Bugesera and Kigali districts.

All this has had a visible impact on the delivery of water and sanitation services. According to data available, by July 2013, 74.5% Rwandans had access to clean drinking water as compared to 41% in 2003. At least 74.6% had access to sanitation services in 2013 (Esteves, et al, 2013).

As a result of these efforts, Rwanda ranks among the first African countries to achieve the Millennium Development Goals (MDGs) on sanitation and even surpass them. MDG 7 calls for reduction by a half the proportion of people without sustained access to safe drinking water and basic sanitation services by 2015.

These achievements in the provision of water and sanitation services have greatly improved people's livelihood and significantly reduced the incidence of water-borne diseases especially among children.

Information Communication Technology (ICT)

ICT: Putting Rwanda on the world map

Rwanda has registered significant gains in the installation of ICT infrastructure that is now connecting Rwandans to global networks. The national fibre optic backbone network connects Rwanda to international sea cables and will facilitate increased affordability and access to the Internet across the country. A national data centre has been developed, which allows Rwanda to centralise her information storage, management and protection, as well as take advantage of cloud computing opportunities.

A Communication, Navigation Surveillance and Air Traffic Management system (CNS-ATM) has been deployed, which will greatly transform air travel, not just for Rwanda, but the region at large.

Broadcasting masts that are transforming broadcasting nationally have been deployed at Rwanda's highest peak of Karisimbi, thereby fast tracking Rwanda's migration from analogue to digital transmission to beat the ITU dealine of 2015.

Due to the ICT infrastructure, a number of well known international mobile telecommunication companies have entered Rwanda's growing market. By 2013 Rwanda had three telecom operators, namely MTN-Rwanda, TIGO and Bharti Airtel Ltd, with mobile telephone penetration as of March 2015 standing at 70.8% of the population, with the number of subscribers now above seven million, according to the Rwanda Utilities Regulatory Agency (RURA).

Due to the national fibre optic network that covers the whole country, and the highest mobile telephone penetration in the region, Kigali City dwellers are now able to access free Internet via Wi-Fi enabled devices through the new government-backed 'Smart Kigali' project. The project symbolises another step towards achieving Rwanda's prospects of becoming a regional IT hub.

In the same spirit, and with its vision of transforming Rwanda's economy from agrarian to knowledge-based status, the government of Rwanda signed a US$ 140 million deal with Korea Telecom (KT) Corp of the Republic of Korea in June 2013 to provide 4G Long Term Evolution (LTE) Broadband networks across the country, especially in areas where Internet connectivity is low. The contract was considered to be one of the biggest Foreign Direct Investments (FDI) ever embarked on by Rwanda in ICT. 4G LTE is now operational in the country.

In recognition of his strategic leadership and promotion of ICT usage for poverty eradication, the United Nations Secretary General nominated President Kagame to co-chair UN's Broadband Commission for Digital Development in 2010.

Rwanda's ICT journey has developed from humble beginnings going back to 1998 when the country's first ever ICT policy, the Rwanda ICT for Development (ICT4D), was mooted.

Commonly known as the National Information and Communication Infrastructure Plan (NICI), it was designed to implement the necessary policies and plans capable of addressing Rwanda's developmental challenges in the information and technology age in order to speed up the country's social economic development process.

In 2005, the RPF government fine-tuned NICI, providing for strategies that would see Rwanda's economy turn from an agrarian to a more knowledge-based one by 2020.

A lot has been achieved since then. In 2009, more than 2,300km of broadband fibre optic telecommunication network was laid across the country to link to undersea cables running along the East African coast. So far, all the 30 districts, nine border posts and several other public and private institutions such as schools and health centres are connected and the network is active, serving different sectors of the economy.

In order to fill the skills gap in the ICT field, Rwanda joined the 'One Laptop per Child' Programme (OLPC) in 2007, becoming the first East African country and the third on the African continent to do so. OLPC is an international programme aimed at introducing computers to the youth. Since then, more than 200,000 laptops have been distributed to more than 140 primary schools.

In addition, the government of Rwanda has partnered with the American Carnegie Mellon University to open a campus in Rwanda. This is aimed at creating the much needed critical mass of science and technology skills, not only for Rwanda's development but also for the African continent. The Carnegie Mellon University-Rwanda (CMU-R) receives students from all over Africa and offers a Master of Science degree in Information Technology.

ICT in Agriculture

ICT initiatives benefiting the agriculture sector include the Agricultural Management Information System (AMIS); an online exchange platform, 'e-Soko', a mobile market information solution that allows farmers and consumers to access market information for agricultural products.

This has empowered farmers to make informed market pricing decisions and ultimately become successful farmers. The e-Soko project won the 2011 public service delivery Technology in Government Award (TIGA). A Land Use Management and Information System has also been implemented to ensure proper usage, planning and management of land.

ICT in Business

ICT initiatives fostering Rwanda's private sector development include: several business and career development support services; online trade information portals; business incubators; online tax calculators; credit reference bureau; a land administration and management information system; electronic case management system; and improvements in online banking and e-transaction regulatory system.

These initiatives have greatly improved Rwanda's business environment. In 2010, Rwanda was the top global reformer in the World Bank's 'Ease of Doing Business' ranking, moving up from 143rd in 2009 to 67th, the biggest jump ever recorded by any country. Currently, Rwanda is marked 46th in World Bank' Ease of Doing Business and Africa's best reformer in 2014. Online business registration was key to Rwanda's improved ranking in 2011, where it currently ranks 58th.

Additionally, in order to take ICT closer to the people, 30 Business Development Centres commonly called Tele-centres are operational across the country. Publicly funded, the centres, which are fully equipped with

IT equipment, are supporting and improving the delivery of public and private sector services.

ICT in Health

Numerous ICT initiatives have been implemented in health such as:

OpenMRS – an open-source medical records system that facilitates nationwide tracking of patient data; TRACnet – a system that allows central collection and storage of clinical health information; and Mobile e- Health – a system used by community health workers to collect data for OpenMRS and TRACnet systems. They also include Telemedicine – a system connecting King Faisal Hospital to hospitals in Kabgayi and Musanze; facilitating the sharing of clinical information between urban and rural hospitals, and most importantly, allowing citizens to receive specialised treatment services remotely without travelling to Kigali. These initiatives are transforming healthcare delivery and helping Rwanda achieve Millennium Development Goals (MDGs) in health.

ICT in Governance

ICT initiatives put in place have significantly altered service delivery by public institutions. Such initiatives have supported and empowered the Immigration and Emigration Department in simplifying entry and exit processes, and also eased the obtaining of travel documents. The aim is to enhance immigration control services and this has been effective through the implementation of the electronic visa issuing component by the Immigration Office.

The online visa application process is fully operational and those visitors who do not have access to a Rwandan embassy could apply for the visa prior to their visit to the country. In addition, immigration related processes are now given tracking numbers, enabling applicants to track their application process.

This innovation has seen Rwanda's Immigration and Emigration Department win the prestigious African Association for Public Administration and Management (AAPAM) Innovative Gold Award 2009.

Urban and Rural Settlement

Before 2004, Rwanda had never had a coherent policy incorporating all elements of human settlement. This lack of a policy guideline, coupled with low incomes and absence of support from the government, contributed to the expansion of unplanned and consequently unsafe settlements in both urban centres and rural areas, poor land management and environmental degradation. This already grave situation was exacerbated by the 1994 genocide against Tutsi, where many houses were destroyed and millions of returning refugees found themselves with nowhere to settle.

Based on its conviction that proper housing is a fundamental right for every Rwandan, the government established Rwanda Housing Authority in 2010 with a major mandate of organising the construction industry as a whole and implementing the national housing, urbanisation and construction plans in an organised manner.

This has led to a rapid transformation and promoted urban growth within different parts of the country since 2003, and more particularly Kigali city. The successes are noticeable, as Kigali is ranked among the most organised and cleanest cities in the world.

Building the Capital City

According to experts, master planning is decisive for actualisation of ideas in any development process. As a result, the Kigali Master Plan was created and approved in 2009. The US$1.7 million Kigali Master Plan, once implemented over the next 50 years, will establish a city that is a symbol of Rwanda's culture which serves as an example to modern Africa; of a liveable community that supports a sense of belonging, cooperation and healing and a model of environmental protection which minimises pollution and waste.

According to the plan, the Central Business District will be located in Nyarugenge, Kiyovu, Quartier Mateus, Quartier Commercial, Muhima, and Kimicanga.

Once marked by simple houses, the new Kigali City is to be characterised by skyscrapers housing shopping malls, restaurants, banks, offices and hotels.

Kigali city is already changing, with new buildings coming up that are decisively altering the city's skyline. This is evidenced by the 20-storey Kigali City Tower, which stands in total contrast to the run-down taxi-park that used to occupy the prime land where it stands today. To Kigali City dwellers and visitors, Kigali City Tower not only stands for aspiration and power, but also for hope in a city rapidly becoming one of the most prosperous, cleanest and fastest growing metropolitan centres on the African continent.

The Kigali Master Plan has not only served to construct such magnificent commercial buildings and office space, but it has also led to the building of new estates in different suburbs of the city that serve the middle-income class which is coming up as a result of the country's steady economic growth.

An example is the Gacuriro Vision 2020 Estate which stands on one of Kigali's sprawling hills once occupied by banana plantations dotted with eucalyptus trees.

Such innovative and focused efforts have been recognised internationally, with Kigali City winning the much-sought after UN Habitat Scroll of Honour Award in 2008. It won the award for its many innovations in building a model, modern city symbolised by zero tolerance for plastics, improved garbage collection and substantial reduction in crime. Kigali City is the first authority to win the prestigious award in Africa.

The Kigali Master Plan serves as both a roadmap for expansion of the city and an overall guide for the growth of other provincial towns, all of which have developed their respective city master plans, to address the once unplanned urban settlement that was characteristic of pre-1994 Rwanda.

Umudugudu: Bringing Services Closer to the People

Following the return of millions of refugees in mid-1996 with unplanned rural settlement, the RPF government devised a settlement programme known as *Imidugudu*. This programme was aimed at providing decent housing to all Rwandans and also free land for more organised agricultural use.

According to the Ministry of Local Government and Social Welfare, in the first quarter of 2013, about 74.4% of total households were living in *Imidugudu*/grouped settlement sites. The programme was hailed for having facilitated the provision of basic services such as safe water, electricity, schools, health facilities and communication services.

Another success story through such pro-people programmes is the abolition of grass thatched houses. More than 125,000 families were relocated to decent houses in what was dubbed 'bye-bye *Nyakatsi*', and others in their thousands were resettled from high risk zones, that were prone to devastating floods and landslides that would regularly claim people's lives.

Private Sector Development

Since 1995, the Rwandan economy has been growing rapidly, recovering from the massive economic disruption caused by the Genocide against the Tutsi of 1994.

In the aftermath of the genocide and associated conflicts, between 1996 and 2000, real GDP grew at over 10% per year (IMF, 2008). In the decade starting with 2000, Rwanda was the tenth fastest growing economy in the world. In fact, since 2000 and by the end of the first Economic Development and Poverty Reduction Strategy (EDPRS) period in 2012, Rwanda registered sustained economic growth, poverty reduction and a reduction in income inequality.

This growth, together with one of the most improved business environment climates on the continent, regional integration within the East African Community (EAC), and impressive macroeconomic stability, have laid a strong foundation for continuous economic development.

There is also considerable momentum coming from the establishment of several key institutions in recent years. One milestone was the establishment of the Rwanda Development Board (RDB) in 2008, the agency charged with promoting investment and providing a one-stop-centre for both foreign and local investors to set up operations in Rwanda. RDB brings together all the government agencies responsible for the entire investor experience under one roof, including issues such as business registration, investment promotion, environmental clearances, privatisation, investor after care and specialist agencies which support the priority sectors such as ICT and tourism.

Another important step was the establishment of Rwanda Revenue Authority (RRA) in 1997, with the mission of mobilising revenue for economic development through efficient and equitable tax administration services that promote business growth.

Finally, the Private Sector Federation (PSF) was established in 1999, replacing the former Rwanda Chamber of Commerce and Industry. PSF is an umbrella organisation that coordinates private sector initiatives and promotes and represents the interests of the Rwandan business community. It has made significant achievements in advocacy and pioneering business development services. PSF now serves as an important component of the government's dialogue with the private sector.

In addition, other important steps have been the creation of the Rwanda Bureau of Standards (RBS) in 2002, Rwanda Cooperative Agency (RCA) in 2008, and the Business Development Fund (BDF) in 2011 providing credit guarantees and advisory services to SMEs.

These institutions and others are critical to achieving the development of an efficient private sector spearheaded by competitiveness and entrepreneurship, which is a main aspiration of the Vision 2020. At the same time, the increasing number of institutions involved in private sector development has also highlighted the need for coordination and a clear division of responsibilities within the sector.

For this reason, the government, through the Ministry of Trade and Industry, formulated a five-year Private Sector Development (PSD) Strategy, approved in June 2013. The PSD Strategy is at the heart of the Economic Development and Poverty Reduction Strategy (EDPRS) II, and aims at developing an entrepreneurial, innovative and competitive sector that delivers broad-based and inclusive economic growth resulting in many more and better-paid jobs for Rwandans. It is now the centre of reform initiatives, informs priorities and establishes a framework for monitoring progress.

Industrial Development

Rwanda industry, and agro-processing sector in particular, was more profoundly affected than other areas of the economy during the early 1990s. Whilst agriculture and services began a sustainable recovery immediately after the 1994 Genocide, manufacturing output fluctuated for a further five years before finding a stable growth trend.

There are several reasons for this. Manufacturing is intricately linked to other firms throughout the economy, and these links take a long time to re-establish once broken. Manufacturing requires substantial investment, and investors become afraid to invest when crises begin, and remain nervous long after they have ended. Moreover, the banking sector was heavily burdened with non-performing loans in the 1990s and was not in a strong position to provide the capital that industry needed.

The sector also requires heavy machinery, much of which was physically damaged or destroyed and took a long time to rehabilitate or replace. Specialised technical skills are necessary, and industry was reliant on foreign experts, many of whom left the country in the period leading up to 1994, and were slow to return afterwards. Manufacturing requires reliable electricity and other public services to function, but national electrical supply did not return to pre-1994 levels until 1998.

Agriculture and services operations were much less vulnerable in most of these ways, enabling them to recover more quickly.

All in all, manufacturing and agro-processing collapsed to about half of their 1980s level in 1994-1995, but were saved from greater destruction by the incoming government's decision to reaffirm existing property rights for both Rwandans and foreign nationals, enabling some industrialists to return to their factories and restart production.

Many of the prerequisites for the future success of the manufacturing sector were established early in the recovery process. Between 1995 and 1996, exchange rates were allowed to float, price controls were removed, domestic marketing of tea and coffee was liberalised, interest rate controls were abolished, import duties were reduced from an average of 35% to less than 20%, and a law empowering the government to privatise or liquidate public companies was passed.

Had these reforms not been enacted, it would certainly have constrained the growth of the manufacturing sector in later years. The first dramatic change for Rwandan industry came in 1999, when long-term credit to the private sector leapt more than twentyfold in a single year. This marked the transition from reconstruction to a new phase of business creation and investment in growth.

The next important change came in 2007, spurred by entry into the EAC, which had a profound impact on investors' interest and confidence in Rwanda.

With duty-free access to the regional market and the promise of ever-greater integration of the five economies as the EAC developed agreements in services and investment, Rwanda became a more attractive destination for foreign investment. Machinery imports tripled to US$60m in 2007 over the previous year, and the share of investment in GDP rose from 15% in 2006 to 22% by 2009. Although new firm creation maintained a healthy level during this period, manufacturing growth was and is being driven by large investment groups that have greater access to finance than smaller entrepreneurs.

Although the Government passed legislation as early as 1996 that laid the groundwork for privatisation of state-owned enterprises, this project was not only able to gather real momentum after 2005, but also became a critical factor in attracting large-scale foreign investment to the country. New owners invested heavily in previously state-owned firms such as Kabuye Sugar Works, various rice mills and Pembe Flour Mills.

Even where this process was challenging and required complex restructuring, the resulting privatised firms have become some of the largest and most successful in the country, as in the case of Rwanda Trading Company.

A key component in boosting the sector in the coming years will be to provide serviced land, which is why the government of Rwanda has developed a Special Economic Zone (SEZ) in Kigali, parts of which are already operational.

The SEZ will soon offer 278 ha of serviced land, including ready-to-use factory units. This provides investors primarily with land, electricity, transport infrastructure and market access. To balance industrial development across the country and stimulate job creation outside of the capital, development of four provincial and four district industrial parks has already begun with a total of 826 ha.

The development of this industrial serviced land is a precondition for transforming Rwanda into a diversified middle-income economy where the industrial sector constitutes 26% of the economy, as targeted in Vision 2020.

Doing Business and Attracting Investment

The government of Rwanda has made great achievements in reforming the environment for doing business and attracting investment. In particular, Rwanda has focused on simplifying the legal and regulatory framework, underpinned by zero tolerance for corruption.

Today, it takes only six hours to start a business and this can be done online. The proportion of companies that register online increases continuously, and in 2013 alone almost 4,000 companies chose this option.

Since 2004, 20 business laws have been enacted by Parliament. Government has moved to reform many commercial legal instruments that have made it much easier to do business in Rwanda such as through simplifying land and business registration, easing property and land acquisition, and infrastructure development.

Commercial legislative reforms in enacting business-friendly laws on the flexibility of company formation, competition, negotiable instruments, security interest in movable and immovable property, mortgages, credit information systems, intellectual property, insolvency, electronic transactions, the labour code promoting greater flexibility in the labour market, and so on, have encouraged private investments in the country. Access to finance has also been greatly facilitated by the law of accepting movable property as collateral for the loans.

ICT initiatives fostering Rwanda's private sector development such as online trade information portals, online tax calculators and a land administration and management information system have particularly improved the business environment in Rwanda.

On the administrative side, four commercial courts have been established and the Law Reform Commission and Rwanda Development Board have been established to fast-track the doing business reform agenda and support the investing community.

These efforts have drawn the attention of global financial and governance institutions. This is especially seen in the World Bank's annual *Doing Business* reports previously referred to.

Similarly, in the World Economic Forum's Global Competitiveness Index 2013-2014, Rwanda was ranked the third most competitive economy in Sub-Saharan Africa and was praised for its strong and well-functioning institutions, good security, low levels of corruption and efficient labour markets. Rwanda is now one of the most attractive locations in the region for firms to operate from and to serve local and regional markets, particularly the DRC and Burundi.

Even though areas such as trading across borders and resolving insolvency are still challenges, continuously improving the investment climate remains a key priority of the government of Rwanda.

How have the post-genocide reforms of the business environment translated into actual investments?

Private investment, as recorded by the National Bank of Rwanda (BNR), totalled US$168.4 million in 2013, compared with US$4.7 million in 2003. Net Foreign Direct Investment (FDI) in 2013 was almost 21 times higher than in 2000, in US dollars. Gross fixed capital formation – which determines the capacity of the economy to expand output in the future, by indicating investment in, for example, machinery – has risen steadily as a proportion of GDP post-genocide; from 13% in 1995 to 27% in 2013. It is now relatively high by international standards and above the Sub-Saharan African average (World Bank 2013).

However, attracting investment must go beyond improving the legal and regulatory environment. There are cross-cutting issues related to, for example, a shortage of skills, access to finance, infrastructure and electricity that the government is actively focusing on. Investment builds the capacity of the economy to grow, which is why the Economic Development and Poverty Reduction Strategy (EDPRS) II sets out ambitious targets; private investment as a proportion of GDP must grow from 10 to 15% and FDI from 2.3 to 4.5% between 2013 and 2018.

Trade Development

Trade openness is critical for developing a competitive private sector and economic growth. This is especially true for a small country such as Rwanda, although being landlocked with long distances to sea ports certainly poses some natural barriers to trade. Nonetheless, the Government has been proactive in facilitating trade by, for example, having major border posts open 24 hours a day and introducing the Electronic Single Window in 2012, which simplifies and expedites information flows between traders and Government institutions. The creation of institutions such as the National Agricultural Export Development Board (NAEB), Rwanda Bureau of Standards (RBS) and the Rwanda Development Board (RDB) has also helped the country gain momentum for increasing exports.

An important pillar of the Vision 2020 is to work towards deeper penetration of regional and international markets, which is why Rwanda has taken on an active role in World Trade Organisation (WTO) negotiations, joined the East African Community (EAC) in 2007 and has signed a number of other regional and bilateral trade agreements. The formulation of the Rwanda Trade Policy in 2010 and the National Export Strategy in 2011 (currently being revised), has certainly helped coordinate policy making and implementation between the range of institutions involved in trade.

Accordingly, Rwanda has gradually become a significantly more open economy, post-genocide. Merchandise trade as a percentage of GDP, which can be considered as an indicator of the openness of an economy, was around 20% in the years after 1994. It grew to almost 35% in 2012.

Looking at exports specifically is important; Rwanda's domestic market has been enlarged by her membership to the East Africa customs union, supporting the growth of the private sector. Various trade missions have been conducted outside East Africa taking along members of the business community to explore and connect to new markets. Diversifying exports reduces vulnerability to for example price swings, and exporting firms also tend to be more efficient than non-exporting firms.

Indeed, in the decade after 2002, exports of goods and services averaged annual growth of 17% and improving the trade balance remains a key focus of the Government.

Tea and coffee exports have been instrumental in Rwanda's impressive trade performance. Taking the coffee sector as an example, quality has improved, leading to higher prices being paid at world markets. In coffee, this trend was mainly driven by the growing share of fully washed coffee, owing to an increased number of processing factories and washing stations owned by the private sector.

Although the bulk of exports is still from traditional sectors – minerals, tea and coffee – the share of non-traditional exports is increasing continuously; averaging 23% growth between 2008 and 2013. There has been a rapid expansion of non-traditional exports in particular to member countries of the EAC and to the DRC.

Increasing exports is one of the key pillars of Rwanda's national development. To support the continuous growth of the private sector, in turn critical for job creation and poverty alleviation, the government is determined to achieve 28% annual export growth by 2018.

SME Development and Job Creation

In line with Vision 2020 and the (EDPRS) II, the SME Policy was approved with a vision to create viable, dynamic and competitive enterprises contributing to export diversification and increasing off-farm jobs to 3.2 million by 2020.

The SME sector, including formal and informal businesses, comprises 98% of the businesses in Rwanda and 41% of all private sector employment; though the formalised sector has much growth potential, with only 300,000 currently employed. Most micro and small enterprises employ up to four people, showing that growth in the sector would create significant private sector non-agricultural employment opportunities.

In view of the vital role of the SME sector in reducing Rwanda's trade imbalance, creating employment, diversifying exports and in widening the tax base as the Government pursues the vision to transform the country into a middle-income country by the year 2020, the 8th National Leadership Retreat boldly set SME development as a top priority on the national development agenda.

To expedite the implementation of the SME policy and achieve (EDPRS) II objectives of job creation, the Ministry of Trade and Industry established different programmes to support SME development and achieve government goals. One strategic instrument is the Hanga Umurimo Programme (HUP), which targets mainly start-up and existing SMEs not exceeding three years in business experience and wishing to expand their businesses.

The main strategic objectives of this programme are to foster the growth of an entrepreneurial culture, to empower communities with basic business skills, increase job creation opportunities, and to identify individuals with entrepreneurial aptitude and nurture good and bankable business ideas.

So far the HUP has been widely successful, with over 30,000 business ideas received and close to 24,000 jobs created, testifying to the entrepreneurial spirit among Rwandans.

Rwanda Cooperative Movement

Since 2005, the government has heavily invested in the cooperative sector, as cooperatives are considered important mechanisms for pooling the people's small resources, with a view to encouraging economies of scale. To support the contribution of cooperatives to the objectives set out in Vision 2020, the government formulated the Policy on Cooperatives Promotion in 2006, in which cooperatives are seen as a potential vehicle through which the cooperatives' members could create employment and expand access to finance through Savings and Credit Cooperatives (SACCOs).

Cooperatives would also facilitate access to income-generating activities, develop their business potential, accelerate entrepreneurial and managerial capacities through education and training, encourage value addition, agro-processing and increase savings and investment activities.

It is worthwhile to highlight the milestones that the government of Rwanda has put in place during the last eight years towards the revival and strengthening of cooperatives, so that they could really constitute a key pillar of the country's general economic development.

Firstly, the Task Force on Cooperatives Promotion was established in 2005, which was later transformed into a fully-fledged Rwanda Cooperative Agency (RCA) in 2008.

Secondly, the government has promoted 416 Umurenge Savings and Credit Cooperatives (U-SACCOs) and the special direct government financial support to that programme so far amounts to FRW7.5 billion.

Thirdly, the government has been actively involved in promotion activities, implying a strong mobilisation campaign that has been carried out since 2006 by RCA, in close collaboration with local governments and various central government institutions, in order to bring the dormant cooperative movement into life and respond to its members' needs.

Finally, the enhancement of marketing cooperatives and SACCOs' capacity should be noted. This has been undertaken through various trainings of leaders, employees and members, workshops and study tours within the country and outside of Rwanda to learn best practices from other countries.

From 2005, pre-cooperative associations were transformed into fully legally registered cooperatives, new cooperatives were promoted and registered, cooperative umbrella organisations were established on the basis of their value chains and these all together established the National Cooperative Confederation, the national Apex Body which is now a full member of the International Cooperative Alliance (ICA).

By the end of 2005, legally registered cooperatives countrywide were 919 whereas by April 2014, over 5,800 marketing cooperatives and 465 Savings and Credit cooperatives had been registered. This has been translated to a total investment of almost FRW30 billion. Since July 2013, more than

350 Umurenge SACCOs have become self-sustaining and stopped being subsidised.

Overall, primary production cooperatives alone have more than 455,000 individual members and SACCOs over 2.3 million members. Since the end of 2010, the number of SACCO members has doubled and the number of account holders quadrupled. These numbers certainly testify to the improvements in savings culture among Rwandans and SACCOs in Rwanda today play a critical role as financial services providers, giving the low income population the opportunity to access financial services.

Going forward, the government has decided to decentralise RCAs' activities for them to be even more accessible to ordinary citizens. The Rwanda Institute of Cooperatives, Entrepreneurship and Microfinance (RICEM) is currently also being established, aiming at providing practice-oriented vocational training to most of Rwanda's population with a relatively low level of education.

Countrywide, cooperatives are also being supported by coaches to design business plans and further professionalise their management systems. SACCOs are also being consolidated, which will culminate in the formation of a Cooperative Bank at the national level.

By further harnessing the culture and spirit of cooperation naturally existing among Rwandans, together with the existence of the political will and institutional framework, major opportunities for the cooperative movement in the future will emerge.

Tourism Development

The tourism sector has experienced a remarkable turnaround since the 1990s. Like with many other sectors, the genocide put a virtual halt to the industry, but it has since then registered significant progress in generating foreign exchange, increasing employment opportunities and attracting investment.

Due to these associated benefits, the government of Rwanda has identified it as a priority sector to achieve Rwanda's development goals as set out in Vision 2020. To this end, the Rwanda Tourism Policy was formulated in 2009, with a view to increasing tourism revenues in a sustainable manner, generating profits for reinvestment and creating jobs. This was to be done by developing new and distinctive market-led products that are clearly positioned and promoted in the marketplace. They would also bring spatial and socio-economic balance to the distribution of tourism benefits.

Indeed, the tourism industry is now playing a significant role in the Rwandan economy. Looking at the first decade of the 2000s, around 20%, or US$ 453 million, of FDI went into the hotels and leisure sector (World Bank and SNV, 2010). The national household survey conducted in 2010/11 (EICV-3) estimated the number of employees in the tourism sector at 23,000, with many more sectors indirectly benefiting from tourism; for example hotels, restaurants, transportation services and retail trade.

The travel and tourism sector has shown an impressive growth and has steadily increased its share of total services exports. Compared with US$ 19 million in 1993 (World Bank and SNV, 2010), US$ 303 million was generated in the travel and tourism sector in 2014. This corresponds to 66% of total services receipts (MINECOFIN, 2014).

Other numbers, too, show a significant growth. In 2013, Rwanda had an occupancy of 7,968 rooms (NISR, 2013), an increase from slightly more than 650 rooms in 2003 (World Bank and SNV, 2010). Rwanda hosted 2,406,039 visitors in 2013, a number that keeps growing year by year; the total number of arrivals increased by more than 50% from 2007 (RDB, 2010 and 2013).

While the vast majority of visitors are from neighbouring countries such as Uganda, Tanzania, Burundi and the Democratic Republic of Congo, the number of tourists from non-neighbouring countries increased by 6% in the year 2013.

These numbers have attracted substantial investments in recent years and as an example, several international hotel chains are now constructing four- or five-star hotels. These include Serena hotels, Marriot hotels, Raddisson Blu hotels, Sheraton and others.

The most well-known attraction for visitors to Rwanda is the rare mountain gorillas in the Virunga Volcanoes in the northern part of the country. Revenues from gorilla trekkers alone account for around 85% of all revenues generated by national parks, and *Kwita Izina*, a naming ceremony of newly born baby gorillas, has become a popular event on the international tourism calendar. This event attracts not only tourists but also international celebrities.

Mindful of the need to avoid putting excessive stress on the environment, the government increased the price of the gorilla permit in 2013, from US$500 to 750. For this reason, even though the number of visitors and therefore pressure on the gorillas lessened, park revenues increased by 15% from the previous year.

Considering the importance of gorilla trekking to overall tourism earnings, and that most tourists stay only a few days in the country, the government is actively involved in promoting a diversification of Rwanda's tourism offer. RDB has initiated proactive marketing strategies which include, among others, Rwanda's participation in major international tourism fairs. Government has also begun encouraging visits based on the cultural heritage and history of Rwanda and promotion of national parks and lakes.

Many tourist attractions have come up since 2003. These include the Akagera National Park in the eastern part of the country and Nyungwe National Park, the largest protected mountain rainforest that offers a rare and important habitat for many species, especially primates and birds.

Moreover, in 2013, the government formulated a Sub-Master Plan for Tourism along the Kivu Belt, an area that offers many untapped opportunities. This plan identifies a selected number of landmark investments for future development of tourism, and highlights five key tourism investment zones along the Kivu Belt.

The country's three national parks, although relatively small in total area, cover over 8.7% of the country's total area and represent a vital natural heritage. They are, and will remain at the very frontline in protecting this natural wealth, the ecosystems, the goods and ecological services they provide. For this reason, the government designed the Rwanda Wildlife Policy in 2013, seeking to primarily ensure the sustainability and protection of Rwandan wildlife and improve institutional capacity and the skills in wildlife management and conservation.

To specifically ensure the effective management of protected areas, the Concessions Management Policy from 2013 helps to lay down the foundations for tapping expertise of the private sector to increase the productivity of tourism in protected areas, as well as providing revenues to the Government.

While the number of leisure tourists has grown more than the number of business tourists, there is substantial untapped potential also in the area of Meetings, Incentives, Conventions and Exhibitions/Events (MICE). Totalling revenues of US$ 49 million in 2013, there are estimates that the MICE sector could triple by 2017, making it a key niche market.

The Rwanda MICE Tourism Strategy from 2014 focuses on, among other things, increasing MICE sales and accelerating new tourism revenue growth, marketing Rwanda as a preferred MICE destination, and promoting private investments.

An important component of this niche is the Kigali Convention Centre that will be ready in 2016, offering premium conditions for international events like conventions, exhibitions, festivals and cultural happenings. It includes a hall seating up to 2,600 persons and a five-star hotel with 292 rooms.

This diversification of the tourism sector, along with the notable pace of development of the already existing offers, will prove key to achieving Rwanda's development goals as set in the Vision 2020.

Emerging Mining Industry

Another important sector of Rwanda's economy that has been revived over the past two decades is the mineral sector. Over the past 10 years the global demand for minerals of all types has fuelled the growth of the broader extractive industries and also become a powerful economic catalyst of local, regional and national economies. For Rwanda, successful expansion of the mining sector is a key component of long-term economic success. Currently, key minerals being extracted and traded in Rwanda include cassiterite (tin), coltan (niobo-tantalite), wolframite (tungsten), beryl, amblygonite, monazite and gold.

Historically, Rwanda's mineral sector suffered from a long colonial history of inefficient 'artisanal' mining. As a result, the industry has gone through multiple transformations - from nationalisation in 1986 to privatisation under the RPF in 2008.

Since privatisation, the government has updated the regulatory legal framework to comply with international standards and in a bid to fight illegal exploitation and trade of mineral resources, the government has introduced mineral certification mechanisms. Consequently, mineral exports from Rwanda are reaching the international market and foreign direct investment from North America has entered the mining sector, introducing modern technology to the industry. Examples are Simba Gold Corp (SGD) and Desert Gold Ventures Inc. (DAU) both based in Vancouver-Canada.

In terms of its contribution to the Rwandan economy, the mineral sector, while accounting for less than 1% of GDP, is increasingly becoming an important source of export revenue for Rwanda. In 2014, the mineral sector generated export revenue of US$ 203 million directly. In total, the sector accounted for 29% of merchandise exports (National Bank of Rwanda, 2014). Data available indicates that by 2013, 558 mining sites were being operated by 231 private companies and cooperatives providing employment across the country (MINIRENA, 2013).

The recent global demand for Rwandan minerals has also boosted corporate profit taxes in the sector. According to data from the Rwandan Revenue Authority, these taxes have more than quadrupled in the last two years. The ability of Rwanda to efficiently extract and sell mineral resources to international markets is therefore central to Rwanda's continued drive for increased self-reliance through reducing the balance of trade deficit and increased foreign exchange earnings.

However, new US legislation (Dodd-Frank) has created challenges to the future development of the industry. The legislation requires manufacturers using minerals originating in the DRC or an adjoining country to "submit a report to the Securities Exchange Commission that includes a description of the measures it took to exercise due diligence on the conflict minerals' source and chain of custody" (SEC Release No. 34-67716). The compliance date with the rule began on 1 January 2013, with first reports due by 31 May 2014.

While Dodd-Frank was introduced to address conflict minerals in the DRC, the impact on the mining sector in Rwanda and the wider Great Lakes region due to geographical proximity and insufficient tagging capacity presents a real risk to the continued export of minerals from the region.

ITRI and the Rwanda Geology and Mines Department (GMD) are working together to implement the ITRI iTSCi tagging regime in order to comply with Dodd-Frank requirements. Over 100 tag miners have been employed to monitor the movement of minerals with the aim of increasing the number to 300. Five senior inspectors have also been employed to oversee implementation of the system of tracing mine sites and minerals through systematic tagging.

Rwanda was the first country in the region to comply with the OECD requirements on mineral traceability through tagging, a factor that has enabled the country to continue exporting minerals even in the face of the new international restrictions imposed by the Dodd-Frank Act.

Whilst great progress has been made over the past 20 years in transforming the mining sector, challenges still remain. The legacy structure the industry has operated under continues to be the greatest barrier to growth. Challenges created by the large artisanal mining population with limited skills and equipment will continue to preoccupy the sector leadership with a view to modernising the sector. Attracting large investors into the sector will also remain a key focus.

Conserving the Environment

Rwanda, under RPF leadership, has been able to maximise land usage, despite being the most densely populated country in Africa, while at the same time conserving the environment. The government recognises that in order to succeed in eradicating poverty Rwanda's natural resources and environment, which the majority of Rwandans depend on, must be judiciously safeguarded.

In this regard, important measures have been taken to halt deforestation, prevent soil erosion, overgrazing, misuse of wetlands and poor waste management, all linked to negative impact on human health and wealth. One of these measures was the ban on plastics.

Plastic-Free Nation

In 2006, Rwanda enacted a law banning the manufacture, importation and use of non-biodegradable plastic bags. The main concern was to address the disastrous environmental consequences linked with such plastic material which include, among many others:
- Providing a breeding ground for disease spreading vectors,
- Preventing water penetration into the soil, leading to low agricultural production,
- Causing death of livestock when ingested,

- Releasing toxic fumes into the air when burnt,
- Clogging drainage channels.

Since 2003, Kigali, Rwanda's capital city, has been described as Africa's greenest and cleanest city. As a result, various delegations from across the globe have been coming here on working visits to learn about the impact of banning plastic.

Following the ban, many jobs have been created locally; the youth and women are involved in the basket weaving industry where they make environmentally friendly bags from cloth, banana fibres and palm leaves as alternatives to plastic bags.

Protecting Swamps

In the last 20 years Rwandans have come to understand and appreciate the various ecosystems and the need to protect the 860 swamps in the country that cover 278,536 hectares of land. They have learnt that development, environment and social welfare are intertwined, with protection of wetlands and swamps being vital for water conservation and sustainable development.

It is for this reason that farmers around the four selected critical ecosystems of Akagera, Rugezi, Rweru-Mugesera and Kamiranzovu were introduced to sustainable agricultural technologies in order to increase agricultural productivity, improve their livelihood and ensure the protection of wetlands under the Integrated Management of Critical Ecosystems (IMCE) Project.

The approach has directed farmers to move from traditional agricultural methods that had previously degraded the ecosystems and they are assisted to adopt modern agricultural technologies. This has resulted in a significant increase in agricultural production in the country and greatly contributed to the long term conservation of biodiversity in various parts of Rwanda.

Land Management

An efficient system of land administration and land management secures land ownership and promotes investment in land for social-economic development and poverty reduction, which is why the RPF government vigorously promoted the reforms in land ownership that led to the guarantee of security of tenure for all landholders in Rwanda.

This principle was affirmed by passing on land ownership rights to Rwandans, something that Rwandans had never ever dreamed of. As of 2013, all land in Rwanda, which is around eight million plots of land, was registered and every landholder is in possession of a land title. Apart from tenure security, other benefits of land registration are that people are able to use land titles as collateral to secure loans or credits from financial institutions and land disputes that were mainly common in different parts of the country have sharply decreased.

Forests Conservation

Although rich in biodiversity, Rwanda had been hit hard by deforestation over the years due to various reasons. These include over-farming due to overpopulation, poor exploitation of forests like burning trees for charcoal, cutting forests for timber and lack of sustainable conservation techniques like land terracing.

In 1994 the return of almost a million refugees who had to be resettled led to neglect of forest conservation efforts, leaving Rwanda's forests almost completely destroyed, with the number of animals living in those forests at a record low level.

To deal with this, conservation was made a national priority and strategies towards ending soil degradation, and safeguarding rivers and forests were adopted. Accordingly, since 2003, the RPF government has scaled up several reforestation programmes in line with the national environmental policy that was formulated and adopted in late 2003, to ensure sustainable protection and management of the environment and natural resources in Rwanda.

Gishwati Forest typifies both the degradation of forests and their restoration and conservation. Gishwati Forest is a protected reserve in north-western Rwanda which was and still is an important catchment area that had remained intact with its forest cover up to 1986. However, during President Habyarimana's regime, Gishwati was cleared for subsistence and livestock keeping to the extent that by 2001, only a small circular patch of natural forest remained with an area of 1,500 acres of the forest's original 250,000 acres.

This had resulted in great loss of biodiversity, catastrophic soil erosion and degradation and dangerous landslides that claimed hundreds of lives annually.

In 2007 Gishwati Rainforest was chosen as the site for a national conservation park sponsored by President Paul Kagame and the Great Ape Trust – an American Scientific Research Centre. This initiative saw the launch of Gishwati Area Conservation Programme (GACP). Gishwati is being reforested as part of Rwanda's policy which aims to have 30% of the country under forest cover by 2020. To achieve this, strategies are underway that will see 67 million tree seedlings planted to restore the state of Gishwati natural forest. Since 2007, there has been a 67% increase in the size of Gishwati Forest. The local chimpanzee population increased dramatically by 46% between 2008 and 2011, and many research and conservation initiatives have been employed within the reserve.

The Great Ape Trust has launched a pilot tourism programme which will offer guided hikes and visits with handcraft producers, traditional healers and beekeeping. All these are geared towards the economic development of the communities around Gishwati Forest.

Gishwati Forest has largely been restored and is commonly referred to as the 'Forest of Hope'. The forest epitomises Rwanda's commitment to conservation, reforestation and community development through ecotourism.

Such efforts are not only concentrated in Gishwati area, but they are also widely spread across Rwanda, from the low-lying dry savannah areas of Bugesera and Umutara in Eastern Province to the hilly areas of Musanze and Nyabihu of Northern and Western provinces respectively. These initiatives have seen the forest cover countrywide increase from 10% in 2009 to more than 22% in 2011.

In recognition of these efforts, Rwanda's National Forest Policy won the famous Future Policy Award in 2011. The award, given out by the United Nations World Future Council, celebrates policies that create better living conditions for the current and future generations.

Home-grown Solutions

Vision 2020 Umurenge Programme (VUP)

After the reconstruction and stabilisation period and having made considerable progress, it was time for RPF to take stock and reassess the relevance of policies and strategies already in place and embark on a new era towards the long journey of promoting sustainable and inclusive socio-economic development.

It is in that context that the second medium-term poverty reduction strategy known as the Economic Development and Poverty Reduction Strategy (EDPRS 2008-2012) was developed. Formulated after the adoption of the social protection policy (2005), the EDPRS came as a real tool to implement the policy with Vision 2020 Umurenge Programme (VUP) as one of its three flagship programmes.

The VUP's prime objective was to release the productive capacities of the poor. It built on past experiences which showed that isolated interventions by sector ministries, donors or NGOs were not sufficient to lift people out of extreme poverty.

The VUP was launched in 2008 and now comprises three main components namely: public work built on Haute Intensité de Main d'Oeuvre (HIMO) or Labour-Intensive Public Works; financial services in the form of the *Ubudehe* credit scheme model and thirdly, direct support to improve access to social services and to provide for households with no members qualifying for public works or credit packages. Such support is unconditional but beneficiaries are expected to engage in appropriate skill acquisition activities.

After being piloted in 30 sectors, the VUP has been scaled up in 240 sectors for direct support and 150 sectors for public works and financial services. Plans are underway to have the programme cover the entire country in 2015/2016.

Agaciro Development Fund (AgDF)

The Agaciro Development Fund is Rwanda's first solidarity fund, based on voluntary donations. *Agaciro* is a Kinyarwanda word which can be loosely translated as "dignity". This Fund has been initiated by Rwandans to fast-track and own their development. This will also improve the level of financial autonomy of Rwanda as a nation. The fund will be financed by voluntary contributions from Rwandan citizens in Rwanda and abroad, private companies and friends of Rwanda. The Agaciro Development Fund sets the tone that Rwandans will work together to drive their own development.

The Agaciro Development Fund will finance key priority projects for the nation as identified by Vision 2020. During the annual campaign, Rwandans will be consulted to decide which priorities to be financed and the outcome of these consultations will be validated at the *Umushyikirano* (National Dialogue Council).

The AgDF is an independent fund. It is a national campaign intended to galvanise all Rwandans to take a more active role in the nation's development. The fund showcases Rwandan solidarity as well as the opportunity for high levels of accountability related to implementation.

Top: Genocide suspects at a Gacaca court trial
Bottom: Abunzi during a session

Top: President Kagame lights a torch at the Genocide Memorial Centre in Gisozi

Bottom: President Kagame and First Lady Jeannette Kagame pay their respects after laying a wreath on a grave during the Genocide Commemoration period

Kigali Street

Top: A RwandAir plane at Kigali International Airport, Kanombe

Middle: Kivu Watt Project, 25MW are to be produced

Bottom Gishoma Peat Power Plant, expected to produce 15MW

Top: Fibre optic being laid across Kigali, Rwanda

Bottom: A slum of the old Kigali

Top: Present-day Kigali city at night

Middle: Old Bus Park in Kigali, where Kigali City Tower now stands

Bottom: Housing quarters at Gaculiro

The Kigali City Tower in present-day Kigali

Top: New Kigali City Hall in present-day Kigali

Middle: Present-day Kigali

Bottom: Remera Round-about in Kigali

Top: Kigali Convention Centre under construction in Kimihurura

Middle: Kigali is rapidly expanding, with a lot of ongoing construction

Bottom: Nyabarongo hydro power station to produce 28MW

Top: Gakiriro, one of the rapidly growing Kigali surburbs

Bottom: Real Estate developments; a sign of confidence in the country's security and future

Top: The Rwanda Development Board Headquarters in Kigali

Bottom: Serena Hotel Kigali

Top: A game lodge at Akagera National Park

Bottom: Tourists experiencing the canopy walk in Nyungwe Forest National Park

A waterfall at Nyungwe National Park

Top: Zebras and Waterbucks in Akagera National Park

Middle: Giraffes in Akagera National Park

Bottom: Gorillas, a big tourism attraction in Rwanda, enjoying their bamboo shoot meal

Miners at Rutongo mining site in Rwanda

14

Social Welfare

Investing in Rwanda's people is the only way to lead the nation beyond recovery to self-sufficiency.
President Paul Kagame

People First

The RPF, basing on its liberation struggle political ideology, strongly believes that well educated and healthy Rwandans are the cornerstone of sustainable national development and prosperity. This is well articulated in its nine-point political programme, specifically in point number six which stresses that it will strive for the promotion of the social welfare of all Rwandans. Since 2003 the RPF-led government has put the following high on its agenda: access to education, healthcare services, job creation, eradication of poverty, proper settlement and promotion of culture and sports.

Education

Primary and Secondary Education

Like many other sectors in Rwanda, the pre-1994 education system was characterised by institutionalised discrimination. In order to have an education system that would produce Rwandans with skills and knowledge and be able to compete in the national, regional and international labour market, the government put in place a system that fosters national unity and reconciliation. The first step towards this was to abolish classification of all Rwandans by assumed ethnic group affiliation.

As indicated in Vision 2020, education is one of the six pillars on which the vision rests. To fulfil this national vision objective, the government committed itself to providing Universal Basic Education. To this end a nationwide Nine-Year Basic Education Programme (9YBE) which offers six years of primary education and three years of secondary education to all Rwandan children free of charge was introduced in 2009. The Universal Nine-Year Basic Education has registered a sharp increase in student enrolment in both primary and secondary schools. According to Ministry of Education records, in the 2002-2003 academic year the total number of pupils in 2,203 primary schools was 1,636,563 while in the 2012 academic year the schools had increased to 2,594, accommodating 2,394,674 pupils, a 46% increase in the number of pupils.

At secondary level, in the 2002-2003 academic year, the total number of students in 405 schools was 179,153, while in the academic year 2012 the schools had increased to 1,466, with 534,712 students (Ministry of Education Statistical Yearbook 2012). This is a record increment of 198.4% between 2003 and 2012 (National Institute of Statistics of Rwanda & UNDP: MDG Country Report 2007). The programme gained momentum following the schools construction campaign which saw thousands of new classrooms built across Rwanda through *Umuganda*, a voluntary community service. All Rwandans, including President Paul Kagame, other senior government officials, and some foreign dignitaries visiting Rwanda participated in the construction of the schools without waiting for any sort of aid. This programme won for Rwanda the prestigious Commonwealth Education Good Practice Award. Rwanda won the award despite being a new member of the Commonwealth because of the role the Nine-Year Basic Education initiative played in accelerating Universal Primary Education.

Rwanda has the highest primary school enrolment in Africa. Gender parity at primary level has been achieved with girls' net enrolment standing at 98% in 2012 while boys' net enrolment is at 95% (Ministry of Education Statistical Yearbook 2012).

Technical and Vocational Education and Training (TVET)

An independent evaluation of the Poverty Reduction and Strategy Programme (PRSP) in 2006 identified an acute skills gap in various sectors of the national economy. It became necessary to focus on technical and vocational education and training (TVET). A national framework for TVET was established to regulate and coordinate all training programmes that emphasised hands-on training as opposed to the theoretical education system.

It was for this reason that the Workforce Development Authority was established in 2009 with the responsibility of promoting the development and upgrading of skills and competencies of the national workforce in order to enhance competitiveness and employability through TVET. TVET is designed to be accessible to students at all levels with multiple entry and exit points for all levels, from university graduates to people who never attended school.

Under the new system a student can easily upgrade from vocational level to university studies, as opposed to the previously limited system under which vocational training was terminal. Enrolment in TVET schools almost doubled, from 51,773 in 2010 to 93,024 in 2014. In 2014 Rwanda had 365 TVET schools; each district had at least four schools. The target is to enrol 60% of students who complete 9YBE into the TVET system by 2017.

To realise the full potential of TVET, Five Integrated Polytechnic Regional centres have been created. They offer higher training programmes in Information and Communication Technology (ICT), mechanical engineering, civil engineering and mining engineering. Another aim of the centres is to serve as models to other TVET centres in the country and the region. This highlights the necessary link between the world of work and training institutions provided by TVET.

TVET graduates with hands-on training will easily be absorbed into the labour market, thus filling the gaps within the market, but also reduce unemployment in Rwanda, particularly among the youth. TVET is already reducing unemployment addressing the shortage of chefs, plumbers, carpenters, travel guides and other technicians, thereby building skills in the key economic sectors that will make Rwanda a service-based economy by 2020.

The importance of this kind of education has been underscored by the appointment of a minister of state in the Ministry of Education responsible for Integrated Technical and Vocational Education Training.

Tertiary Education

Since the RPF came to power, the government has focused on tertiary education and the number of universities has also grown from 1 to 32, seven of them being public and 25 private with a total population of 84,448. Public universities have a total involvement of 40,731 students at undergraduate and graduate levels, while the private iniversities have 43,717. (MINEDUC 2013)

The seven public universities were merged into one multi-campus University of Rwanda (UR) in September 2013. According to the new set-up, the University of Rwanda is composed of six colleges which incorporate specific similar study programmes in former public institutions. The philosophy behind this is to transform the country's higher education system by increasing assets, promoting equality, ensuring high quality of education and providing infrastructure of advanced quality. According to education experts, the outcomes of such reforms will lead to transformative learning and interdependence of institutions. The National Council for Higher Education (NCHE) was established in 2005 to monitor and maintain quality education assurance in Rwanda's universities, especially privately administered ones. Since its inception, NCHE has helped to ensure Rwandan universities meet international standards and many institutions have upgraded their standards as a result of the critical watchdog role played by NCHE.

In addition, the government merged five institutions formerly independently affiliated to the Ministry of Education to create the Rwanda Education Board (REB) in 2010. Among the departments of REB is the Higher Education Student Loan Department, formerly the Student Financing Agency of Rwanda (SFAR). For sustainability, the beneficiaries of the student loan scheme have to repay the loan on completion of their studies. This innovation has helped more Rwandans access higher education inside the country and abroad, many of whom would not have otherwise had a chance to do so.

Teacher Training and Development

With the record high enrolment of students in both primary and secondary schools in the history of Rwanda, especially due to the 9BYE and the 12YBE, teacher demand has increased dramatically. In response to this national demand, teacher training institutions offering various programmes have been established and strengthened countrywide. Kigali Institute of Education (now the College of Education of the University of Rwanda), which was founded in 1999 has been offering various programmes in the field of teacher education, ranging from certificate to PhD in partnership with universities well known worldwide. Eleven Teacher Training Colleges (TTCs) were also created to cater for primary school teacher needs.

Due to these initiatives, the number of teachers in public primary and secondary schools has increased from 4,175 in the 1994/1995 academic year to 40,159 in 2013. (Statistical Year Book 2014)

ICT to Access Modern Education

The government of Rwanda views the Rwandan people as the nation's most precious natural resource in the country's development journey to middle-income level by 2020. In this digital age, they must possess ICT skills and leverage them to drive Rwanda's economy. Therefore, right from pre-school to university level, there must be strategies to develop their skills and talents if they are to be the strong foundation for Rwanda's development.

This is well articulated under the pillar of human resource and a knowledge-based economy of Vision 2020. The plan has three horizontal areas; the third being science and technology, including Information and Communication Technology (ICT).

It is under this strategy that the Rwandan government has deployed the use of ICTs in the country's education system, the most famous being the One Laptop per Child Programme for all primary school pupils. Presiding over the launch of the programme in 2008, President Paul Kagame said:

> Our goal is to continue raising means and ways to provide all primary school children with this important learning tool. We are going to turn the dream of all our children owning a computer into reality; it is possible to achieve this. (*President Paul Kagame's Speech at the launch of the "One Laptop per Child" Project in October 2008*)

According to the Ministry of Education, from 2008 to 2013, 207,026 laptops were distributed to 407 primary schools across Rwanda. The target is to have distributed at least 1,000,000 laptops by 2017 to primary school pupils. This means more Rwandan youth will have access to the life-changing opportunities that the Internet and computer skills can bring. Not only have primary schools witnessed ICT systems deployed for usage, but secondary schools have also benefited almost equally.

A good number of secondary schools, more particularly those identified to serve as centres of excellence in science subjects, are now furnished with Internet-connected computers, which assist both teachers and students in their work.

Another innovation made possible by ICT is that candidates, parents and head teachers can now access exam results on REB's website or via short text messages (SMS) on their mobile phone without leaving their homes or offices whereas previously they would be forced to travel long distances to local administrative offices or to the headquarters of the Rwanda Education Board (REB) to check their national examination results.

Healthcare for All

Rwandans are the fundamental resource on which Rwanda's future development hinges. This belief in people and self-reliance is fundamental to the RPF and originates from the liberation struggle when it relied on Rwandans from all walks of life for fighters, logistics like finances, food, medicine, clothing and so on. Since then government has vowed to provide healthcare to all Rwandans, through the provision of preventive, curative and rehabilitative healthcare, thereby contributing to the reduction of poverty.

President Paul Kagame has on several occasions spoken of a transformed Rwanda, a nation where people are happier, healthier and live longer lives. To achieve this dream, several strategies under eight strands have been put in place since 2003 and have borne good results.

Financial Accessibility

The number of Rwandans covered by health insurance schemes (RSSB-Medical Benefits, MMI, CBHI and others), in particular, the adherence to Community Based Health Insurance (CBHI) increased from 7% in 2003 to more than 80% today (Ministry of Health 2015). Set up to provide medical insurance to rural and poor Rwandans in 1999, the country's insurance health scheme, Mutuelle de Santé or Community Based Health Insurance, which is available to all Rwandans, has greatly improved access to healthcare. In the spirit of self-reliance, which is a national value among Rwandans the poor are helped by their communities to pay their medical insurance costs.

The success of this innovation has turned Rwanda into an international example on universal healthcare.

The medical benefits of RSSB cover public officials, civil servants, their spouses and children who are all insured under a public health insurance scheme.

A clear indication of the RPF-led government's commitment to healthcare for Rwandans is that the public budget allocation to this sector has increased from 5.9% in 2003 to 16.05% in 2013, thus fulfilling the goals set by the Abuja Declaration.

In order to ease and streamline the procurement and distribution of drugs and other health-related equipment, Centrale d'Achats des Medicaments Essentials du Rwanda (CAMERWA) has been strengthened and merged with other agencies to form the Rwanda Biomedical Centre (RBC). Similarly, district and hospital pharmacies have been created and provided with pharmacists and other skilled staff for better management, while 30 trucks have been availed for the transport and distribution of drugs. A system to monitor stock outs has been put in place, and is being computerised.

Distribution and Access to Health Services

The number of hospitals in the country increased from 34 in 1994, to 48, including four national referral hospitals: Centre Hospitalier Universitaire de Kigali (CHUK), Centre Hospitalier Universitaire de Butare (CHUB), King Faisal Hospital (KFH), and the Kanombe Military Hospital. King Faisal Hospital has acquired international accreditation. The other three national referral hospitals are also undergoing an accreditation programme. The programme to build new hospitals and to renovate/expand existing ones is ongoing. Similarly, the number of health centres has increased from 184 in 1990 to 465 in 2013 (Ministry of Health 2013).

One of the major milestones in the health sector in Rwanda under RPF leadership, has been the launch of the ambulance service – Emergency Medical Assistance Service (SAMU) – which was launched in 2007, when it was only operational in Kigali City with only three ambulances. In 2010, ambulances reached all 30 Districts and the fleet has grown to over 180 ambulances. For emergency transport, at least five ambulances are deployed in districts mainly for the referral of patients. A water boat ambulance has also been deployed on Lake Kivu.

Community Health Programme

Instituted in 1995, the Community Health Programme (CHP) was initially conceived as a response to the major public health problems that had developed as a result of war and genocide against the Tutsi in Rwanda. The foundation of the CHP was, and continues to be, a cadre of community health workers (CHWs). Initially the CHWs provided basic services, such as health education and sensitisation on immunisations, sanitation and hygiene. Over the years, the CHW package increased to include the community-based nutrition programme (CBNP); home-based management of malaria; directly observed treatment (DOTS) for tuberculosis; community performance-based financing (c-PBF) pilot phase; integrated community case management (ICCM) of malaria, pneumonia, and diarrhoea; community health workers' cooperatives (CHWC) and PBF; community-based provision of contraceptives (CBP) and community maternal and newborn healthcare (c-MNH); infant and young child feeding and community-based nutrition programmes (CBNP); and community non-communicable diseases (NCDs). Currently, there are two types of CHWs: the binome (one male and one female per village) and the ASM (agente de santé maternelle), who is focused on maternal and child healthcare. Communities elect both types of CHWs as volunteers using a standard set of criteria. Today, there are 45,000 CHWs, three CHWs per *mudugudu*. CHWs are trusted and respected community members. They are also recognised and appreciated by their supervisors and other implementing agencies. Other motivation sources include community performance-based financing and CHW cooperatives as well as in-kind incentives.

Human Resources for Health

The number of health workers at different levels has increased dramatically under the leadership of RPF. The number of doctors deployed in the public health sector has increased from 112 in 1996 to 684 in 2013. Among them, 171 are specialists. A total of 8,985 nurses are currently deployed across Rwanda compared to 742 in 1996. Also, 492 midwives are working in various public health facilities, a category of staff that did not exist in Rwanda before the creation of Kigali Health Institute in 1996. Mental health professionals are also being trained at the University Central Hospital (CHU) and Institute of Agriculture, Technology and Education of Kibungo (INATEK).

Efforts are focused on training specialised doctors and upgrading A2 nurses from high school diploma to A1 (undergraduate diploma), in order to develop human resources for the health sector. To achieve this, five new nursing schools and distance learning programmes have been launched. For medical specialisations, most personnel are trained in Rwanda through a Memorandum of Understanding signed between the government of Rwanda and some American universities, while others are sent abroad. In 2013 some 240 doctors were undergoing specialised training.

Improvement of Health Services

In general, prevention and clinical services for Maternal and Child Health and other clinical services have been strengthened with the equipment of health facilities, the construction of maternity wards, emergency transport, construction of more health facilities, creation of neonatology services, the strengthening of family planning services, availability of commodities, construction of health posts, community-based provision, and other long term methods.

After the 1994 Genocide against the Tutsi, Rwanda had the highest child mortality and lowest life expectancy at birth anywhere. Less than one in four children were fully vaccinated. Twenty years later, Rwanda is likely to be the first country in Africa to achieve the Millennium Development Goals for health set by the United Nations. Child mortality has fallen by more than two-thirds since 2000, and Rwanda's immunisation campaign is one of the strongest in the world with persistently high administrative coverage of more than 90% for all children vaccinated with 10 vaccines, and with 11 vaccines for girls aged 12 and above. Rwandans are now living better lives than ever before in the history of Rwanda.

Interventions to Fight Malnutrition

There has been progress towards reducing child and maternal malnutrition in the country. Wasting has decreased from 4.6% in 2005 to 3% in 2010, while rates of underweight and stunting that were 18% and 51% (2005) have been reduced to 11.4% and 44%, respectively (Demographic Health Survey 2010). Iron-deficiency anaemia also declined from 51.5% to 38.1% among children under five, and from 26% to 17% among women. These strides and successes are related to enhanced community-based nutrition (CBN) programmes.

Fight against HIV/AIDS

HIV prevention is done through Voluntary Counselling and Testing (VCT) and some 11,765,368 tests have been carried out so far in almost all health facilities. The Prevention of Mother to Child Transmission (PMTCT) is covered at 90% and 98% of all pregnant women are tested. The transmission of HIV from mother to child has reduced from 10.8% in 2004 to 1.9% in 2012, and the new infections have been reduced by 50%. By June 2013, some 122,972 patients were on antiretroviral treatment, up from only 4,189 in 2003. The coverage of antiretroviral treatment was 91.6% in 2013. Due to these strong and strategic efforts, in 2013 HIV prevalence was 3% (DHS, 2005), compared to 5.8% in 1992. Rwanda is now one of the African countries with the lowest HIV prevalence (Ministry of Health 2013).

Fight against Malaria

Malaria prevention is mainly carried out using long lasting insecticide treated mosquito nets; indoor residual spraying for high risk zones and the treatment of cases by artemisin-combination therapies (ACTs), along with a strengthened health system. The possession of mosquito nets increased from 18.2% in 2005 to 82% in 2010 in households. Seventeen percent of children used treated mosqito nets in 2005 and 70% in 2010, while 71% of pregnant women used them in 2010.

As a result, there has been a reduction of 85% in the number of malaria cases and deaths. The rate of malaria cases treated after laboratory confirmation was 99% in 2012 before treatment compared to 40% in 2005.

Management of Tuberculosis

This has dramatically improved with treatment success at 88.6% in 2013 which is higher than the recommended WHO level of 85%. The TB mortality rate was reduced by 78% between 1997 and 2010, while the prevalence and incidence were reduced by 71% (DHS 2012).

Non-communicable Diseases

The new priority of the health sector is to prevent and treat non-communicable diseases like cancer, heart, and renal diseases. For this purpose, referral hospitals have been equipped with diagnostic equipment. Dialysis equipment has been installed in the Central University Hospital of Butare (CHUB) and King Faisal Hospital (KFH) and the Central University Hospital of Kigali (CHUK) is also being equipped to offer care to patients in need of dialysis.

A cancer centre was established in Butaro district Hospital in the Northern Province and capacity is being built in terms of human resources. For cervical cancer, prevention is carried out with the provision of HPV vaccine to young girls between 12 and 15 years, and means have been put in place to detect cervical cancer as early as possible.

With the aim of strengthening preventative care and early treatment of diseases, most especially non-communicable diseases, women who are 35 years old or above and men who are 40 years old or above and enrolled in the community-based health insurance scheme, are allowed to voluntarily have an annual medical check-up from an agreed health facility.

National Referral Hospitals

National Referral Hospitals have been deliberately strengthened to improve tertiary healthcare by deployment of more specialists and more skilled nurses, improvement of diagnostic capacity and provision of updated equipment. King Faisal Hospital was accredited in 2013 and was recently equipped with its first MRI machine. It also has a dialysis unit. To reduce pressure on King Faisal Hospital, other national referral hospitals have undergone a similar process. The vision of the government of Rwanda under the leadership of the RPF is to have King Faisal Hospital turned into a regional medical centre, attracting patients from the greater East African region.

All these efforts have led to an improved healthcare system in Rwanda, which, by 2013 had raised life expectancy to 64 years up from 39 years in 1990. According to Ministry of Health data, the maternal mortality deaths per 100,000 births have dramatically decreased to 487 in 2010 from 1,071 in 2000 (Demographic Health Survey, 2010) (DHS 2010).

Social Security

Studies worldwide reveal that significant progress can be made in improving standards of living in the developing world if social security is considered in social-economic and poverty reduction programmes. The RPF shares this view and has clearly indicated that it will tirelessly strive to provide a quality insurance scheme to all Rwandans since it is one of the pillars of national development and poverty reduction.

It was thought prudent to revamp the Social Security Fund of Rwanda to better serve Rwandans who now live longer and happier lives. In 2010 the government merged the Social Security Fund of Rwanda that had been created in 1962 and Rwanda Health Insurance Fund (RAMA) to form the more vibrant and business-oriented Rwanda Social Security Board (RSSB).

Currently the Board has a range of products on its menu, which include medical insurance coverage, pension and work related accidents compensation. On a daily basis, the Board's services and products touch hundreds of thousands of lives of Rwandans. Under the Board, workers from the public and private sector are protected from social insecurity as they are provided with a range of benefits. These include old age, invalidity, genocide survivors, work injuries and work-related ailment compensation and health insurance.

Due to improved professional management of the board and its assets, in addition to the benefits members are getting, members have been joining various social security schemes in increasing numbers since 2003. According to RSSB data, in March 2010 membership stood at 13,067 but by the last quarter of 2012, the figure had increased to 265,660. The interpretation is that more members means greater benefits. In the same quarter, for example, members of pension schemes had contributed FRW 10.45 billion and the Board distributed benefits to members amounting to FRW 2.3 billion. For medical care, they contributed FRW 9 billion and the board distributed FRW 2.75 billion to members.

RSSB Investment

RSSB is currently the largest institutional investor in Rwanda. In order to generate funds for the various schemes in a more sustainable manner, RSSB has a diverse investment portfolio, the most famous one being real estate countrywide as well as shares and government bonds.

As a social security fund, the large part of RSSB's investment is in social housing. The most recent project was the resettlement of more than 150,000 people from Kigali's lower Kiyovu to a new settlement of 250 low-cost houses in Batsinda, Kigali. RSSB is also planning to build 150 residential houses and guest houses for the less fortunate residents of Nyagatare town, Eastern Province.

In addition to providing such services for the benefit of its members in terms of returns, RSSB has also invested in catering for middle-income earners, whose number is growing as Rwanda's economy continues to grow. The Board, together with the former Rwanda Housing Bank, which has been merged with Rwanda Development Bank (BRD) constructed 234 residential houses in Gacuriro in Kigali city, which have given the City a facelift.

RSSB's investments have had a positive economic impact on Rwanda's economy and uplifted the social welfare of her people. In 2009, for instance, RSSB, the then CSR, created 2,123 jobs through direct investment and 245 more jobs through indirect investment. More importantly, the more money RSSB raises through investments, the more money there is for its members to benefit from.

FARG: Offering Assistance to Needy Genocide Survivors

In the spirit of Rwanda's self-reliance strategy, from 2003 the Genocide Survivors Support and Assistance Fund (FARG) was revamped. The fund provides a variety of support for genocide survivors ranging from paying for education and medical expenses to building houses and providing direct financial assistance to the most vulnerable. To achieve this, the government has decided to contribute 6% of Rwanda's annual budget to the Fund.

The funding to FARG has been growing. The Genocide Survivors Support and Assistance Fund (FARG) spent FRW 3.7 billion in 2003 on education, and by 2010, spending on education had more than tripled to FRW 11.6 billion. On health related matters, FARG spent FRW 603 million in 2003, but in 2010, the Fund had at its disposal FRW 758 billion to cater for its members (http://www.farg.gov.rw/). In 2003 FARG spent only FRW 263 million for shelter provision to genocide survivors, but in 2010, it spent FRW 1.8 billion for the same cause.

Teachers' Welfare

Along with other developments in education, there has been improvement in teachers' welfare. President Paul Kagame personally advocated for the establishment of a Teachers' Savings and Credit Cooperative. And so Umwalimu Savings and Credit Cooperative (Umwalimu SACCO) was born in 2006 and started operating officially in 2008. By the last quarter of 2012, Umwalimu SACCO had registered 36,000 members out of 60,000 teachers in the country. Out of the 36,000 members, 34,000 had already got loans from the Cooperative.

Many teachers have improved their livelihoods and economic standing in their communities through the Umwalimu SACCO. As a result, this has greatly improved teacher retention, stability and effective curriculum instruction.

In a similar effort to improve teachers' welfare, the Ministry of Education, in collaboration with district administrations, had by 2013 constructed more than 400 teachers' houses across the country, each with a capacity to accommodate eight teachers.

Impact of Social Protection Reforms

Rwanda has made important gains in reducing poverty. In a period of five years (2006-2011) more than one million people were lifted out of poverty. Poverty was reduced by 12 percentage points from 57% to 45% and extreme poverty from 36% to 24% (Statistical Year Book 2014). Inequality also reduced in the same period where the Gini-coefficient declined from 0.51 in 2005/06 to 0.49 in 2010/11.

Several social protection programmes, notably VUP, Ubudehe and Girinka (One Cow per Poor Family Programme) have led to this remarkable reduction. They have helped to increase the livestock holdings and durable assets of extremely poor beneficiary households. For example, more than

147,000 cows have been distributed to the poor families since the beginning of the programme.

The social protection system in Rwanda has evolved to different sectors. In the health sector, 92% of Rwandans currently access health insurance. As earlier indicated, the maternal mortality rate reduced from 2,300 per 100,000 live births in 1994 to 210 in 2015. The One Cow per Poor Family Programme has allowed the creation of wealth – production assets for poor families – while also reducing malnutrition in children.

Under VUP 89,011 households had been employed in public works by mid-2013, while 43,671 households had received direct support and 181,229 households benefited from financial services. Financial inclusion increased to 72% from 48% in 2008.

Sports for a Healthy Nation

The government of Rwanda, and President Kagame in particular, support the development of sports in the country. This is because they recognise the value of sports for people, especially keeping them healthy for nation building. This factor can be traced back to the liberation war when, during ceasefire periods, the RPF fighters would take time off their military training and drills to engage in various sports and games, especially football. Upon assuming office, therefore, the RPF put Rwanda on an ambitious road to build her image as a serious player on both the regional and global sports scenes.

Today Rwanda has various sports initiatives at all levels, from school children to public servants. Rwandan sports teams have participated in regional, continental and world sporting events such as FIFA's Under-17 World Cup that took place in Mexico in June 2011. For the first time in her football history, Rwanda also participated in the finals of the African Cup of Nations in Tunisia in 2004 alongside some of Africa's best footballing nations like Nigeria, Cameroon, Ghana, and Tunisia.

Rwanda has also hosted international sporting events. For instance in 2011 the country hosted the African Under-17 Championship in Kigali and Rubavu on the shores of Lake Kivu. President Paul Kagame's support for sports goes beyond Rwanda and extends to the region. Since 2002, he has personally sponsored the Confederation of East and Central Africa Football

Associations' Club Cup competition (CECAFA Club Cup) which was later named after him. He provides cash prize awards to the tune of US$ 60,000 for the Cup winner and two runners-up. Since 1998 some Rwandan clubs have won the cup four times, with Rayon Sport winning in 1998 and APR FC in 2004, 2007 and 2010.

Cycling: New Success in Rwanda

A new sport in Rwanda is taking root. Rwanda had not participated in cycling as a sport at national or global level. This changed with the birth of Team Rwanda in 2005, when Tom Ritchey, a former 1970s cyclist made his first visit to Rwanda and was impressed by the large number of cyclists and the prominence of bicycles in the daily lives of Rwandans.

Ritchey and his fellow Americans, following the passion they saw among Rwandan cyclists in their daily lives carrying bags of coffee and other agricultural products to markets and factories, decided to set up a national team and within about six weeks, the team was up and running. In 2006 the team entered the nine-day Cape Epic in South Africa, the biggest mountain bike race in the world.

In 2009, the Tour of Rwanda was born, and it has become an International Cycling Race. It was included on the International Cycling Union (UCI) Calendar. Tour of Rwanda is attracting teams from Africa and Europe. Because of these efforts, Rwandans have participated in various competitions, including the 2012 London Olympics.

Other sports

Sport in Rwanda today is not limited to football and cycling. There has been resurgence in such sports as volleyball and basketball at all levels for both men and women. Over the last decade, national teams in both have regularly appeared in continental tourneys and competed with Africa's best for honours.

Rwanda's mountainous terrain is well-suited for endurance sports like cycling and distance running. It is therefore no wonder that, as described above, Rwandan cycling is making steady progress on the international scene.

Equally, Rwandans are increasingly taking part in international competitions in long distance running, from 10 kilometres to the marathon,

The country's runners may not be where Kenyan and Ethiopian athletes are at the moment, but it may not take long before they get there.

Home-grown Solutions

One Cow per Poor Family: Girinka Munyarwanda

The programme was adapted from the traditional Rwanda solidarity practice of giving each other a cow as a pact of friendship and support in the event of misfortune or when people were in dire need. In Rwandan culture, a cow is a symbol of wealth and it provides an avenue to break free from poverty.

In an effort to reduce child malnutrition and improve the poor living conditions of thousands of Rwandans, which he had identified in many parts of Rwanda, President Paul Kagame initiated the programme. Since its inception, the Girinka programme has helped curb malnutrition, break down social barriers, improve agricultural output, support reconciliation efforts and greatly improved the welfare of hundreds of thousands of Rwandans. This is so because Girinka beneficiaries are selected by community members who nominate the most deserving, based on their poverty level.

Umuganda

In traditional Rwanda, members of a community would meet and jointly support one of their members in building a house, digging a garden or working on any community project. That is *umuganda* in the traditional set-up. It would not only forge a very strong bond of unity among community members but also help them overcome certain challenges.

It is from that background that *umuganda* resurfaced and was adapted to today's context. Every last Saturday of the month, everyone, regardless of social status or gender comes together to participate in a five-hour community work programme. They dig rain water trenches, clean roads, streets and slash grass in their surroundings or build houses for vulnerable children. Through *umuganda*, hundreds of classrooms, health centres and local government offices have been constructed.

Umuganda is also an egalitarian exercise. Ordinary men and women, senior government officials, the President himself and sometimes high ranking dignitaries on state visits work together, shoulder to shoulder with ordinary folk. In time it might even be one of Rwanda's exports as

Rwandans on various peacekeeping missions across the world introduce it where they serve, like they have done in Darfur.

Ubudehe: People's participation in Identifying Problems and Solutions

Ubudehe is an old Rwandan traditional practice in which communities would come together to identify general problems and devise solutions by working together towards their set goals. The *ubudehe* practice with a modern touch in recent years has strengthened government service delivery in poverty reduction.

It is under this practice that communities identify the most needy and vulnerable members among them, who are then chosen to benefit from various programmes like acquisition of livestock, which has seen many people's livelihoods improve considerably.

Ubudehe not only addresses poverty, but also enhances decentralisation and reconciliation policies. This is because it enables communities to come together and play an active role in finding solutions to their peculiar problems. The programme won the United Nations Better Management: Better Public Service Award in 2008. Up to 150 countries participated and 12 programmes were nominated. According to the judges, *Ubudehe* stood out for its people-centred characteristics that empowered the communities to play an active role in solving their own social-economic challenges.

15

Journey Ahead: Thinking Big

Things in Rwanda get better every day but we should also understand that the tasks ahead get even harder.
President Paul Kagame

Vision 2020 for Economic Transformation

The government of Rwanda (GoR) adopted Vision 2020 in 2000 with the primary objective of transforming Rwanda into a middle-income country through a knowledge-based economy by the year 2020. The basic goals of Rwanda's Vision 2020 are:
- Rapid economic growth to middle income status
- Increased poverty reduction
- More off-farm jobs, more urbanisation
- Reduced external dependency
- Private sector as the engine of growth

The expected outcome of the vision is a united Rwanda that is both regionally and globally competitive. The vision is being implemented through the medium term planning framework that began in 2002 with the first Poverty Reduction Strategic Plan (PRSP I). This has since been followed by the Economic Development and Poverty Reduction Strategy (EDPRS 1) which covered the period 2008-2012. In line with this objective, Vision 2020 targets were revised recently, and EDPRS 2 is aligned to these.

According to the revised targets, Rwanda aims to achieve at least 11.5% average GDP growth per annum, and also reduce poverty to below 30%.

During EDPRS 2, the private sector in Rwanda is expected to take the driving seat in economic growth and poverty reduction. This strategy will also focus government efforts on transforming the economy, the private sector and alleviating constraints to the growth of investment.

Under EDPRS 2, the government of Rwanda expects to address the challenges confronting medium and long term development aspirations and pursue the numerous available opportunities such as:

- the youthful labour force,
- domestic, political and economic stability;
- improving literacy and numeracy of the population;
- the existing decentralised structures for development and service delivery;
- increased regional integration;
- Rwanda's alertness and pro-activeness in environment mainstreaming.

These will be effected through the four strategies of economic transformation, rural development, productivity and youth employment, and accountable governance.

This targets accelerated economic growth (11.5% average) and restructuring of the economy towards more services and industry.

To ensure that poverty is reduced from 44.9% to below 30% by 2018, focus will be placed on increased productivity of agriculture which engages the vast majority of the population.

An important part of development is ensuring that growth and rural development are underpinned by appropriate skills and productive employment, especially for the growing youth population. To fulfil this requirement, one of the main objectives of EDPRS 2 is the creation of at least 200,000 new jobs annually.

Regional Integration

Rwanda's long-term development vision, as articulated in the Vision 2020, lays out a roadmap for the country's future development, founded on six pillars, the last of which is regional and international economic integration. It implies an open, liberal trade regime, minimising barriers to trade as well as implementing policies to encourage foreign direct investment, adopting policies to promote competitive enterprises, exports and entrepreneurship and economic zones for ICT-based production in trade and commerce.

Rwanda is a member of the Economic Community of Great Lakes Region (CEPGL), East African Community (EAC), COMESA and the Commonwealth and has applied to rejoin the Economic Community of Central African States (CEEAC).

Regional integration is important for economic growth, political stability and socio-cultural development. Rwanda sought to expand and open its market for trade and labour and promote the private sector development and to be competitive in a bigger market that promotes the tourism industry.

As a landlocked country, Rwanda wanted to be a linked economy (gateway to the sea) and cut down the cost of transport by removing non-tariff barriers along the transport corridors and also promote export.

Rwanda also looked at cooperation in infrastructure development (road network, railways, ports) and becoming a strong voice in the international arena.

Regional integration is also a framework for conflict resolution, promotes peace and security and foreign policy coordination and enhances internal confidence and trust vis-à-vis other countries.

Rwanda has strong cultural and historical ties and similarities with her neighbours and has always sought to strengthen them even further by promoting free movement of people and labour, increasing socio-cultural activities such as sports, the arts, and educational exchanges.

East African Community (EAC)

The EAC is a community of partner states that include Burundi, Kenya, Rwanda, Uganda and the United Republic of Tanzania and has its headquarters in Arusha, Tanzania.

EAC member states agreed on four stages of integration, namely: the Customs Union, the Common Market, the Monetary Union and the Political Federation.

The Customs Union started on 1 January 2005, the Common Market on 1 July 2010 and a protocol on Monetary Union was signed on 30 November 2013 to be effective after 10 years of preparations. The roadmap for the East African political federation is under discussion.

The Northern Corridor Integration Projects

The Heads of State of the Republics of Rwanda, Kenya and Uganda held a tri-lateral meeting on 25 June 2013 in Entebbe, Uganda during which they agreed on a number of issues pertaining to regional infrastructure development, energy, trade facilitation and the East African Political Federation. This was in line with the principle of variable geometry in the East Africa Community, providing for co-operation in a variety of areas and at different speeds among a sub-group of members in a larger integration scheme.

They noted that non-tariff barriers continue to hinder intra-EAC trade and full implementation of the EAC Common Market Protocol. They also noted the delays in the clearing of goods at Mombasa port and Malaba border post and agreed to take immediate measures to decongest the port of Mombasa and expedite clearance by Uganda Revenue Authority at Malaba border post in order to improve transport on the Northern Corridor.

The measures agreed on to facilitate trade in the region include among others the development of a mechanism for clearing and paying customs duties in the country of destination before goods arrive at the point of first entry i.e. Mombasa port. The Revenue Authority of each country will send proof of payment to Mombasa port in order to expedite the release of goods from the port.

They also agreed to establish a mechanism for mutual recognition of quality standards within the EAC framework and other internationally recognised standards in which Kenya, Rwanda and Uganda are members.

In the tri-lateral meeting, the three Heads of State of the Republics of Rwanda, Kenya and Uganda agreed to fast track the following projects:

- Railways: to revamp the existing railway network, to construct a new standard gauge railway line and extend it to Rwanda, and to jointly mobilise resources.
- Oil pipelines: Develop an oil pipeline for finished products from Eldoret to Kampala and extend it to Rwanda. Develop a crude oil pipeline from Uganda to Kenya through South Sudan.
- Oil refinery: Explore the possibility of EAC partner states to invest in the oil refinery to be constructed in Uganda.
- Electricity: To enhance electricity generation and distribution by exploring and utilising the resources within each partner state,

including exploring other alternatives sources like renewable, nuclear and geothermal energies
- Single customs territory: To establish a single customs territory where goods will be cleared at the first point of entry and circulate freely within the three member states.
- Fast-track the East African political federation: By setting up a committee that will draft an EAC political federation framework that will be considered and discussed by all relevant parties.
- Use of national identity cards as travel documents allows the citizens of the three countries to cross borders using the identity cards in order to ease the movement of persons and services.
- The single tourist visa: Fast-track the establishment of a single tourist visa to promote the tourism industry in the region and work on a formula to share revenues from the single tourist visas.

Progress Reports on Northern corridor Projects

In the summit of Heads of State held in Kigali on 28 October 2013, the Republic of South Sudan joined the initiative on infrastructure projects.

New projects were considered to fast-track the integration process including:
- Commodities exchange
- ICT
- Air space management and connectivity
- Defence, peace and security cooperation
- Human resource capacity building in relevant areas.

Standard Gauge Railway (SGR)

The preliminary Engineering design study for Kampala-Kigali section is ongoing. The feasibility study for Nairobi-Malaba-Kampala is complete, the ground breaking ceremony for the construction of the Mombasa-Nairobi section was held on November 28, 2013 and the construction was to start in October 2014. It will be completed in four years from the starting date. The train and track under construction will be operated using electricity.

Oil Refinery

Rwanda expressed its interest to participate in the Uganda oil refinery in October 2013. A cost-benefit analysis is being undertaken in order to enable Rwanda decide on investing in the project.

Oil Pipeline

The feasibility study for the Kampala-Kigali oil pipeline section was concluded in August 2014. The procurement for an EPC contractor for the Eldoret-Kampala- Kigali pipeline is ongoing and is set to be complete by March 2017.

Power Generation and Transmission

An MoU for the promotion and sustainability of the development of power generation and interconnection of transmission and distribution systems in Rwanda, Uganda and Kenya was signed in October 2013.

Interconnection transmission lines of 220 KV between Rwanda and Uganda are under construction (NELSAP project). This will allow trading of power between Rwanda, Uganda and Kenya from April 2015.

The Kawanda-Masaka-Mbarara sections in Uganda will be upgraded from 132 KV to 220 KV by March 2017 and the standardisation of the transmission lines to 400 KV in the partner states as directed by the Summit is under study and set to be complete by June 2018.

Single Customs Territory

The single customs territory was launched in October 2013 and is now operational.

In Kenya, cargo destined to Uganda and Rwanda is weighed once at Mariakani near Mombasa.

In Uganda, only two weighbridges are remaining between Busia/Malaba and Katuna.

Existing ICT systems of the revenue authorities in the three countries have been integrated and interface with the port of Mombasa ICT system developed.

Similary, electronic cargo tracking systems along the Nothern Corridor (Kenya and Uganda using their own systems, Rwanda using the COMESA system) have been interconnected.

Police roadblocks were eliminated, the number of customs declarations reduced from three to one and customs security bonds also reduced from three to one.

As a result of all these measures, time spent to move along the corridor reduced from 18 days to four days from Mombasa to Kampala and from 21 days to six days from Mombasa to Kigali.

The Rwanda and Uganda Revenue Authorities have deployed staff at Mombasa port and the latter has also opened offices in Kigali and Kampala to facilitate payment of port fees.

Single Tourist Visa and Use of IDs

The use of IDs for Rwandans and Kenyans, voter cards for Ugandans who have not yet been issued IDs and student cards for students as travel documents and the single tourist visa (valid in Kenya, Rwanda and Uganda) started on 1 January 2014.

The East Africa single tourist visa fee of US$ 100 is shared by the three countries (US$ 30 for each country plus US$ 10 administrative cost paid to the issuing country). The visa is valid for 90 days and is a multiple entry visa.

Defence, Peace and Security Cooperation

The Mutual Defence Pact and Mutual Peace and Security Pact were signed by the Heads of State at the Kampala Summit on 20 February 2014. The organs and structures to implement the two pacts were approved by the Heads of State in their meeting in Kigali on 3 July 2014.

Air Space Management

Partner states agreed to liberalise the air transport sector as one of the strategies to lower the cost of travel in the region. An MOU on cooperation in air space management was to be signed in October 2014 during the 7th Summit.

ICT Project

In order to lower roaming charges and eliminate surcharges on regional traffic, partner states agreed to establish a One Network Area and necessary preparations were made for its launch by October 2014.

Confronting Challenges

Economic Challenges

As outlined in previous chapters, remarkable socio-economic progress was made in the last decade, exceeding all expectations. The economy grew steadily and poverty reduced significantly, uplifting one million people out of poverty. These outcomes were driven mainly by an increase in agricultural output, social protection programmes, robust exports and strong domestic demand.

However, despite high rates of growth, structural transformation of the economy towards higher productivity industry and services were limited during the EDPRS 1 (2008-2012). The private sector mainly consists of small enterprises that are constrained by limited skills and access to finance. The number of large competitive businesses is limited. The demographic trend requires 200,000 off-farm jobs to be created annually, a challenge closely linked to the need to spur the movement of people away from scarce agricultural land to higher productivity in non-agricultural sectors. Moreover, Rwanda's fiscal space is limited and still relies on external aid to complement national budget resources for development programmes. In the medium term, this will continue to affect the speed of government to leverage and support socio-economic development. However, focus will be on harnessing the private sector to fill the gap.

Transforming the economy requires addressing a number of cross-cutting challenges. Firstly, the main constraint to private sector growth and investment is related to infrastructure and in particular, electricity. Electricity consumption per capita is lower in Rwanda than in many other EAC countries. Projections indicate that achieving the targets for economic and industrial growth, which will require an increase in electricity consumption, means that energy supply will have to rise at over 27% per year until 2020. Other infrastructure-related issues are the availability of land, the high cost of transportation to sea ports and an inefficient logistics system all adding the significant costs of both importing and exporting of goods.

Apart from purely infrastructural issues there are also challenges of increasing market access, reducing barriers to trade by neighbouring countries, and developing promotion activities to link producers with markets. This is especially important for the much-needed increase in non-traditional exports which is a key objective of the government.

Secondly, private sector growth and competitiveness is constrained by low skills and labour productivity. Currently, capacities are still low with only about 4% and 3% of the work force with upper secondary and university qualification respectively. The number of formal sector firms reporting inadequate skills as a major constraint has doubled since 2006, indicating that this is a growing problem.

Lack of skills is a particular issue for large firms with more than 100 employees, 45% of which reported an inadequately educated workforce as a constraint in 2011. The 2009 National Skills Audit reported an average 61.5% skills deficit and severe skills gaps in the private sector in Rwanda. The percentage of firms identifying an inadequately educated workforce as a major constraint has doubled since 2006. Evidence consistently shows that training in the workplace environment and training closely linked to the requirements of private sector firms, provides the best chance of overcoming skills deficits.

If Rwanda is to engage in high value industries, then the education and skills level of its work force has to be improved. The young generations also have to be equipped with skills to participate in not only the local economy but in the region and globally. Thirdly, the level and quality of entrepreneurship is low in Rwanda, as evidenced by a relatively small number of businesses. The Establishment Census of 2011 estimated that there are over 123,000 firms operating in Rwanda, which is around one business per 100 people (1.2%). A higher business density reflects high rates of formal entrepreneurship and hence lower barriers to formalising business activity. The more businesses form, the likelihood of new investment and competition in markets will increase and this will in turn drive up efficiency and innovation, thus driving up productivity and growth.

But SMEs in particular are also constrained by access to finance, including high interest rates and collateral requirements compared to similar countries. Many entrepreneurs need support in formulating business propositions, loan applications and record keeping, further limiting their access to finance.

Finally, although as shown in previous chapters there has been a substantial growth of FDI in recent years, challenges remain in terms of diversifying investment as well as increasing the proportion of pledged investments that get operationalised. The data for the past decade shows that FDI in Rwanda is dominated by a very small number of large investments; the top 10 investment pledges made up 72% of total investments in the period from 2000 to 2009. More investment in a wider range of sectors will be required, particularly in the manufacturing, agro-processing and finance sectors. Problems that investors face tend to relate to post-registration and insufficient investor after care, as well as infrastructure-related constraints as elaborated on above. Addressing these issues is critical to ensure an increase in the proportion of registered investment that gets implemented.

A complete structural change of the economy is the key ambition of the government of Rwanda. Given that the major aspiration of Vision 2020 is to transform Rwanda's economy into a middle-income country, or US$1,240 per capita by 2020, an annual growth rate of at least 11.5% will be required. As stated in Vision 2020, this will not be achieved unless Rwanda transforms from a subsistence agriculture economy to a knowledge-based society, with high levels of savings and private investment, thereby reducing the country's dependence on external aid. Even if Rwanda's agriculture is transformed into a high productivity sector, it will not, on its own, be a sufficient engine of growth. There has to be an exit strategy from reliance on agriculture into the service and industrial sectors.

Indeed, Vision 2020 sets out explicit targets for industry to grow by 14%, and the service sector by 13.5%, annually until 2020. Exports should grow by 28%, and there is a need to create 200,000 jobs, annually. For these ambitious targets to be achieved a structural transformation of the economy is mandatory.

This is even more explicit in the (EDPRS) II, running from 2013 to 2018, where a key principle is the economic transformation for accelerated economic restructuring and growth striving for middle-income status. This strategy is based on the premise that a country's journey to economic transformation is impossible to achieve without strategic and pro-active involvement of the public sector in catalysing private sector growth. At the same time, the government clearly puts the private sector at the forefront of this transition. It envisages the development of an efficient private sector spearheaded by competitiveness and entrepreneurship. Based on these

considerations, the (EDPRS) II outlines five key objectives for economic transformation:
- Increasing the domestic interconnectivity of the economy through investments in hard and soft infrastructure;
- Increasing the external connectivity of the economy and boosting exports;
- Transforming the private sector by increasing investment in priority sectors;
- Transforming the economic geography of Rwanda by facilitating and managing urbanisation and promoting secondary cities as poles of economic growth; and
- Pursuing a 'green economy' approach to economic transformation.

The majority of these issues are cross-cutting and form the basis for a number of explicit targets. Exports in relation to GDP will have to increase from 14.6 in 2012 to 27.2% by 2018 and the share of non-traditional exports to 60% of all exports. FDI should grow from 2.3% to 4.5% of GDP and private investment from 10% to 15%. Implementing programmes that address the challenges outlined in the previous section will prove key to achieving these targets.

Building infrastructure for Rwanda's connectivity to the region and globally and building a critical mass of skilled people will take the biggest share of the journey ahead.

Major projects have been embarked on and will continue to be monitored for effective implementation over the next decade. These include building a robust national airline that connects the world to Rwanda, development of a modern international airport in Bugesera district, investing in the development of the standard gauge railway linking Rwanda to the ports of Mombasa and Dar-es-Salaam, investing in the development of the refined oil products pipeline linking Kigali to the port of Mombasa, and investing in the trans-national electricity transmission line linking Rwanda to Kenya via Uganda for importation of cheaper power, among others.

Centres of excellence for critical skills development will also take centre stage. This will include the full establishment of Carnegie Mellon University in Rwanda, the development of the labour pool for ICT as well as strengthening the now merged University of Rwanda. Upgrading the

TVET system to generate a critical mass of specialised technical skills will continue to be a major area of focus.

Finally, the role of the private sector in this journey cannot be over emphasised. The (EDPRS) II period is the time when the Rwandan private sector is expected to take the driving seat in economic growth and poverty reduction. Government will continue to focus its efforts on transforming the economy, the private sector and alleviating constraints to the growth of investment.

Security challenges

Rwanda's post-genocide recovery and development has had to confront and overcome serious threats to its national security. The same forces that killed over a million people, caused a humanitarian crisis in DRC and led to regional instability for the last two decades still maintain the same genocide ideology and remain poised to attack Rwanda. With sanctuary from sympathetic states and organisations as well as continued indifference by the international community, these genocidal forces pose a threat to Rwanda and the region at large.

FDLR, RNC and other name-mutating organisations united by the same genocide ideology and political opportunism attempt to conduct acts of terror in Rwanda. These terror outfits skilfully disguise themselves as legitimate political organisations. Rwanda knows too well that a group which maintains genocide ideology, commanded and led by killers of millions of Rwandans does not suddenly become a legitimate political organisation simply by changing name. It is for this simple fact that Rwanda maintains its vigilance in defence of the nation.

Rwanda's current and future security remains assured. For over two decades, Rwanda has built a strong national defence, and effective regional and international alliances. Through mechanisms such as the International Conference of the Great Lakes Region (ICGLR), the East African Standby Force and other mechanisms, Rwanda continues to contribute to regional security and development of the Great Lakes Region, Africa and beyond. Rwanda strives to remain a stable and prosperous country at peace with herself and her neighbours.

Political Challenges and Future Perspectives

The political challenges that Rwanda is faced with are of a varied nature; some are brought by the very nature of our political history and others by our current and future perspectives.

Managing the identity question is one specific challenge that Rwanda has dealt with since 1994, considering that the political history of Rwanda has been characterised by a rising number of social conflicts which were ultimately caused by the primacy of deliberately created ethnic divisions among the Rwandan people. These plunged the country into social turmoil over the years and culminated in one of the most horrific human tragedies of the 20th century: the genocide against the Tutsi in 1994. The lack of promotion of a national identity was identified as being responsible for the internal social conflicts among Rwandans and finally, the genocide in 1994.

In addressing these challenges, the government chose to promote the national identity over diversity sensitivities through its various programmes. However, in as far as the unity of the Rwandan people is concerned, the challenge remains how to keep the legacy of the primacy of a national identity and how this will be transmitted to the next generations.

The liberation of the country from bad governance and the genocide in 1994 has made tremendous changes in the lives of all Rwandans. It brought about socio-economic transformation of the country, peace and security, unity and reconciliation among other positive transformations. Since 1994, the government has effectively worked to consolidate the gains of liberation. The challenge now is to provide the next generation with the capacity to protect the gains of liberation and to maintain the momentum towards achieving the national vision.

The liberation of Rwanda is itself one great legacy to all Rwandans. It has brought about peace, security, unity and reconciliation but also social economic transformation for the betterment of all Rwandans. Rwanda, like any other country is evolving in a globalised world system. While this has benefits, it also represents a challenge. The challenge is how to achieve our goals while maintaining partnerships with other countries.

Social Challenges

During (EDPRS) I, there was a significant reduction in extreme poverty, though it remains high and persistent, particularly in rural areas. In 2008-2011, poverty reduced more in rural than urban areas. However, poverty in rural areas still stands at 48.7%, compared to 22.1% in urban areas (EICV). In Rwanda's poorest district, Nyamagabe, 73% of people live below the poverty line.

Women are more affected by poverty than men, with 47% of female headed households being poor compared to 44.9% of all households. A key challenge for (EDPRS) II is, therefore, to ensure sustained growth and poverty reduction nationwide and among all groups. The depth of poverty indicators, i.e. the proportion by which poor households fall below the poverty line, shows that despite improvements, many households in rural areas are far below the poverty line while others continue to be vulnerable to shocks, particularly in the agriculture sector.

Rwanda also continues to have comparatively high inequality. Although inequality, as measured by the Gini coefficient, has reduced in the last five years to a level lower than in 2000/2001 (EICV), it remains high when compared to other Sub-Saharan Africa countries. Inequality will only continue to reduce if Rwanda can ensure that the poor, particularly in rural areas, have access to the benefits of economic growth and jobs, and that they are not left behind in Rwanda's development story.

Farm workers make up 60% of the working age population. This represents 3.5 million people whose main occupation is farming. They are mostly poor, live in rural areas, have low education, and are underemployed, working an average of around 26 hours per week. Vision 2020 targets employment of half the Rwandan workforce off-farm by 2020, up from just 28% today. This is because non-farm workers are five times more productive than farm workers, and are 50% less likely to be in poverty. Reaching this goal will require creating an additional 200,000 non-farm jobs every year.

Basic financial literacy courses will also be provided, focusing on short "rule of thumb" courses on financial access and management, which have been proven to increase earnings. More than three million people are targeted to be reached out by literacy courses and the national financial literacy campaign.

Rwanda is one of the most densely populated countries in Africa and land is perhaps Rwanda's scarcest resource. Current population density in Rwanda stands at 415 people per square km (NISR 2012). This demographic reality, whilst an opportunity, carries risks and pressures for the economy. The scarce land available is dominated by smallholder farms. Smallholders in rural areas hold four to five plots that make up a mean land size average of approximately 0.59 hectares, with the median value at 0.33 hectares. This restricts both the productivity of land and the ability of rural populations to escape poverty. This enhances the need for modern farming methods to increase agricultural productivity, increased off-farm employment to release land for scaled-up agriculture, and leveraging the process of urbanisation.

The largest group of people not working are young people, who make up 11% of the working age population. The demographic trend necessitates 200,000 jobs to be created each year for new entrants into the workforce, meaning that Rwanda will need to see a significant increase in both formal and informal jobs over the period of (EDPRS) II.

A key emerging challenge in Rwanda is unemployment amongst skilled youth especially in urban areas. Although the number of the unemployed is relatively small, it represents an important waste of human capital, and suggests that graduates may not be obtaining the skills that firms need.

An attitude change regarding employment is necessary in reducing underemployment and unemployment amongst the young in Rwanda. Youth attitudes towards work are still poor. Young people tend to look down on certain jobs such as blue-collar in preference for white collar office jobs. This further translates into a negative attitude towards learning skills related to those perceived blue-collar jobs. There is also lack of an entrepreneurship culture among Rwandan youth.

A national Youth Mentorship programme will be developed, with the goal of raising awareness amongst the youth about the opportunities that are available in both the private sector and through government schemes, and to inculcate a culture of hard work, entrepreneurial spirit and independence. Modelled on the successful community health worker programme, local government will coordinate a network of successful entrepreneurs to provide regular monthly guidance sessions with youth in which they can impart knowledge and skills.

Only when Rwanda's job market entrants are used productively in the economy will Rwanda's growth be sustained and accelerated.

Pupils exhibiting to President Kagame the use of laptops under the One Laptop per Child Programme

Top: Students at the Educational Institute for the blind demonstrate how to use a computer as a learning aid - Nyaruguru, 20 February 2013

Middle: President Kagame and Mrs Kagame listen to a Gashora Girls student's view in Bugesera, 3 July 2012

Bottom: President Kagame and Mrs Kagame pose with Gashora Girls Academy students in Bugesera, 3 July 2012

Top: Students at FAWE Girls' School

Middle: TVET students doing practical work

Bottom: School children enjoy milk, provided by the One Cup per Child feeding programme

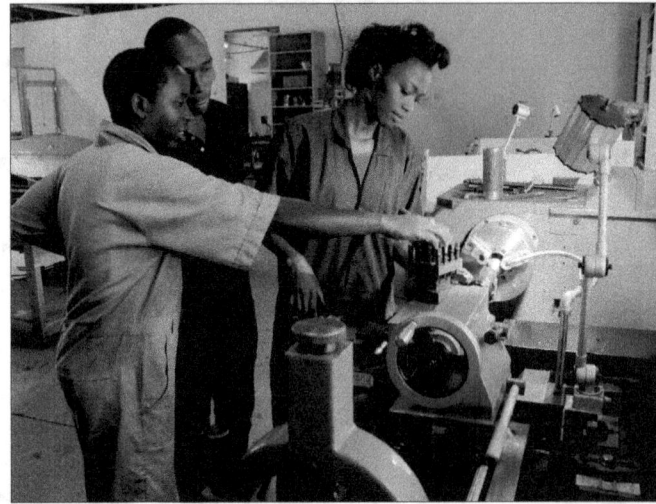

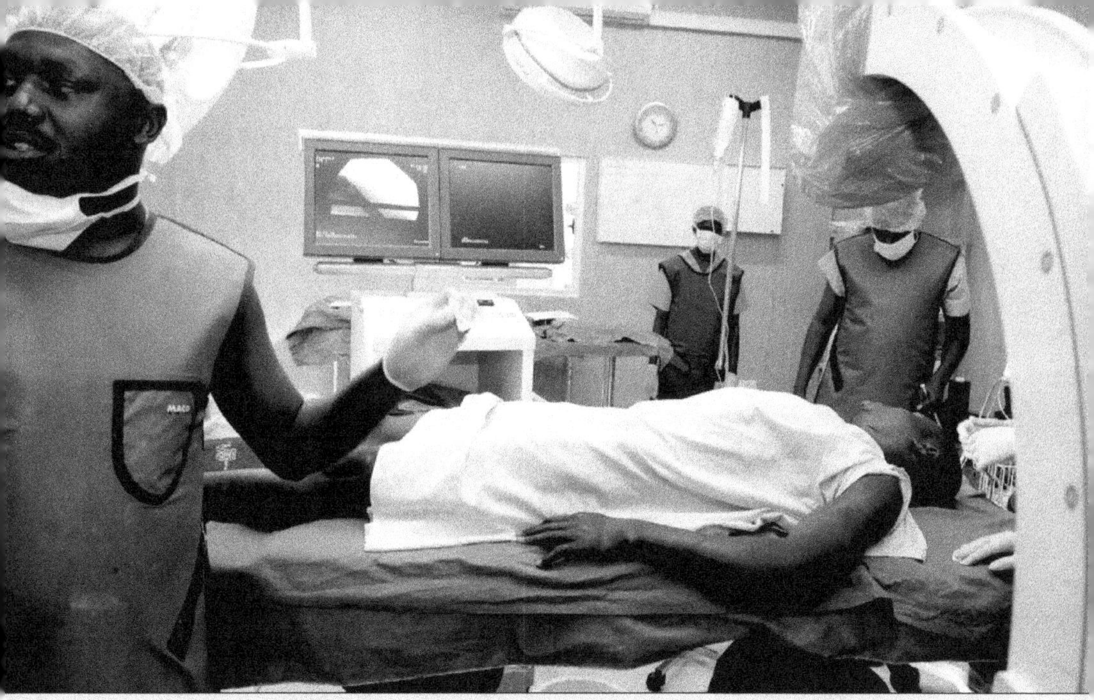

Top: A patient being attended to at King Faisal Hospital, Rwanda's largest referral hospital

Bottom: President Paul Kagame waves to health workers during a meeting at Amahoro Stadium, Kigali

Top: Graduates of the Itorero ry'igihugu at a pass-out ceremony

Middle: Rwanda National Police in support of home-grown initiatives in Nyamasheke during Police Week activities, 2011

Bottom: RDF soldiers participating in community work (Umuganda)

Top: President Paul Kagame with the top performers during the Imihigo ceremony in Kigali, 12 September 2014

Bottom: Rwandan soldiers arrive in Darfur for a peacekeeping mission

Top: From left to right President Salva Kiir, President Yoweri K. Museveni, President Paul Kagame, and President Uhuru Kenyatta at a Summit on the Northern Corridor projects, 2014

Bottom: President Paul Kagame welcoming US President George Bush during his visit to Rwanda, 2008

Top: President Paul Kagame greets President Nicolas Sarkozy of France at Élysée Palace, 2010

Bottom: President Paul Kagame meeting with Prime Minister of Israel Benjamin Netanyahu in Davos, 23 January 2014

Top: President Kagame meets Tony Blair during Business Leaders breakfast held in Davos, 22 January 2014

Bottom: President Kagame meeting with President Goodluck Ebele Jonathan in Kigali, 6 October 2011

Top: President Kagame's London Trip for the Commonwealth Flag-raising Ceremony - London, 8-11 March 2010

Bottom: Hoisting the Rwanda flag at the Commonwealth Flag-raising Ceremony in London, 8-11 March 2010

Top: Participants at the Rwanda Day in Atlanta, 20 September 2014

Middle: First Lady Jeannette Kagame and participants enjoy a light moment during President Kagame's address in Atlanta, 20 September 2014

Bottom: A participant receives an award from President Paul Kagame on Rwanda Day in Chicago - 11 June 2011

Top: A children's choir entertains participants on Rwanda Day in Chicago - 11 June 2011

Bottom: Participants dance to morale-boosting songs during the closing session of the 11th National Dialogue - Kigali, 7 December 2013 (Day 2)

Top: Rwandan voters queue up ready to cast their vote during national elections, 2010

Bottom: Women Members of Parliament take the oath of office

Valens Ndayisenga wins Tour du Rwanda, 23 November 2014

Bibliography

Amnesty International (2004). Rwanda: 'Marked for death': rape survivors living with HIV/AIDS. *Available at* http://web.amnesty.org/library/Index/ENGAFR470072004 [Accessed 16 April 2004]

Chrétien J. P. (2000). *L'Afrique des Grands Lacs. Deux mille ans d'Histoire.* Paris: Aubier.

Clark, P. and Kaufman, Z. D. (eds.) (2009). *After Genocide: Transitional Justice, Post-Conflict Reconstruction and Reconciliation in Rwanda and Beyond*, New York: Columbia University Press.

Dallaire, R. (1994). Fax to Maurice Baril, 11 January New York

Dallaire R. (1994). *Request for Protection for Informant:* Fax sent from UNAMIR in Kigali on 11 January to Baril, UN's Department of Peace Keeping Operations in New York

Dallaire R. (2003). *Shake Hands with the Devil: The Failure of Humanity in Rwanda.* Toronto: Random House, Canada.

Definition et Identification de l'ENI [Enemi], document circulated with the letter of Nsabimana to Liste A, September 21, 1992.

DFID. (2007). *Governance, Development and Politics*, London

Elshtain B. J. (1995). *Women and War.* New York: Basic Books.

Esteves, M., et al. (2013). *Financing of the water, sanitation and hygiene sector in Rwanda.* Case study commissioned by WaterAid, produced by Development Finance International (DFI). *Available at*: https://www.wateraid.org/.../Rwanda%20the%20financing%20of%20t. [Accessed 12 May 2013]

European Commission. (2003). *Communication on Governance and Development.*

Gallup. (2012). *Global States of Mind: New Metrics for World Leaders.* Washington D.C. *Available at*: https://www.gallup.com [Accessed 12 May 2015]

Gallup. (2012). *Latin Americans Least Likely Worldwide To Feel Safe. Available at*: https://www.gallup.com/poll/156236/latin-americans-least-likely-worldwide-feel-safe.aspx.

Gallup. (2013). *Global States of Mind. Available at*: https://www.gallup.com/poll/165497/global-states-mind-2013.aspx.

Genocide Chronology. *Available at*: https://www.google.com/search?q=genocide+chronology&ie=utf-8&oe=utf-8.

ICTR. (2008). *Proceedings of the International Criminal Tribunal for Rwanda*, The Prosecutor v. Théoneste Bagosora et al., Case No. ICTR-98-41-T, p 46, (18 December 2008).

Inger, A. and Jensen, B. S. (1993). The Psychosexual Trauma of Torture. In: Wilson, P. J. and Raphael, B., (eds) *International Handbook of Traumatic Stress*. New York: Plenum Press.

Inger, A. (1989). Sexual Torture of Political Prisoners: An Overview. *Journal of Traumatic Stress* 2(3), 305–18.

International Food Policy Research Institute (IFPR) (2013). Global Hunger Index www.ifpri.org/ghi/2013/summary

International Monetary Fund (IMF) (2008). *Rwanda: Poverty Reduction Strategy Paper*. IMF Country Report No. 08/90.

James Munyaneza (2007) *Kagame receives 2007 Africa Gender Award*. The New Times. Available at http://www.newtimes.co.rw/section/article/2007-12-12/2022/

Kagame, A. (1943). *Inganji Kalinga*, Kabgayi.

Kagame A. (1972). *Un abrégé de l'ethno-histoire du Rwanda*. Butare: EUNR.

Kanimba, M. and Mesas, T. (2003). *Rwanda: a Journey through the National Museum Collection*. Paris: Maisonneuve et Larose.

Kanimba, M, (2002). Peuplement ancien du Rwanda: A la Lumière des Récentes Recherches. *Peuplement du Rwanda: Enjeux et Perspectives*. Editions de l'Universite Nationale du Rwanda.

Kinzer, S. (2008). *A Thousand Hills – Rwanda's Rebirth and the Man who Dreamed it*. New Jersey: John Willey & Sons, Inc.

Legatum Prosperity Index Rank. (2012). World Rankings *Available at* .http://knoema.com/LPIR2012/legatum-prosperity-index-rank-2012?country=1001060-rwanda. [Accessed 12 May 2015]

Lemarchand, R. (1970). *Rwanda and Burundi*. Washington, London: Pall Mall.

Lijphart, A. (1999). *Patterns of Democracy. Government Forms and Performance in Thirty-six countries*. Connecticut: Yale University Press

Linda, P. (2010). *The Crisis Caravan: What's Wrong With Humanitarian Aid?* New York: Metropolitan Books.

Mamdani M. (2002). *When Victims Become Killers: Colonialism, Nativism, and the Genocide in Rwanda*. Kampala: Fountain Publishers, Dar es Salaam: E&D Limited.

Melvern L. (2000). *A People Betrayed: The Role of the West in Rwanda's Genocide*. London: Zed Books.

Melvern, L. (2006). *Conspiracy to murder. The Rwandan Genocide*. London, New York: Verso.

Mugesera, A. (2004). *Imibereho y'Abatutsi kuri Repubulika ya mbere n'iya Kabiri (1959-1990)*, Kigali: Les Editions Rwandaises.

Mukamunana, R, Brynard, P.A. (2005). The role of civil society organisations in policy making process in Rwanda. *Journal of Public Administration*, Vol. 40 No. 4.1 pp 665-676.

Muvunanyambo, A. (2011). *Umurage w'u Rwanda Gakondo: Ingoma Renge Nyiginya*. Kigali: Graphic Print Solutions Ltd.

Muzungu, B. (2003). *Histoire du Rwanda précolonial*. Paris: L'Harmattan.

Neugebauer R, Fisher PW, Turner JB, Yamabe S, Sarsfield JA, and Stehling-Ariza T (2009): Post-traumatic stress reaction among Rwandan children and adolescents in the early aftermath of genocide. *International journal of Epidemiology* 38(4): 1033-45.

Ndiaye, W. B. (1993). Report of 11 August 1993 by the United Nations Special Rapporteur Bacre Waly Ndiaye on Extrajudicial, Summary or Arbitrary Executions and Addendum of 7 April 1993 of the Rwandan offices of the President and Prime Minister.

Nkunzumwami, E. (1996). *La tragédie Rwandaise. Histoire et Perspectives.* Paris: L'Harmattan.

Organisation of African Unity (2000). *Rwanda the Preventable Genocide*; The Report of the International Panel of Eminent Personalities (IPEP) to Investigate the 1994 Genocide in Rwanda and the Surrounding Events.

Owen, M. (2001). 'Widows Expose HIV War Threat'. *Worldwoman News*, 12 June.

Pagès, A. (1993). *Un royaume hamite au centre de l'Afrique*, Bruxelles: Marcel Hayez.

Prunier, G. (1995). *The Rwanda Crisis 1959-1994: History of a Genocide*. Kampala: Fountain Publishers.

Prunier, G. (1997). *The Rwanda Crisis: History of a Genocide*. London: Hurst &Co. revised edn. (1999).

Republic of Rwanda (2003). *Constitution of the Republic of Rwanda*, Kigali

Republic of Rwanda (2010) Demographic and Health Survey - Final Report. *Available at* www.statistics.gov.rw› Publications › Survey reports

Republic of Rwanda (2012) Gacaca Report 2012. Rwandapedia.com

Republic of Rwanda. (2008). Joint Governance Assessment Report, Kigali.

Republic of Rwanda, MINADEF. (2008). Constitution of the Republic of Rwanda. *Available at* http://mod.gov.rw/fileadmin/user_upload/PDF_Documents/Constitution_of_the_Republic_of_Rda.pdf

Republic of Rwanda, MINAGRI (2012) Annual Report *Available at* http://www.minagri.gov.rw/fileadmin/user_upload/documents/Reports/Final_AnnualReport_FY2010_2011updated.pdf

Republic of Rwanda, MINAGRI, (2013). *Grow Africa 2013 Progress Report. Available at* http://www.minagri.gov.rw/.../user.../Grow_Africa_2013_Progress_Report.pdf [Accessed 12 May 2012]

Republic of Rwanda, MINECOFIN (2014). *Macroeconomic Framework Dataset*, Kigali

Republic of Rwanda, MINEDUC (2012) *Education Statistics. Available at* http://www.mineduc.gov.rw/.../user.../2012_Education_statistical_yearbook.pdf.

Republic of Rwanda, MINICOM, (2013). Rwanda Kivu Belt Tourism Sub Master Plan. Prepared by *Horwath HTL Interconsult GmBH. Available online at* http://www.westernprovince.gov.rw/uploads/media/Rwanda_Kivu_Belt_Sub_Master_Plan_01.pdf

Republic of Rwanda, MINIRENA (2013). Potential for Investment in Rwandan Mining Sector. *Available at* http://www.slideshare.net/miningontop/20130626-rwanda-presentation-mining-on-topafricalondon-summit

Republic of Rwanda (2014) *National Bank of Rwanda (BNR) Data*, Kigali

Republic of Rwanda (2013) National Bank of Rwanda (BNR). *Balance of Payments since 1998*. *Available at* http://www.bnr.rw/index.php?id=212)

Republic of Rwanda (2007) National Institute of Statistics of Rwanda & UNDP: *MDG Country Report*, Kigali

Republic of Rwanda (2012) National Institute of Statistics Rwanda Year Book. *Available at* http://statistics.gov.rw/system/files/user_uploads/.../YEAR%20 BOOK_2012.pdf

Republic of Rwanda (2014) National Institute of Statistics, *Mortality*. *Available at* http://statistics.gov.rw/system/files/user_uploads/files/books/Mortality.pdf

Republic of Rwanda (1999): Official Gazette of the Republic of Rwanda, *Available at* http://www.migeprof.gov.rw/uploads/media/MATRIMONIAL_REGIMES_LIBERALITIES_AND_SUCCESSIONS-2.pdf

Republic of Rwanda, Rwanda Development Board (RDB), (2010). *Highlights of Tourist Arrivals in Rwanda* – 2009. *Available at* http://www.rdb.rw/fileadmin/user_upload/Documents/tourism%20conservation/Rwanda_Arrival_Statistics__2009.PDF

Republic of Rwanda, Rwanda Development Board (RDB), (2013). *Tourism Report 2013*. *Available at* http://www.rdb.rw/fileadmin/user_upload/Documents/tourism%20conservation/statistics/tourism_report_2013.pdf

Republic of Rwanda (2014): *Rwanda Governance Scorecard*. Rwanda Governance board, Kigali

Republic of Rwanda. (2010). Rwanda National Report Submitted in Accordance with Paragraph 15 (a) of the Annex to the Human Rights Council Resolution 5/1 in the Framework of the Universal Period Review *Available at*: http://www.undp.org/content/dam/rwanda/docs/demgov/RW_UPR%20Report%20submitted%20by%20the%20GoR.pdf

Republic of Rwanda, Supreme Court (2015) *Judicial Reforms*. *Available at*: http://www.judiciary.gov.rw/fileadmin/Publications/Reports/Achievements 2004-2014.

République Rwandaise (1992) Note au Chef EM AR from Anatole Nsengiyumva, Kigali, July 27, 1992. Objet: Etat d'esprit des militaries et de la population civile.

Reyntjens F. (1985). *Pouvoir et droit au Rwanda. Droit public et évolution politique, 1916-1973*. Tervuren: MRAC.

Rusagara, K.F. et al. (2009). *Resilience of a Nation: A History of the Military in Rwanda*. Kigali: Fountain Publishers Rwanda.

Ryan, O. (2004). *Rwanda's struggle to rebuild the economy*. BBC News. *Available at* http://www.news.bbc.co.uk/2/hi/bussiness/3586851.stn

Saoti.over-blog.com *Available at* http://www.zoominfo.com/CachedPage/?archive_id=0&page_id=5157139815&page_url=//saoti.over-blog.com/35-index.

html&page_last_updated=2010-12-28T19:11:45&firstName=Paul&lastName=Dijoud [Accessed March 11, 2015]

Sebasoni, S. (2000). *Les origines du Rwanda*. Paris: L'Harmattan.

Stanton, H. G. (2013). *The Ten Stages of Genocide*. US State Department.

Stefan, E. (2002). HIV/AIDS and the Changing Landscape of War in Africa. *International Security*, 27 (2), 159–177.

The Legatum Institute (2012). *The 2012 Legatum Prosperity Index*, London

The Linda Melvern Rwanda Genocide archive, The Hugh Owen Library, University of Wales.

The New Times. (2009). President and Mrs. Kagame to be honoured in the US. *Available at* http://www.newtimes.co.rw/section/article/2009-06-02/8739/

The Prosecutor v. Théoneste Bagosora et al., Case No. ICTR-98-41-T. 18 December 2008.

UNDP (2006). *Governance Indicators, A User's Handbook*.

United Nations (1999). UN Report of the Independent Inquiry into the Actions of the United Nations During the 1994 Genocide in Rwanda published on 16 December 1999.

United States Committee for Refugees and Immigrants. (1997). *US Committee for Refugees, World Refugee Survey 1997 - Democratic Republic of Congo (formerly Zaire)*, *Available at* http://www.refworld.org/docid/3ae6a8a70.html [Accessed 13 March 2015]

USAID, Office of Democracy & Governance: Governance, *Available at* http://www.usaid.gov/our_work/democracy_and_governance/technical_areas/dg_office/gov.html

Uvin, P. (1998). *Aiding Violence: The Development Enterprise in Rwanda*. West Hartford: Kumurian Press.

UNICEF (2012). *Education*. *Available at* http://www.unicef.org/rwanda/education.html

Vansina, J. (2001). *Le Rwanda ancien. Le royaume nyiginya*. Paris. Karthala.

Vansina, J. (2004). *Antecedents to Modern Rwanda: The Nyiginya Kingdom*. Oxford: James Currey, Kampala: Fountain Publishers.

Wallis, A. (2006). *Silent Accomplice. The untold story of France's Role in the Rwandan Genocide*. London: I. B. Tauris.

World Bank and SNV (2010). *The Success of Tourism in Rwanda – Gorillas and more. Background paper for the African Success Stories Study*. *Available at* http://siteresources.worldbank.org/AFRICAEXT/Resources/258643-1271798012256/Tourism_Rwanda.pdf

Index

Abatwa (Pygmies) 3, 14
African Union 85, 115, 129
Africa's First World War 84
agricultural
  intensification 157
  productivity 186, 239
agriculture
  modernised 152
  subsistence 234
agriculture(al)
  cash crops 156
  export 176
  irrigation 150
  market 167
  productivity 186, 239
agro-forestry 151
Akagera National Park 182, 202, 204
AMASASU 53
anti-Semitism 67
armed groups 68, 84, 85, 92
Armée pour la Libération du Rwanda (ALiR) 83
Arusha Peace Agreement 41, 42, 74, 75, 87, 139
bad governance 105, 237
Bagogwe people 40, 49
Bagosora, Théoneste (Col.) 53, 55
Bahutu
  political party 39
Bahutu extremists 40, 52, 53, 57, 58
Batutsi 11, 12, 13, 15, 16, 18, 19, 25, 29, 34, 36, 38, 39, 40, 41, 42, 49, 50, 51, 52, 53, 54, 55, 56, 57, 58, 62, 88, 91, 92, 93, 96, 112, 169
  refugees 18, 25, 41
Bayingana, Peter (Mayor) 35
Broad Based Transitional
  Government (BBTG) 75, 106
  Parliament (BBTP) 90
Bulk Water Supply Project 164
Bunyenyezi, Chris (Maj.) 35

Business Development Fund (BDF) 172
Buyoya, Pierre 35
child mortality 215
Christian Democratic Party (PDC) 38
commemorative activities 141
community
  health workers 214
  justice. *See also* Gacaca courts
conventional warfare 35
crimes of genocide 96
Crop Intensification Programme (CIP) 149, 150
Dallaire, Romeo (Gen.) 41, 42, 53
Declaration
  Abuja 213
  Cordoba 67
Demobilisation, Disarmament, Rehabilitation and Re-Integration (DDRR) 68
Democratic Forces for the Liberation of Rwanda (FDLR) 84
Democratic Republic of Congo (DRC) 69, 161, 163, 164, 175, 177, 184, 236
discriminatory education policies 77
divide and rule policy 89
domestic food security 148, 149, 150, 157
Dragons 'Abakozi' 55
economic
  recovery xiv, 95, 102
  stability 145, 226
  transformation 157, 234, 235
education infrastructure 77
ethnic
  affiliation 105
  divisions 237
  group 208
female headed households 120, 238
First World War 12, 13, 84

Food and Agriculture Organisation (FAO) 148
food security 145, 147, 148, 149, 150, 157
Forces Armées Zairoises (FAZ) 35
foreign aid 91, 96
fundamental change 73
Gabiro military barracks 34
Gacaca
  Courts 142
genocide(al)
  forces 236
  ideology 141, 236
  survivor(s) 135, 144, 218, 219, 220
  suspects 135, 140, 142
Girinka programme 133, 152, 153, 223
Global Hunger Index (GHI) 146
good governance 111
Government of National Unity (GNU) 90
grass-roots leadership 94
Great Lakes region 184, 236
Habyarimana, Juvenal (Maj.Gen.)
  President 21, 48, 187
  regime 139
health service delivery 77
high-value crops 157
home-grown solutions 130, 142, 188, 223
human
  resources 215, 217
  rights 136, 139, 140, 144
humanitarian
  assistance 81
  crisis 236
'Impuzamugambi' 56, 57
'Inkotanyi-cyane' 8
institutionalised
  discrimination 50, 207
  hatred 105
'Interahamwe' militia 38, 40, 41, 42, 51, 55, 56, 57, 75, 82, 83, 84, 85, 92
Internally Displaced Persons/People (IDPs) 37
international
  betrayal 62
  community 31, 36, 39, 40, 41, 62, 76, 81, 82, 83, 142, 236
  organisations 81, 111, 128, 129
  peacekeeping force 84
International Criminal Tribunal for Rwanda (ICTR) 85
'Inyenzi' (Cockroach) 18, 25, 27, 30
irrigation
  agriculture 149. *See also* agriculture irrigation
Jewish Holocaust 67
Kagame, Paul 44, 48, 188, 208, 211, 212, 220, 221, 223, 243, 245, 246, 247, 250
Kanyarengwe, Alexis 48
Kayibanda, Gregoire (Gen.) 21
Kigeli, Mwami IV (King) 4, 5
land
  consolidation 149
  husbandry 102, 146, 149, 150, 151
  issues 93
liberalisation programme 154
Liberal Party (PL) 38
liberation struggle 207, 212, 221
Lusaka Ceasefire Agreement 84, 85, 86
maternal mortality rate 221
mental health interventions 65
militia camps 82, 83
Millennium Development Goals (MDGs) 164, 168
Mitterrand, Francois (President) 31
mountain gorillas 181
multi-party politics 55, 106
Museveni, Yoweri 28, 30, 35
national
  reconciliation 89, 117
  strategic reserve 149
  unity 27, 75, 81, 88, 93, 94, 96, 99, 100, 105, 113, 116, 117, 118, 131, 144, 207
National Information and Communication Infrastructure Plan (NICI) 166
National Park

Akagera 182, 202, 204
Nyungwe 182, 203
National Resistance Army 27
National Resistance Movement/Army (NRM/NRA) 28
National Unity and Reconciliation Commission (NURC) 93, 100, 116
Nsabimana, Deogratias (Col.) 38
N'sele Ceasefire Agreement (1991) 35, 36, 39
Ntaryamira, Cyprien 42
nutritional security 147
Nyarubuye Roman Catholic Church 58
Obote, Milton 28, 30
Opération Turquoise 62
'Option Z' 30
Organisation for Security and Cooperation in Europe (OSCE) 67
Organisation of African Unity (OAU) 34, 35, 36, 63, 84
political
  parties 16, 18, 37, 39, 41, 56, 62, 74, 88, 93, 106, 112, 113
  values 87
  violence 112
poverty reduction 97, 122, 146, 147, 157, 164, 171, 186, 189, 218, 224, 225, 226, 236, 238
Pretoria Accord (2002) 85, 86
private investment 176, 234, 235
Prunier, Gerard 50
public health insurance 213
Radio-Télévision Libre des Mille Collines (RTLM) 51
Rassemblement Démocratique pour le Rwanda (RDR) 81
reconciliation policies 224
resilience 258
rural development 147, 226
Rwanda Armed Forces (FAR) 51
Rwanda Defence Force (RDF) ix, 126
Rwanda Demobilisation and Reintegration Commission (RDRC) 68
Rwanda Development Board (RDB) 171, 176, 258
Rwandan
  domestic courts 85
Rwanda National Police (RNP) 126
Rwanda Patriotic Front (RPF) ii, ix, xi, xii, xiii, 26, 27, 49
Rwanda Revenue Authority (RRA) 115, 171
Rwanda Transport Development Agency (RTDA) 160
Rwigyema, Fred 35
Salim, Ahmed Salim (Dr.) 34
sanitation services 160, 164, 165
satellite farming 150
Second Congo War 83
self-imposed exile 92
social
  challenges 238
  -economic challenges 224
  welfare 28, 107, 112, 124, 131, 186, 207, 219
  wounds 67
Social Democratic Party (PSD) 38
socio-economic development 73, 92, 99, 189, 223, 232
soil
  conservation 146
  erosion 151, 185, 187
Southern African Development Community (SADC) 84
Stanton, Gregory (Prof.) 51
staple crop production 149
subsistence 146, 152, 157, 187, 234
sustainable development 97, 105, 116, 145, 165, 186
sustainable socio-economic development 99
transmittable diseases 77
trauma counsellors 67
Turquoise Zone 75

'Ubudehe' programme 104, 189, 220, 224
'umuganda' (solidarity camps) 127, 130, 133, 208, 223, 244
Union Démocratique du Peuple Rwandais (UDPR) 74
United Nations Assistance Mission for Rwanda (UNAMIR) ix, 41, 42, 53, 55, 62, 255
United Nations Peacekeeping Mission to Congo (MONUC) viii, 86
Urugwiro Consultations 87, 88, 92, 95, 96, 97, 99

Uwilingiyimana, Agathe 38, 42, 57
Virunga volcanoes 181
'war tax' 82
water-borne diseases 77, 165
water harvesting 151
Week of Mourning 142
wife-inheritance 119
World Bank 68, 95, 111, 115, 123, 163, 167, 175, 181, 259
World War I 12
'zero network' 53, 55

www.ingramcontent.com/pod-product-compliance
Lightning Source LLC
Chambersburg PA
CBHW070827300426
44111CB00014B/2475